# Digital Library Creation

# Digital Library Creation

G.K. Sampath Kumar

ADHYAYAN
ADHYAYAN PUBLISHERS & DISTRIBUTORS
NEW DELHI (INDIA)

*Published by*
**ADHYAYAN PUBLISHERS & DISTRIBUTORS**
4378/4B, 105, J.M.D. House, Murari Lal Street
Ansari Road Darya Ganj, New Delhi - 110002
Ph.: 011-23263018, 011-23277156, Fax: 011-23280028
Email: adhyayanpublishers@yahoo.com

Digital Library Creation


Edition 2011
ISBN 978-81-8435-236-8



Printed in India

Published by Harish Chandra Yadav for Adhyayan Publishers & Distributors, Laser Typeseting at A.V. Rao and Printed at Tarun Offset Printers, Delhi

# Preface

A digital library is a library in which collections are stored in digital formats and accessible by computers. The design and development of digital libraries depend on computer, communication and other technical skills. Successful digital libraries leading to a global digital environment can only happen when enough practitioners have the skills to design, build and manage them.

There are several advantages of a digital library over a conventional library. These include minimising storage space and cutting down costs of library maintenance and resource distribution. A digital library is also not merely an automated conventional library, where the resources are electronically catalogued and are available only for browsing purposes. Although conventional libraries do preserve sociocultural ambiences within their spaces, a digital library can provide more equitable and widely distributed access at lower costs. It may be most appropriate means of organising intellectual artifacts that cannot be represented or distributed in printed formats, such as audio/video multimedia content.

This book offers all the knowledge and tools needed to construct and maintain a digital library. It provides information regarding the nature and growth of digital libraries, the technological infrastructure, digital library collections, digitalisation and document management, organisation of digital information, information retrieval, users, interfaces and user-centered digital libraries, archiving and preservation, the impact of digital libraries on the information professions, etc. in detail. It is a perfectly self-contained resource for individuals, agencies, and institutions wishing to put this powerful tool to work in their burgeoning information treasuries.

***G.K. Sampath Kumar***

# Contents

# 1

# Introduction to Digital Library

A digital library is an organization, which might be virtual, that comprehensively collects, manages and preserves for the long term rich digital content, and offers to its user communities specialized functionality on that content, of measurable quality and according to codified policies. The first use of the term *digital library* in print may have been in a 1988 report to the Corporation for National Research Initiatives The term *digital libraries* was first popularized by the NSF/DARPA/NASA Digital Libraries Initiative in 1994. These draw heavily on As We May Think by Vannevar Bush in 1945, which set out a vision not in terms of technology, but user experience. The term *virtual library* was initially used interchangeably with *digital library*, but is now primarily used for libraries that are virtual in other senses.

A distinction is often made between content that was created in a digital format, known as born-digital, and information that has been converted from a physical medium, e.g., paper, by digitizing. The term hybrid library is sometimes used for libraries that have both physical collections and digital collections. For example, American Memory is a digital library within the Library of Congress. Some important digital libraries also serve as long term archives, for example, the ePrint arXiv, and the Internet Archive.

Many academic libraries are actively involved in building institutional repositories of the institution's books, papers, theses, and other works which can be digitized or were 'born digital'. Many of these repositories are made available to the general public with few restrictions, in accordance with the goals of open access, in contrast to the publication of research in commercial journals, where the publishers often limit access rights. Institutional, truly free, and corporate repositories are sometimes referred to as digital libraries.

The function of conventional libraries has been described as fourfold: collection; organisation and representation; access and retrieval; and analysis, synthesis, and dissemination of information. Collection includes techniques for understanding what information resources are of use to a client population and for cost-effective storage and preservation of such resources. Organisation and representation have to do with classifying and indexing information resources in ways relevant to their potential users. Access considerations include design of physical space and organisation of materials within such space to respond effectively to user needs and expectations. Information retrieval has been addressed, of course, in the design of systems specific to that task. Analysis, synthesis and dissemination functions include responding to reference questions, producing evaluative reviews, and devising community outreach programmes. Librarians and information scientists have developed techniques, procedures, and systems for addressing each of these functions for many kinds of data and presentation. Digital library does not add any qualitatively new roles to these, nor does it omit any of these roles. Although DL implementation may well depend on the local context and technologies chosen, there are commonly accepted constraints which must be maintained to please users. DL research has focused on automating activities carried out by librarians, such as automatic indexing and classifying and expert systems for reference desks.

Conventional cataloguing presumes people are involved and can only assign a few keywords; digital catalogues can support long keyword and key phrase (or even word sense) sets with weights, long user queries, ranked retrieval, etc. Information search via hypertext illustrates that indices can be implicit rather than explicit, giving users a seamless blend of primary and secondary works. Further, some current library activities may become irrelevant; for instance, circulation problems originating in a fixed number of copies of each work simply disappear. Thus, DL involves not only automation of each traditional library activity and service, but also calls for redefinition of services, new groupings of services or replacements of groups of services with other solutions. Whether one judges the differences between digital and conventional libraries to be intrinsically qualitative or merely quantitative, the quantitative factors are so immensely different that it will often be better to treat them as qualitative. On the positive side, the potential ease of integration of information in different modes from mutually remote repositories creates new social possibilities.

A digital library is a machine readable representation of materials which might be found in a university library together with organising information intended to help users find specific information. A digital library service is an assemblage of digital computing, storage, and communications machinery together with the software needed to reproduce, emulate, and extend the services provided by conventional libraries based on paper and other material means of collecting, storing, cataloguing, finding, and disseminating information. A full service digital library must accomplish all essential services of traditional libraries and also exploit digital storage, searching, and communication. Public, private, professional, school, commercial, and other kinds of library emphasize different services, different kinds of information, and different service styles. While any digital library instance may thus offer only partial services, the technology suite from which library instances are assembled must permit assembly of a full service library. In addition, this suite must shield the user who wishes to draw on multiple libraries from inter-library differences which are irrelevant to him.

Digital library is having the benefits of improved control and plasticity are not only improved data quality, but also more freedom and reduced bureaucracy for individual users. Only a librarian may add to the collection of a conventional library, because of the discipline essential to create a quality catalogue. In a digital library, cataloguing discipline and search restrictions to authorised data can be automatically enforced. It can thus allow each patron and author a wider range of services than is practical with a conventional library.

## 1.1. Digital Library Software

Digital libraries are created by software which includes the following module classes:

— *A document storage subsystem* is a resource manager that creates a library abstraction implementing all the essential data storage, retrieval, protection, communication, and search functions as primitive operations which do not depend on the interpretation of the data handled. It is middleware that integrates more basic resource managers, such as database managers, video servers, cache managers, and file managers.

— *Network directory and security servers* are intimately related resource managers which help users locate protected resources, limiting each user to what each resource and item owner permits. A name or directory service maps names to locations and other descriptors. Authentication and authorisation services combine to control access to what is permitted.

— *A billing subsystem* is a component or set of components which collects and validates subject and account information, rate information and resource consumptions, and submits these to a charge-back subsystem.

— *A source selector* and fuser is an application enabler which partitions a query among as many libraries as the query implies, calls on query managers to execute the queries, and assembles the results to hide those inter-library differences that the user considers irrelevant.

— *A search engine* is a resource manager which accepts a query and returns item descriptors, but not usually copies of the items themselves. There may be primitive search engines that operate only on certain kinds of database and also more complex search engines which partition queries among simpler query engines and combine results using joins and selections which are beyond the simpler engines. Part of a search engine might be an external query optimiser intended to overcome the performance problems inherent in multiple, separated library catalogues.

— *A filter service* is a separately programmed bit-stream to bit-stream transformation that can be linked into a resource manager or an application enabler for functions like encryption, compression, and partial object access.

— *A link engine* is an application enabler which interprets a hypermedia link and calls on resource managers to manipulate a copy of the item indicated, possibly by launching separately-provided application programme, and possibly invoking library services to provide integrity holds on the primary copy of the item.

— *A preview/thumbnailer* is an application enabler which collects from one or more libraries a set of small data objects, or creates each such thumbnail from a library item, to present these to a user for selection. Each thumbnail remains bound to the associated item so that selecting it can be used to drive item retrieval or some other action.

— *A presenter or renderer* is an application enabler which prepares an object for manipulation in a client machine, possibly assembling item parts from one or more libraries. Each tool is specific to an object class, i.e., is selected when the user asks to render an item of the class at hand. There is no clear boundary with a filter or a format converter which edits a set of files to create another set of files representing a subset of the same information, typically executing close to the data source or sink.

— *Data analysis tools*, browsers, navigators, and authoring and editing services are application enablers.

— *Source/sink servers* are resource managers such as scan servers, print servers, and fax servers.

— *Indexing tools, document analysers, and other tools* to recognise patterns and structure are application enablers for creating search indices automatically. An actor or active agent is a persistent process which monitors database state and sends to principals filtered information about changes. Alternatively, an active agent is a network process which creates other active agent instances at remote locations, with each instance collecting filtered information from databases.

Resource managers and application enablers are essentially passive and cannot distinguish active agents from human users. Triggers, a database feature in which an incoming message causes not only database changes and/or responses to its source, but also messages to a third party, share some of the characteristics of actors. Both triggers and actors are dependent on store-and-forward network services because the message target may not be active when the message is ready for delivery. Some of these components can and must be adopted from activities not labelled DL. Such components certainly include those for naming, authentication, and many kinds of search engine.

Requirements for document storage services are many, some broadly applicable elements are summarised below.

— *Distribution:* People are often distant from needed information, frequently in locations for which high speed links are not affordable. Such recipients of large items often want delayed delivery at times of day when communication tolls are low.

— *Performance:* Updating a stored document is likely to be a rare event and not subject to stringent responsiveness objectives. In contrast, retrieval should be rapid, and search to identify which items are worth retrieving should be even more rapid.

— *Large and small items:* Item sizes range from about 103 bytes for ASCII notes to 107 bytes for high resolution pictures. Digital video and audio items are even bigger and must be delivered with controlled pacing.

— *Accessibility from all workstation platforms:* Different people will have different kinds of personal computer because of history, function needed, or personal preference. Increasingly, individuals may use more than one machine type. Library service must be accessible from whatever workstation is chosen for other reasons.

— *Catalogue service from all kinds of operating system platform:* A large enterprise may have different kinds of database server in different locations, and should be able to provide compatible library catalogue services from these database servers.

— *Support for all kinds of item storage:* Custodians should be able to house items as economically as possible within their operational and policy constraints. They should be able to add capacity using the currently most effective storage medium hierarchy and attach this wherever needed to minimise communication costs and maximise responsiveness.

— *Low administration overhead:* Installation and custodial responsibilities for a library should require only a small addition in time and training for data administrators. Installation and use of the workstation portion of library services should be easy given only 'shrink wrap' materials, without help from specialists.

— *Joining libraries to other databases:* People want easy use of library data in unanticipated ways, joining library catalogues to enterprise databases and combining data across agencies and sometimes across administrative jurisdictions. People want to do particular correlations on short notice and with low cost.

— *Application independence:* The utility of stored data is hampered by anything that tailors it to one application or one usage paradigm in preference to alternatives. Cataloguing documents is economical primarily under the presumption of future pertinence to multiple, unanticipated applications.

— *Open subsystem:* Emerging workstation application packages—text, graphic, image, and audio editors, spreadsheets, CAD packages, and industry support packages such as those for hospitals and for doctors offices—are potential sources and sinks for large numbers of electronic documents.

— *Standard interfaces and protocols:* The previous requirements imply a long term commitment to an application programming interface for library services, and to how the storage system exploits underlying communication services.

## 1.2. Advantages of Digital Libraries

The advantages of digital libraries as a means of easily and rapidly accessing books, archives and images of various types are now widely recognized by commercial interests and public bodies alike.

Traditional libraries are limited by storage space; digital libraries have the potential to store much more information, simply because digital information requires very little physical space to contain it. As such, the cost of maintaining a digital library is much lower than that of a traditional library.

A traditional library must spend large sums of money paying for staff, book maintenance, rent, and additional books. Digital libraries may reduce or, in some instances, do away with these fees. Both types of library require cataloguing input to allow users to locate and retrieve material. Digital libraries may be more willing to adopt innovations in technology providing users with improvements in electronic and audio book technology as well as presenting new forms of communication such as wikis and blogs; conventional libraries may consider that providing online access to their OPAC catalogue is sufficient. An important advantage to digital conversion is increased accessibility to users. They also increase availability to individuals who may not be traditional patrons of a library, due to geographic location or organizational affiliation.

- *No physical boundary*. The user of a digital library need not to go to the library physically; people from all over the world can gain access to the same information, as long as an Internet connection is available.
- *Round the clock availability*. A major advantage of digital libraries is that people can gain access 24/7 to the information.
- *Multiple access*. The same resources can be used simultaneously by a number of institutions and patrons. This may not be the case for copyrighted material: a library may have a license for "lending out" only one copy at a time; this is achieved with a system of digital rights management where a resource can become inaccessible after expiration of the lending period or after the lender chooses to make it inaccessible (equivalent to returning the resource).
- *Information retrieval.* The user is able to use any search term (word, phrase, title, name, subject) to search the entire collection. Digital libraries can provide very user-friendly interfaces, giving clickable access to its resources.
- *Preservation and conservation.* Digitization is not a long-term preservation solution for physical collections, but does succeed in providing access copies for materials that would otherwise fall to degradation from repeated use. Digitized collections and born-digital objects pose many preservation and conservation concerns that analog materials do not.
- *Space.* Whereas traditional libraries are limited by storage space, digital libraries have the potential to store much more information, simply because digital information requires very little physical space to contain them and media storage technologies are more affordable than ever before.

— *Added value*. Certain characteristics of objects, primarily the quality of images, may be improved. Digitization can enhance legibility and remove visible flaws such as stains and discoloration

## 1.3. Problems of Digital Libraries

Technological standards change over time and forward migration must be a constant consideration of every library. Migration is a means of transferring an unstable digital object to another more stable format, operating system, or programming language.Migration allows the ability to retrieve and display digital objects that are in danger of becoming extinct. This is a rather successful short-term solution for the problem of aging and obsolete digital formats, but with the ever-changing nature of computer technologies, migration becomes this never-ending race to transfer digital objects to new and more stable formats. Migration is also flawed in the sense that when the digital files are being transferred, the new platform may not be able to capture the full integrity of the original object. There are countless artifacts sitting in libraries all over the world that are essentially useless because the technology required to access the source is obsolete. In addition to obsolescence, there are rising costs that result from continually replacing the older technologies. This issue can dominate preservation policy and may put more focus on instant user access in place of physical preservation.

Some people have criticized that digital libraries are hampered by copyright law, because works cannot be shared over different periods of time in the manner of a traditional library. The republication of material on the Web by libraries may require permission from rights holders, and there is a conflict of interest between them and publishers who may wish to create Web versions of their content for commercial purposes.

There is a dilution of responsibility that occurs as a result of the spread-out nature of digital resources. Complex intellectual property matters may become involved since digital material isn't always owned by a library. The content is, in many cases, public domain or self-generated content only. Some digital libraries, such as Project Gutenberg, work to digitize out-of-copyright works and make them freely available to the public. An estimate of the number of distinct books still existent in library catalogues from 2000BC to 1960, has been made

Some digital libraries acquire a license to "lend out" their resources. This may involve the restriction of lending out only one copy at a time for each license, and applying a system of digital rights management for this purpose.

The ability to find works of interest in large libraries is directly related to how well they are catalogued. While cataloguing electronic works digitized from a library's existing holding may be as simple as copying moving a record for the print to the electronic item, with complex and born-digital works requiring substantially more effort.While full text search can be used for some searches, there are many common catalog searches which cannot be performed using full text.

## References

Conway, Paul, *Preservation in the Digital World,* Washington, D.C.: Commission on Preservation and Access, 1996.

Fox, E. A., *Source Book on Digital Libraries*, Virginia Tech, Department of Computer Science, 1993.

Ioannidis Y. Digital libraries at a crossroads. *International Journal of Digital Libraries*, 5(4):255-265, August 2005.

Gopal Krishan, *Digital Libraries in Electronic Information Era*, Authorspress, New Delhi, 2000.

Rajashekar, T.B., *Digital Libraries, Information Studies,* October, 1995.

# 2

# Foundations of Digital Libraries

Digital Libraries represent the meeting point of many disciplines and fields, including data management, information retrieval, library sciences, document management, information systems, the web, image processing, artificial intelligence, human-computer interaction, and digital curation. This multidisciplinary nature has led to a variety of definitions as to what a Digital Library is, each one influenced by the perspective of the primary discipline of their proposer(s).

The concept of Digital Library has evolved substantially since the early idea of it as a system for providing access to digitised books and other text documents. The DELOS Network of Excellence on Digital Libraries, for example, now envisions a Digital Library as a tool at the centre of intellectual activity having no logical, conceptual, physical, temporal, or personal borders or barriers to information. Generally accepted conceptions have shifted from a content-centric system that merely supports the organisation and provision of access to particular collections of data and information, to a person-centric system that delivers innovative, evolving, and personalised services to users.

Conceptions of the role of Digital Libraries have shifted from static storage and retrieval of information to facilitation of communication, collaboration, and other forms of dynamic interaction among scientists, researchers, or the general public on themes that are pertinent to the information stored in the Digital Library. Moreover, expectations of the capabilities of Digital Libraries have evolved from handling mostly centrally located text to synthesising distributed multimedia document collections, sensor data, mobile information, and pervasive computing services.

This vision of Digital Libraries seems to resonate well with the concept of "Information Space" as established within the field of Computer Supported Cooperative Work (CSCW). Snowdon, Churchill, and Frecon have developed future visions about "Connected Communities" and "Inhabited Information Spaces", with the latter being closely related to the vision of Digital Libraries, in that ubiquitous information is a prerequisite for CSCW.

The variety of conceptions of what a Digital Library is has had a substantive impact on attempts to define and bound the term 'Digital Library'. Since 2006 the term has been generally used to refer to systems that are heterogeneous in scope and provide diverse types of functionality. These systems include digital object and metadata repositories, reference-linking systems, archives, content administration systems (mainly developed by industry), and complex systems that integrate advanced digital library services (mainly developed in research environments). This "overloading" of the term 'Digital Library' results in Digital Library services and systems that do not deliver interoperability and reuse of content and technologies.

Given the current level of maturity and substantial knowledge and experience that have been accumulated in recent years, the time is certainly ripe to lay the necessary foundations for overcoming these challenges by facilitating integration of relevant research results and improving system development methodologies. In order to respond to this need, and following the example of other IT research areas, the members of the DELOS Network of Excellence on Digital Libraries have published the Digital Library Manifesto.

The Manifesto establishes principles to underpin the field and lead to the development of reference documents that will capture the full spectrum of concepts playing a role in Digital Libraries. The Manifesto exploits the collective understanding of Digital Libraries developed by European research groups, including those that are partners in DELOS, and the results of DELOS working meetings.

## 2.1. DIGITAL LIBRARIES : THREE-TIER FRAMEWORK

A Digital Library is an evolving organisation that comes to existence through a series of development steps that bring together all necessary constituents.

Figure 2.1 presents this process pictorially and indicates three distinct notions of "systems" developed along the way: Digital Library, Digital Library System, and Digital Library Management System. These correspond to three different levels of conceptualisation of the universe of Digital Libraries.

*Figure 2.1. DL, DLS, and DLMS: A Three-tier Framework*

These three system notions are often confused and are used interchangeably in the literature; this terminological imprecision has produced a plethora of heterogeneous entities and contributes to making difficult the description, understanding and development of digital library systems.

As Figure 2.1 indicates, all three systems play a central and distinct role in the Digital Library development process. To clarify their differences and their individual characteristics, the explicit definitions that follow may help.

### 2.1.1. Digital Library (DL)

A possibly virtual organisation that comprehensively collects, manages, and preserves for the long term rich digital content, and offers to its user communities specialised functionality on that content, of measurablè quality and according to codified policies.

### 2.1.2. Digital Library System (DLS)

A software system that is based on a defined (possibly distributed) architecture and provides all functionality required by a particular Digital Library. Users interact with a Digital Library through the corresponding Digital Library System.

### 2.1.3. Digital Library Management System (DLMS)

A generic software system that provides the appropriate software infrastructure both (i) to produce and administer a Digital Library System incorporating the suite of functionality considered foundational for Digital Libraries and (ii) to integrate additional software offering more refined, specialised, or advanced functionality.

A Digital Library Management System belongs to the class of "system software". As is the case in other related domains, such as operating systems, databases, and user interfaces, DLMS software generation environments may provide mechanisms to be used as a platform to produce Digital Library Systems. Depending on the philosophy it follows, a DLMS belongs to one of the following three types:

— *Extensible Digital Library System*. A complete Digital Library System that is fully operational with respect to a defined core suite of functionality. DLs are constructed by instantiating the DLMS and thus obtaining the DLS. Thanks to the open software architecture, new software components providing additional capabilities can be easily integrated. The Delos DLMS is a prototypical example of a system based on this philosophy.

— *Digital Library System Warehouse*. A collection of software components that encapsulate the core suite of DL functionality and a set of tools that can be used to combine these components in a variety of ways (in Lego-like fashion) to create Digital Library Systems offering a tailored integration of functionalities. New software components can easily be incorporated into the Warehouse for subsequent combination with those already there.

BRICKS and DILIGENT are two prototypical examples of systems that are based on this philosophy.

— *Digital Library System Generator*. A highly parameterised software system that encapsulates templates covering a broad range of functionalities, including a defined core suite of DL functionality as well as any advanced functionality that has been deemed appropriate to meet the needs of the specific application domain. Through an initialisation session, the appropriate parameters are set and configured; at the end of that session, an application is automatically generated, and this constitutes the Digital Library System ready for installation and deployment. The MARIAN framework equipped with the 5SL specification language represents an example of this process.

Although the concept of Digital Library is intended to capture an abstract system that consists of both physical and virtual components, the Digital Library System and the Digital Library Management System capture concrete software systems. For every Digital Library, there is a unique Digital Library System in operation (possibly consisting of many interconnected smaller Digital Library Systems), whereas all Digital Library Systems are based on a handful of Digital Library Management Systems. For instance, through DILIGENT it is possible to build and run a number of DLSs, each realising a DL serving a target community. The DL is thus the abstract entity that "lives" thanks to the software system constituting the DLS.

## 2.2. Digital Libraries Universe

Despite the seeming richness and diversity of existing digital libraries, in actuality, there is only a small number of core concepts defined by all systems. These concepts are identifiable in nearly every Digital Library currently in use. They serve as a starting point for any researcher who wants to study and understand the field, for any system designer and developer intending to construct a Digital Library, and for any content provider seeking to expose its content via digital library technologies.

Six core concepts provide a foundation for Digital Libraries. Five of them appear in the definition of Digital Library: Content, User, Functionality, Quality, and Policy; the sixth one emerges in the definition of Digital Library System: Architecture. All six concepts influence the Digital Library framework.

### 2.2.1. Content

The Content concept encompasses the data and information that the Digital Library handles and makes available to its users. It is composed of a set of information objects organised in collections. Content is an umbrella concept used to aggregate all forms of information objects that a Digital Library collects, manages, and delivers, and includes primary objects, annotations, and metadata. For example, metadata have a central role in the handling and use of information objects, as they provide information critical to its syntactic, semantic, and contextual interpretation.

### 2.2.2. User

The User concept covers the various actors (whether human or machine) entitled to interact with Digital Libraries. Digital Libraries connect actors with information and support them in their ability to consume and make creative use of it to generate new information. User is an umbrella concept including all notions related to the representation and management of actor entities within a Digital Library. It encompasses such elements as the rights that actors have within the system and the profiles of the actors with characteristics that personalise the system's behavior or represent these actors in collaborations.

### 2.2.3. Functionality

The Functionality concept encapsulates the services that a Digital Library offers to its different users, whether classes of users or individual users. While the general expectation is that DLs will be rich in capabilities and services, the bare minimum of functions would include such examples as new information object registration, search, and browse. Beyond that, the system seeks to manage the functions of the Digital Library so that they reflect the particular needs of the digital library's community of users and/or the specific requirements relating to the information resources it contains.

### 2.2.4. Quality

The Quality concept represents the parameters that can be used to characterise and evaluate the content and behavior of a Digital Library. Quality can be associated not only with each class of content or functionality but also with specific information objects or services. Some of these parameters are objective in nature and can be automatically measured, whereas others are subjective in nature and can only be measured through user evaluations (e.g., focus groups).

### 2.2.5. Policy

The Policy concept represents the set or sets of conditions, rules, terms and regulations governing interaction between the Digital Library and users, whether virtual or real. Examples of policies include acceptable user behavior, digital rights management, privacy and confidentiality, charges to users, and collection delivery. Policies belong to different classes; for instance, not all policies are defined within the DL or the organisation managing it. The policy concept supports the distinction between extrinsic and intrinsic policies. The definition of new policies and re-definition of older policies will be a feature of Digital Libraries.

### 2.2.6. Architecture

The Architecture concept refers to the Digital Library System entity and represents a mapping of the functionality and content offered by a Digital Library onto hardware and software components. There are two primary reasons for having Architecture as a core concept: (i) Digital Libraries are often assumed to be among the most complex and advanced forms of information systems; and (ii) interoperability across Digital Libraries is recognised as a substantial research challenge. A clear architectural framework for the Digital Library System offers ammunition in addressing both these issues effectively.

The concepts of Content, User, Functionality, and Policy share many similar characteristics and are all concepts referring to internal entities of a Digital Library that can be sensed by the external world. Introducing the Resource concept, which subsumes the above four, enables us to reason about these characteristics in a consistent manner.

The six core concepts (Content, User, Functionality, Quality, Policy and Architecture) that lie at the heart of DLs need to be considered in conjunction with the four main ways that actors interact with digital library systems.

## 2.3. Main Actors of Digital Library Systems

We envisage actors interacting with Digital Library Systems playing four different and complementary roles: DL End-Users, DL Designers, DL System Administrators, and DL Application Developers.Each role is primarily associated with one of the three "systems" in the three-tier framework.

### 2.3.1. DL End-Users

DL End-Users exploit the DL functionality for the purpose of providing, consuming, and managing the DL Content and some of its other constituents. They perceive the DL as a stateful entity serving their functional needs. The behavior and output of the DL depend on the DL's state at the time a particular part of its functionality is activated. The state of the DL corresponds to the state of its resources, consists of the collections of information objects managed by the DL, the set of authorised users, the DL's functionality, and its set of policies. This state changes during the lifetime of the Digital Library according to the functionality activated by users and their inputs. DL End-Users may be further partitioned into Information Creators, Information Consumers, and Librarians.

### 2.3.2. DL Designers

DL Designers exploit their knowledge on the semantics of the application domain in order to define, customise, and maintain the Digital Library so that it is aligned with the information and functional needs of its potential DL End-Users. To perform this task, they interact with the DLMS providing functional and content configuration parameters. Functional parameters instantiate aspects of the DL functionality that are to be perceived by the DL End-Users, including the characteristics of the result set format, query language(s), user profile formats, and document/data model employed. Content configuration parameters specify third-party resources exploited by the specific DL, e.g., repositories of content, ontologies, classification schemas, authority files, and gasetteers. The values of these parameters configure the way the DL will be presented to the DL End-Users, because they determine the particular Digital Library System instance serving the Digital Library. Of course, these parameters need not necessarily be fixed for the entire lifetime of the DL; they may be reconfigured to enable the DL to respond to the evolving expectations of users and changes in all aspects from policies to content.

### 2.3.3. DL System Administrators

DL System Administrators select the software components necessary to construct the Digital Library System. Their choice of elements reflects the expectations that DL End-Users and DL Designers have for the Digital Library, as well as the requirements that the available resources impose on the definition of the DL. DL System Administrators interact with the DLMS by providing architectural configuration parameters, such as the chosen software components and the selected hosting nodes. Their task is to identify the architectural configuration that best fits the DLS in order to ensure the highest level of quality. The values of the architectural configuration parameters can be changed over the DL lifetime. Changes of configuration parameters may result in the provision of different DL functionality and/or different quality levels.

### 2.3.4. DL Application Developers

DL Application Developers develop the software components of DLMSs and DLSs, to ensure that the appropriate levels and types of functionality are available.

The four roles described above encompass the whole spectrum of actors interacting with digital libraries. Their models of the DL Universe are linked together in a hierarchical fashion. This hierarchy is a direct consequence of the above definitions, since DL End-Users act on the Digital Library, whereas DL Designers, DL System Administrators and DL Application Developers operate on the DLMS and, consequently, on the DLS and DL as well. This inclusion relationship ensures that co-operating actors share a common vocabulary and knowledge. For instance, the DL End-User expresses requirements in terms of the DL model and, subsequently, the DL Designer understands these requirements and defines the DL accordingly.

## 2.4. Reference Frameworks

The digital library universe is complex and comprises multiple elements. The representation of the details of these elements depends upon the introduction of frameworks supporting different levels of abstraction:

— *Reference Model.* As stated in, "A Reference Model consists of a minimal set of unifying concepts, axioms and relationships within a particular problem domain, and is independent of specific standards, technologies, implementations, or other concrete details". Digital libraries need to obtain a corresponding Reference Model in order to consolidate the diversity of existing approaches into a cohesive and consistent whole, to offer a mechanism for enabling the comparison of different DLs, to provide a common basis for communication within the DL community, and to help focus further advancement.

— *Reference Architecture.* The Reference Architecture is an architectural design pattern indicating an abstract solution to implementing the concepts and relationships identified in the Reference Model. There may be multiple Reference Architectures that indicate how to design Digital Libraries Systems built on the Reference Model.

— *Concrete Architecture.* At this level, the Reference Architecture is actualised by replacing the mechanisms envisaged in the Reference Architecture with concrete standards and specifications. For example, a Concrete Architecture may specify that the run-time environment deployed on the hosting nodes will be CORBA or the Web Services Application Framework, and that four specific communicating Web Services will implement the Search functional component.

## References

Borgman C.L. What are digital libraries? Competing visions. *Information Processing and Management*, 35(3):227-243, 1999.

Del Bimbo, A.; Gradmann, S.; Ioannidis, Y. (Eds.) *Future Research Directions*. 3rd DELOS Brainstorming Workshop Report, Corvara, Italy, July, 2004.

Fox, E.A.; Akscyn, R.M.; Furuta, R.; Leggett, J.J. Digital Libraries. *Communications of the ACM*, 38(4):23-28, April 1995.

Fox, E.A.; Marchionini, G. Toward a Worldwide Digital Library. *Communications of the ACM*, 41(4):29-32, April 1998.

Gonçalves, M.A.; Fox, E. 5SL - A Language for Declarative Specification and Generation of Digital Libraries. In *Proceedings of the 2nd ACM/IEEE-CS Joint Conference on Digital Libraries (JCDL '02)*, Portland, Oregon, USA, 2002.

Ioannidis Y. (Ed.) *Digital Libraries: Future Directions for a European Research Programme*. DELOS Brainstorming Report, San Cassiano, Italy, June 2001.

# 3

# Building Digital Library

The library of the future will be digital and have the following features:

— contain all recorded knowledge online (billions of items)

— distributed, maintained globally

— accessible by:

  — any person

  — in any language

  — any time

  — anywhere on earth

  — via the Internet

— act as the information resource for the 21st Century

Building a digital library is a daunting challenge, involving a wide variety of technological, social and policy issues.

This notion of a digital library is radical; most current digital library efforts are aimed at building individual libraries to replace existing physical libraries that are burdened by financial and space constraints. However, the avowed digital library policy of Japan is that "each home will be able to access electronic libraries and electronic museums around the world via networks, allowing users to readily search and obtain worldwide information on books and art based on their own particular interests."

### 3.1. Digital vs. Traditional Libraries

The shift from traditional libraries to the digital is not merely a technological evolution, but requires a change in the paradigm by which people access and interact with information.

A traditional library is characterized by the following:

— emphasis on storage and preservation of physical items, particularly books and periodicals

— cataloging at a high level rather than one of detail, e.g., author and subject indexes as opposed to full text

— browsing based on physical proximity of related materials, e.g., books on sociology are near one another on the shelves

— passivity; information is physically assembled in one place; users must travel to the library to learn what is there and make use of it

By contrast, a digital library differs from the above in the following ways:

— emphasis on access to digitized materials wherever they may be located, with digitization eliminating the need to own or store a physical item

— cataloging down to individual words or glyphs

— browsing based on hyperlinks, keyword, or any defined measure of relatedness; materials on the same subject do not need to be near one another in any physical sense

— broadcast technology; users need not visit a digital library except electronically; for them the library exists at any place they can access it, e.g., home, school, office, or in a car

The total number of different books produced since printing began does not exceed one billion. If an average book occupies 500 pages at 2,000 characters per page, then even without compression it can be stored comfortably in one megabyte. Therefore, one billion megabytes are sufficient to store all books. This is $10^{15}$ bytes, or one petabyte. At commercial prices of $20 per gigabyte, this amount of disk storage capacity could be purchased for $20 million. So it is certainly feasible to consider storing all books digitally.

### 3.1.1. Databases

A database of a billion objects, each of which occupies one megabyte, is large but not inconceivable. Once one is comfortable with sizes of this kind, it is feasible to imagine a thousand such databases, or to envision them all as portions of the same global collection. This amount of storage is sufficient to house not only all books, but all of the following:

— photographs
— legislative material, court decisions
— museum objects
— recorded music
— theatrical performances, including opera and ballet
— speeches
— movies and videotape

### 3.1.2. Distributed Holdings

When information is digitized and accessible over a network, it makes little sense to speak of its "location," although it is technically resident on at least one storage device somewhere, and that device is connected to at least one computer. If the information is available at multiple mirror sites, it is even less meaningful to speak of it being in a "place." While traditional libraries measure their size by number of books, periodicals and other items held, the relevant statistic for a digital library is the size of the corpus its users may access. This means that digital libraries will want to expand their "holdings" by sharing digital links with other libraries. Unfortunately, there seems to be very little sharing of this sort taking place at present.

How can we understand the unwillingness of libraries to share content? The question goes back to the old measure of the size of a traditional library—the number of books it holds. When a library expends funds to assemble digitized works, it loses a portion of its prestige (or thinks it does) by allowing other libraries to copy or access its data. Ultimately, however, *all* material should be accessible from *every* library.

### 3.1.3. Gore's Digital Earth

In 1998, Vice President Gore stated that "A new wave of technological innovation is allowing us to capture, store, process and display an unprecedented amount of information about our planet and a wide variety of environmental and cultural phenomena.... I believe we need a 'Digital Earth.' A multi-resolution, three-dimensional representation of the planet, into which we can embed vast quantities of geo-referenced data". He then called on scientists to create a digital map of the earth at a resolution of one meter. Such a project will require technical innovation beyond that required even for a digital library containing every book ever written. The area of the earth in square meters is about 5 x $10^{14}$. Storing two megabytes of data per square meter (which would include terrain data, imaging, environmental and other pertinent information) will require $10^{18}$ bytes, an amount roughly equal to the amount of digital storage currently present on earth.

## 3.2. Digitization

Ultimately, everything that people are interested in accessing will have to be digitized. The reason is that digital searching will become so easy, inexpensive, fast and ubiquitous that users will not tolerate, or will not access, traditional materials. Capture requires a concerted, shared, worldwide effort. The cost of digitizing is not trivial, so it makes little sense for any work to be digitized more than once. Yet without any registry of digitized works, many books are digitized multiple times, while others are ignored.

Converting text, images and objects to digital form requires much more than digital photography or even high-resolution scanning and requires, instead, the following:

— initial input, either scanning or keyboarding
— conversion to one of a set of standard formats
— optical character recognition (OCR) to capture text characters for searching
— OCR correction (since OCR is inherently error prone)
— creation and input of metadata and cataloging information
— special techniques for non-textual materials, such as music, images, videotape, etc.

Policy issues, discussed below, will determine the resources made available for digitization and how they will be allocated.

If digital libraries are to become truly useful, they must assist users in making the transition from paper books to digital hypermedia. Many people report that they derive a high degree of comfort from books for the following reasons:

— *Portability.* Books can readily be carried, are compact, light in weight and comfortable to read. Anything you can't read in bed will never displace a book.

— *Reliability.* Reading books would still be possible even if every computer on earth were down.

— *Familiarity with the medium.* The pages of a book are easy to turn, the book can be opened to any page, and the linear hierarchical organization of the material is easy to grasp.

— *Low cost.*

— *Ability to annotate.* Comments and corrections can be written in a book; passages can be marked for emphasis or studying, and a book can be resold to recover costs.

A move to electronic libraries will alter the fundamental role of librarians. Far less attention will be paid to acquisitions, cataloging and circulation, and much more to systems, online assistance, navigation assistance and conversion issues. Unless graduate programs for digital librarians are established to create trained personnel, the real risk exists that users, particularly young adults who grew up in a digital generation, will outstrip the ability of librarians to assist them.

## 3.3. E-BOOKS

It will be impossible to displace paper books if reading digital ones is inconvenient. In fact it is likely that an electronic book will have to offer significantly more capability than a paper one to gain wide acceptance. Toward this end, several manufacturers are developing E-books which attempt to mimic the essential features of traditional books while providing huge advantages, such as the ability to store 1,000 electronic books in the space of one paper book and keep the user's place in each.

The worldwide ecological burden imposed by paper books is immense. Tremendous energy and human resources are required to grow and harvest trees, convert them to paper, print and bind books, transport them to warehouses, maintain bookstores and ship the books from the warehouses to the bookstores. The processes of making paper and ink release noxious chemicals, to say nothing of the fuel required to transport boxes of books all over the world. All of this is done merely to disseminate information that could be disseminated electronically with far greater speed and efficiency.

The chief technical barrier to E-books at present is that they do not capture the familiar feel of paper volumes. When this problem is solved, we will then have to face the issue of how content is downloaded to them and paid for.

## 3.4. INTEROPERABILITY

Given that numerous libraries around the world will be developing digital collections, how will it be possible for a user of library A to access and view material housed in library B? The existence of numerous digital libraries will make it essential to share digitized items and ensure that cataloging, searching and retrieval tools at each one can be used readily with materials from others.

### 3.4.1. Formats and Standards

While standards may have the effect of inhibiting innovation, they are essential to interoperability. Agreement must be achieved on such fundamental issues as how text is to be stored. Is it straight ASCII, Microsoft Word, HTML, SGML, XML or something else? What kind of compression will be used? If text is compressed, how will searching be done? How are images, music and videotape to be represented? If agreement is not reached, at least the number of different ways in which works are digitized should be reduced to a number small enough to allow each library to support them.

Digital libraries must also have a second set of intake standards, going not to technology but to quality and reliability, which are discussed later on. Archivists question the permanence of digital materials since they note that electronic documents can be modified readily and the media on which they reside become obsolete at least once each decade. The question then is how an ever-expanding corpus of information will be converted to new media and formats as these evolve.

### 3.4.2. Metadata

This term is often used to mean information *about* an item, rather than the information in the item itself. Examples include the author, title, date of acquisition, price paid, donor, etc. It is particularly critical to capture metadata that is not present in or derivable from the item. For example, the author's date of birth is often not printed in a book but can be important in distinguishing among authors with similar names (particularly parents and children). Libraries may "share" content by simply providing links, but uniform access to the content requires uniform metadata and a procedure for generating and storing it economically. It is of little avail to exchange documents at light speed if they must be held up for months until a human cataloger can prepare metadata.

### 3.4.3. Character Set Representations

This is not merely a question of different alphabets and writing systems, a major hurdle in itself, but also an issue of how characters are represented. For example, there are several widely differing mappings of Chinese characters into ASCII. There is some appeal to having a worldwide universal standard, such as Unicode, but the notion of attempting to list all of the world's glyphs and freeze them in a standard reduces flexibility and tends to overlook obscure or variant writing systems and restrict the development of new ones. Possibly a standard should be developed that permits new character sets so long as the definition of the glyphs and the representation mapping is maintained in an accessible location.

## 3.5. Scalability

A major problem encountered in digital library development is scalability—the expansion of system capabilities by many orders of magnitude. For example, a Web site, even one with huge capacity, may be choked if many people access it at the same time. Assuming that before long approximately a billion people will be able to connect to the Internet, if only one percent of them are interested in a topic (a number that is far too low for subjects of global concern such as the death of Princess Diana), that is a collection of 10 million people. If a server requires 100 milliseconds to grant access to a Web page, then the population would have to wait 12 days for everyone to see the same page. Therefore, technology that seems instantaneous when used on a small scale may become impossibly cumbersome when expanded.

One can imagine speeding up access to a page by adding more servers in response to anticipated demand, but even this numerical solution does not scale. If the problem is delivery of an HDTV movie (which takes 10 seconds to download at 10 gigabits per second), distributing the film to even one million people (a tenth of a percent of anticipated net users and fewer than the attendance at a major film during its first weekend of release), would require 120 days. Increasing the number of servers by an order of magnitude would not make the delay even remotely tolerable.

Bandwidth scalability is largely a hardware and networking problem. Keyword searching presents a problem of an entirely different sort. The commercial Web searchers now index approximately 50 million documents. A search can easily return 1,000 hits. This is a number small enough that a user could consider glancing at all of them to find what he wants. If the corpus being searched contained 50 billion pages (less than the number of pages in all books), a search might return a million hits, which would instead require a lifetime of effort to review. Therefore, building a digital library index, particularly one to be shared among many libraries, is not simply a matter of building a large one. Access methods, screening and navigation tools must also be provided.

Even if a library has a few million books, its staff members can be generally familiar with the nature and extent of its holdings. A library with a billion books and several billion other items would be qualitatively different and probably beyond the ability of any person to master. The sheer volume of transactions, catalog records, new acquisitions and help requests would be overwhelming. This is particularly true if the library permits access by computer programs as well as humans. It is apparent then that new organizational concepts on a grand scale will be required if digital information systems are to scale properly.

## 3.6. Digital Library Systems

A digital library "system" is composed of multiple hardware and software components, including the following:

— scanners
— computers and servers
— storage devices
— media
— catalogs
— converters
— networks
— displays
— multimedia interfaces
— usage measurement software
— human processing procedures
— reference assistants

All of the above are interconnected through networks and gateway software and must be designed for scalability, interoperability and reliability. This is a daunting challenge, particularly since the technology in many of the areas is changing rapidly. A system that uses one speech recognition system for input must be designed so that the recognizer can be replaced with another very quickly. Otherwise, the digital library, potentially one of the most responsive and useful systems in the world, can become fossilized.

## 3.7. Search

The problem of locating items in libraries is frequently referred to as "search," although that word tends to imply that one knows in advance what one is looking for, and possesses handles, indicators or index terms to serve as finding aids. This narrow view ignores the activity of browsing or even the higher-level function of becoming acquainted in general with a library's holdings. Browsing in a traditional library is a physical activity-it involves scanning shelves on which related works have been placed in proximity, and occasionally withdrawing them from the shelves for examination. Browsing in a digital library is a logical activity mediated by a computer. It does not require physical proximity in any sense; indeed, two consecutive items examined may be stored on different continents. The question, then, is how can a library user (not to say the library staff) become familiar with the whole of recorded human information in a way that makes it accessible and useful?

We adopt the term "navigation" to mean moving about in a digital collection. Search is a directed form of navigation in which the goal is defined in advance with reasonable clarity. The result of a search may be an item, a collection of items, or any part of an item, even down to a single glyph. Tools must be provided that enable users to move about at varying levels of granularity within the corpus.

The usual requirement for a search is that the user is looking for a specific piece of information or a summary of what is available about a certain topic. A common case is that the user wants the answer to a specific question, such as when the postcard was invented. Only rarely does such a question translate naturally into a keyword query. Such retrieval is indirect in the sense that the user wants to learn A, but formulates a query B, to which he receives a set of retrieved documents that must be scanned to determine whether the answer to A is among them. It would be far better simply to allow the user to ask question A instead of requiring him to convert it to some query language.

### 3.7.1. Non-Textual Matter

The existence of Web searchers proves that text can be searched without being indexed or cataloged. At least on a microscopic level, documents can be located purely by their content. Many documents consist of text plus other information such as mathematical equations, tables and drawings that themselves cannot be searched directly but can often be located by the presence of related text. Purely non-textual matter is very different. Although substantial progress is being made on video searching (through the use of extensive captioning cues, speech recognition and other aids), content searching of music and visual materials is non-existent or in its infancy. The problem is further complicated by the existence of work that combines media in various ways.

### 3.7.2. Translingual Issues

Most library items, particularly in non-English-speaking countries, are not in English. The central translingual library question is how users may navigate through materials in foreign languages and make effective use of them. Translingual search is currently a research problem for which obvious solutions do not work. A keyword search cannot be made multilingual merely by translating the keywords one at a time. The number of possible translations of each word may be very large, so an explosion in the number of hits may result. This approach also takes no account of idiomatic uses, untranslatable words such as particles, and numerous other language-related phenomena.

An interim solution is the use of translation assistants-programs that offer dictionary entries or partial or suggested translations of text portions. These show great promise for users who are at least partially familiar with the language of the retrieved document.

### 3.7.3. Synthetic Text

A user who is looking for general information on a particular topic is constrained in traditional libraries to go to an encyclopedia (which may have no entry or an outdated one on the topic of interest) or to refer to books that are generally about the subject under consideration. The time necessary for the user to obtain an overview at the appropriate level may be large because of the volume of repetitive material obtained. Programs are needed that are able to scan hits with the particular query in mind and produce abstracts, summaries, translations or analyses of the retrieved material.

## 3.8. Information Reliability

It seems inevitable that the class of works available through digital libraries will include electronic-only publications, ephemeral and unreviewed materials and even fabricated or counterfeit matter. The ease of publishing on the Internet combined with the absence of traditional methods for evaluating reliability makes it likely that library users will be retrieving works of questionable authenticity and value. Issues concerning the Internet and digital materials include:

— *Reliability*. How can a user (or an automated agent) evaluate the reliability of digital materials? What information must be maintained about the source of the item and its creator to facilitate a decision?
— *Version control*. How can changes made to a document be tracked and the appropriate catalog entries updated?
— *Archiving*. What assurance can there be that the digital materials will be retained somehow in their original form for an indefinite period?
— *Authenticity*. How can the genuineness of materials be assured?
— *Reviews*. The system should allow the user to scan reviews of the retrieved work and then add his own reviews or comments to a database.
— *Citations*. How may a user readily learn which works have cited the retrieved work, either favorably or unfavorably?

## 3.9. ECONOMICS

While a huge amount of material is in the public domain and may be freely assimilated into a digital library, the most valuable items are recent and protected by copyright. In order to induce copyright owners to allow their content to be accessed or downloaded from digital libraries, mechanisms need to be developed to compensate them appropriately. In the most extreme case, an author might himself produce but a single electronic copy of a work. In order to justify his effort, he might have to sell it for $100,000. Such a sale would be impossible if the buyer were not able to charge for use of the material, and in fact charge enough to make a profit.

Fortunately, digital libraries theoretically permit precise measurement of the use made of content. A secure browser, for example, might prevent copying, printing or retransmission of material. Automated permission systems can be developed whereby users can pay directly for certain kinds of licenses. These in turn require metadata concerning the collection of rights the library has obtained for the item.

However, the implementation of charging requires another paradigm shift. The cost of building and maintaining traditional libraries is borne by governments, foundations and corporations, but hardly ever by individuals directly. Usage of materials is free, despite the high cost of maintenance. Note that authors receive substantial money on account of libraries, because currently each library that wants a book must purchase a copy of it, and the authors of popular books receive large royalties. In the digital world, the following are necessary to preserve this revenue stream:

— centralized organizations finance

— subscription fees

— fees for individual use

## References

Gore, Albert. The digital earth: Understanding our planet in the 21st century. Speech delivered at the California Science Center, Los Angeles, California. January 31. 1998.

Ioannidis, Y.; Maier, D.; Abiteboul, S.; Buneman, P.; Davidson, S.; Fox, E.; Halevy, A.; Knoblock, C.; Rabitti, F.; Schek, H.; Weikum, G. Digital library information-technology infrastructures. *International Journal of Digital Libraries*, 5(4):266-274, August 2005.

MacKenzie, M.; Laskey, K.; McCabe, F.; Brown, P.; Metz, R. *Reference Model for Service Oriented Architecture*. OASIS Committee Draft 1.0, February 2006.

Șchek, H.-J.; Schuldt, H. DelosDLMS - Infrastructure for the Next Generation of Digital Library Management Systems. *ERCIM News*, No. 66, July 2006.

Snowdon, D.N.; Churchill, E. F.; Frecon, E. (Eds.) *Inhabited Information Spaces - Living with your Data*. Springer, London 2004.

MITI. *Program for advanced information infrastructure*. Japan Ministry for International Trade and Industry. May. 1994.

# 4

# Digital Library Architecture

The purpose of a digital library is to provide coherent organization and convenient access to typically large amounts of digital information. The following principles provide working definitions of a digital library from both a conceptual and a practical standpoint:

— A digital library is an integrated set of services for capturing, cataloging, storing, searching, protecting, and retrieving information.

— Digital library services bring order where data floods and information mismanagement have caused much critical information to be incoherent, unavailable, or lost.

— Digital library architecture emphasizes organization, acquisition, preservation, and utilization of information.

— Digital library systems are realizations of an architecture in a specific hardware, networking, and software situation.

## 4.1. Capabilities of Digital Library Systems

Digital library systems compose a family of automated systems that together provide a comprehensive capability to manage the digital content of an enterprise. It is useful to divide the capabilities of digital library systems into the following areas:

— capture or creation of content

— indexing and cataloging (metadata)

— storage

— search and query
— asset and property rights protection
— retrieval and distribution

Content exists in multiple sizes, formats, and media, each with accompanying technical challenges. Content may be structured or unstructured. It may have exact, precise meaning; or it may be fundamentally ambiguous. Content may directly or indirectly support a business process or function.

A digital library architecture shows how capabilities are realized and related, and does this at several levels. Digital library architectures show how business processes or functions are enhanced; they show how technology components fit together and how, in detail, components interoperate with each other.

Such functions and relationships, when reduced to a particular software and hardware implementation, lead to operational digital library systems.

## 4.2. Digital Library Functions

Digital library functions, insofar as they purport to organize information, may be compared with traditional library functions. Consider digitization, which technically is the conversion of analog to digital formats. A common human artifact, such as a bound book, loses value when simply scanned into bits. In a library context, where organization, access, protection, and preservation are important business functions, digitization technologies are starting points for a complicated set of computational processes that in the first instance reconstruct the cultural, conventional, and intuitive significance, structure, and external relationships that defined the original artifact. Additionally, digitization and other processes may be able to add value and support certain fiduciary responsibilities that resemble functions of traditional libraries.

In a similar way, other core capabilities of traditional libraries can be transposed to the digital domain. Cataloging is transposed to the generation of metadata, and is an area where much work needs to be done to develop automated, multidimensional indexing and cataloging procedures. Just as the public card catalog is a gateway to the holdings of a conventional library, search of content and metadata is the gateway to a digital library. Circulation in a conventional library transposes to network access, retrieval and delivery.

The fiduciary responsibilities of traditional libraries are related to issues of copyright protection and intellectual property rights. Table 4.1 relates digital library capabilities to well-known capabilities of traditional libraries. The point is that traditional libraries have established uniform business processes and highly interoperable data formats which support especially bibliographic catalogs, item ordering, and interlibrary loan. Although many of these procedures pre-date "digital" libraries, digital library design can benefit from the comparisons.

*Table 4.1. Comparison of Digital and Traditional Library Capabilities*

| Digital Library Capability | Traditional Library Capability |
|---|---|
| Capture | Acquisitions and collection development |
| Catalog and Index | Cataloging rules and bibliographic control |
| Store | Stacks, inventory management and shelf lists |
| Search | Public card catalog |
| Protect | Patron privileges and circulation rules consistent with public law and policy |
| Retrieve | Loan management and interlibrary loans |

Having made these comparisons, it must be emphasized that neither in the United States nor in Japan is the digital library regarded as a technology related to library automation or the provision of integrated library systems for operating traditional libraries. None of the digital library projects visited in Japan either utilized or were based on library automation technologies. On the contrary, the panel saw digital library technologies, which very strikingly enabled the digital library capabilities enumerated in this chapter, creating new lines of business in both public and private endeavors.

## 4.3. Architecture for Digital Libraries

In the following paragraphs an architectural approach to the digital library will be developed, which is based on taking the fundamental capabilities, introduced above, as the fundamental requirements the architecture must satisfy. We begin with the following notional architecture for digital libraries:

— A digital library approach to information management depends fundamentally upon a distinction between data and metadata. Metadata provide external classifying and organizing relations for data that may be unstructured, complex, or very large.
— Middleware services such as search, asset protection, and retrieval processes depend on metadata. Since metadata refers to data, which may be stored in separate hierarchical storage subsystems, integrity of reference must be maintained between metadata and data.

Figure 4.1 illustrates these fundamental distinctions between data management and metadata management, and between ingestion and utilization of content.

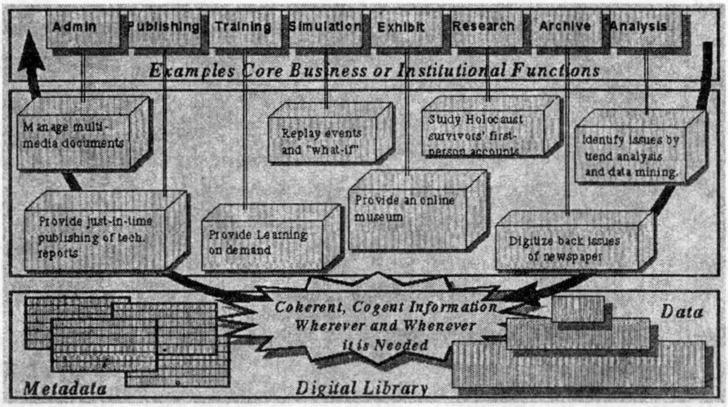


*Fig. 4.1. Notational architecture—building blocks of information to enhance existing functions and enable new operational capabilities.*

### 4.3.1. Operational Architecture

Operational architecture is an information management system represented in terms of the business processes it supports, and how information related to conduct of the business processes passes through the system's components.

The example shown in Figure 4.2 is an enterprise that conducts training by utilizing an extensive computer-based simulation system. The operational (business) processes, most obvious in the example, depend on the timely and well-organized capture of training information as it happens, and both contemporaneous and retrospective search and retrieval of information from a training event. Although the information is generated in several different enterprise domains (eight in the example), effective utilization of information often depends on cross-domain searches and retrievals. Therefore, digital library services must provide information interoperability in middleware.

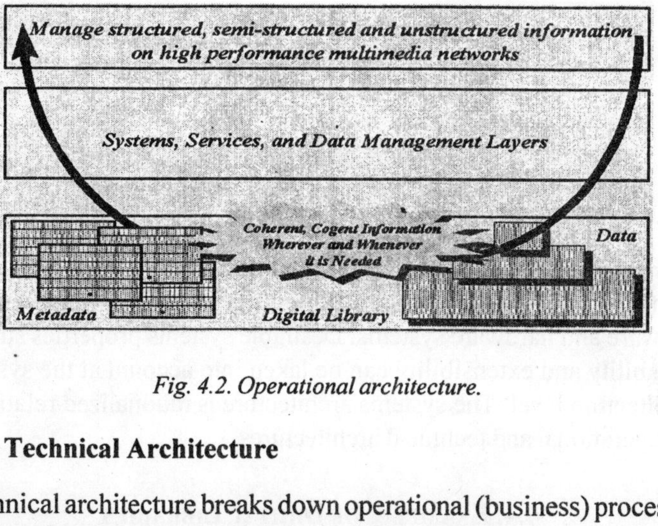


*Fig. 4.2. Operational architecture.*

### 4.3.2. Technical Architecture

A technical architecture breaks down operational (business) processes into functional components and capabilities (Figure 4.3). Hardware and software implementations are still not resolved.

The utilization of digital library materials depends on the existence of metadata to give an efficient and accurate view of content. Metadata must be created as content is added to the digital library. Metadata and data must be bound together logically, and there must be a robust underlying technology to manage the logical connection through time, across platforms, and over geographical separations, all on a networked, distributed system.

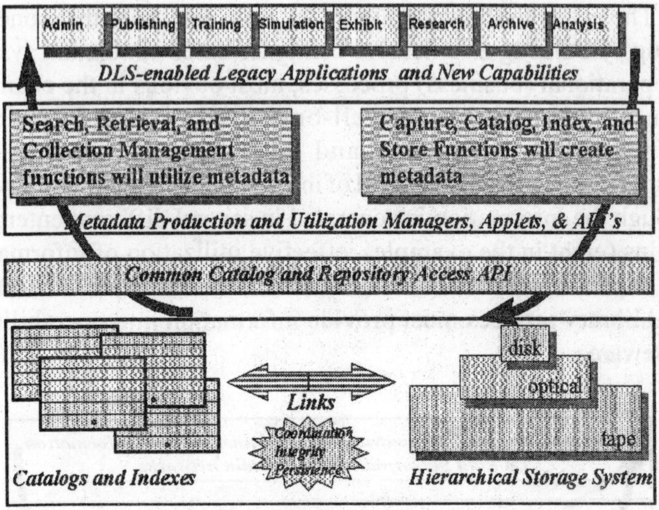


*Fig. 4.3. Technical architecture.*

### 4.3.3. Systems Architecture

A systems architecture shows the technology enablers and their interrelationships.A fully detailed systems architecture resolves into software and hardware systems. Desirable systems properties such as scalability and extensibility can be taken into account at the systems architecture level. The systems architecture is rationalized relative to the operational and technical architectures.

## 4.4. Examples of Digital Libraries

This section will show how specific examples of digital libraries in Japan align with the design principles and the reference model sketched. It will try to represent each case on its own terms, leaving general comparisons and evaluations until the end of the chapter.

### 4.4.1. Nara Institute of Science and Technology

This section begins with the digital library at the Nara Institute of Science and Technology (NAIST). NAIST's digital library is functional today and exhibits all the characteristics of the generic digital library reference architecture. The presence and management of both data and metadata is especially apparent in the NAIST technical and operational architectures. The reader is directed to the site visit reports for descriptive information about NAIST.

#### *4.4.1.1. Capture and Catalog*

The acquisition or capture process at NAIST is based on local conversion of print materials to digital form. Semi-automated means are used to prepare journals for scanning. For journals, article-level bibliographic data are produced; the articles are scanned and passed through optical character recognition systems for both English and Japanese texts. NAIST uses external cataloging services from NACSIS, a national service, which provides bibliographic records for many Japanese libraries.

#### *4.4.1.2. Protect*

NAIST does not use technologies beyond user login to protect content. NAIST relies on publisher agreements to manage copyright issues.

#### *4.4.1.3. Search and Distribution*

The NAIST interface for query and retrieval is mainly Web-based, but there are specialized video presentation and editing workstations.

NAIST's digital library mission subsumes traditional research library missions, and practically all library capabilities are partially or fully realized with digital technologies. NAIST includes all core capabilities of a digital library and was the most complete example of a digital library that we saw.

From an architectural standpoint, NAIST's digital library aligns with the reference model, with emphasis on multimedia as the content rather than an abstract content type such as "library holdings" or "library objects." Implementation is largely through integration of off-the-shelf components running on commercially available systems, servers, and networks.

NAIST's systems include five main subsystems and interconnections to campus and external networks:

— The input system includes capabilities to digitize materials, especially journals and technical literature. There are color and monochrome scanners, digital cameras, and microform conversion equipment, and capability to convert already digitized materials for storage and retrieval in the NAIST digital library.

— A video subsystem supports special conversion and delivery requirements for quality of service for video ingestion and playback. Commercial (SGI Challenge XL) equipment is used.

— The main storage subsystem is controlled by an SGI Challenge XL. A hierarchical storage system is used with hard disk, optical, and tape capacity.

— The retrieval subsystem includes World Wide Web serving, and some special client-server capabilities that utilize SGI Indy workstations.

— A business support subsystem manages the administrative computing for the digital library.

NAIST adopts mainline technologies and builds most digital library services upon a readily available commercial base. The panel did not find, however, that the NAIST digital library, or any other Japanese example was either built upon or extended the capabilities of conventional, commercial automated library systems. NAIST's operational concept is very advanced. Remarkably, NAIST's system implementation is very conventional.

**4.4.2. Nikkei (Nihon Keizai Shimbun)**

Nikkei demonstrates how digital library technologies provide support for new and expanded lines of business where information management is central to core business functions. Nikkei's systems illustrate the following principles:

— Nikkei has designed and built a comprehensive system for organizing digital information.

— The architecture and system design are driven by business processes.

— Well-managed digital information permits creation of new lines of business

— The recent history of Nikkei online services illustrates commercially viable scaling and market segmentation

The reader is directed to the site visit report for further details about the scope of Nikkei's newspaper and information businesses.

News gathering corresponds to the acquisition function of a digital library, but in the Nikkei situation, one sees that capture technologies, such as scanning, are secondary. Instead, the emphasis is on information gathering by a worldwide staff of reporters. The Nikkei automated systems are sharply focused on converting information into information-intensive products and services that are distributed via print, broadcast, and online media.

Nikkei has mastered the problem of building a system for management of digital information that can very easily adapt to new technologies (e.g., Internet). This achievement appears to derive from an operational architecture that is explicitly designed to re-purpose and leverage information that is derived from or complementary to the newspaper production system. But in leveraging its core capabilities, Nikkei is pursuing new lines of business, such as being the Japanese supplier of AOL.

#### *4.4.2.1. PLES*

PLES is the PaperLess Editing System that prepares material for publication. PLES processes the information produced by the worldwide staff of 1,400 reporters, data gathered from wire services, and other internal archival and current information resources. Interestingly, it uses a text-to-speech system for copyediting. It is believed that multi-modal editing (both listening and reading) is more accurate than simply reading copy. PLES also includes a complete graphics input system, including scanners and digital format conversions.

#### *4.4.2.2. ANNECS*

ANNECS is the computer-based publishing system. Not only does it perform typesetting and layout, but also routes its data to other Nikkei businesses. Nikkei's approach to leveraging and reuse of information works because they have digital information which can inter-operate with a variety of systems, and which can be effectively reused in other lines of business besides publishing.

Nikkei illustrates very clearly how interoperability in data and middleware can leverage information assets into many lines of business with different market targets, different selections of information, and different application-level interfaces and capabilities. The architectural and systems approaches seen in Nikkei information systems are the clearest and most advanced examples of digital library approaches to the organization of information for commercial purposes that the panel saw in Japan.

### 4.4.3. Japan's National Museum of Ethnology

Japan's National Museum of Ethnology is a leader in utilizing technology for many aspects of museum operations, which are detailed in the site report. The museum is a good example of systems and architecture because all technologies at the museum are specifically designed and implemented to automate or enhance internal museum procedures.

The museum utilizes 3D imaging and measurement technologies to partially automate the acquisition process. Digital library technologies are extending the capabilities of the museum, and over more than two decades, an elaborate local system to support museum functions has evolved, which features the following:

— digital library technology used to manage holdings of a museum
— support for:
  — online asset management
  — multimedia support for exhibition
  — indexing, cataloging, and search of scholarship
  — virtual collections for Internet communities
— example of a local museum solution

The museum's current systems design places technologies for individual museum functional capabilities such as video exhibits, kiosks, scholarship, asset management, and Internet on a high performance local network. This system is not designed as a single unified or comprehensive museum system. In that sense the design is conservative. However, the scale of the system relative to the museum's overall mission is very impressive, because nearly everything at the museum is strongly supported by technologies that map clearly to the digital library reference models.

#### 4.4.4. IBM Tokyo Research Global Digital Museum

One of the visions of digital library is global virtual collections. Working with the National Ethnographic Museum and the British Museum, IBM's Tokyo Research Laboratory has designed and implemented a global virtual museum focused on problems of K-12 museum education. The virtual museum includes the following characteristics:

— features architecture and system for worldwide virtual museum
— creates shared abstractions of collections that are managed differently
— focuses on K-12 museum education as a line of business

One of the problems a virtual collection must address is a data architecture that makes the different legacy systems of the various museums interoperable in the virtual collection space. The Global Museum Project defines data abstractions and user-level operations that allow teachers to create virtual collections for instructional purposes, and students to annotate, select, and present their own personal collections.

#### 4.4.5. Fujitsu Multimedia Library

Japan's technology providers are very focused on multimedia systems. Fujitsu's vision represents some of the architectural and systems issues that must be faced in order to build full-service, scaleable multimedia digital libraries, as indicated below:

— vision of modern system for scaleable multimedia management
— representative of technology companies seeking to provide core technologies at middleware level

From the top down, heterogeneous media requires changes in search and storage subsystems. Improvements in database technology for managing metadata must be complemented by advances in multimedia object stores. Multimedia distribution raises quality of service issues and requires resource management at the systems level. Finally, many device improvements will drive the multimedia library, especially devices that extend information management to new areas of internetworking, consumer electronics, home devices, and collaborative workspaces.

### 4.4.6. Japan's Second Generation Digital Library Project

In Japan, a second national digital library project is underway, funded by the Ministry of International Trade and Industry (MITI), and conducted by the Information Technology Promotion Agency (IPA) and Japan Information Processing Development Center (JIPDEC).

The purpose is to develop a reference architecture that will drive development and utilization of advanced technologies for information management. Only an overview of a preliminary version of the next generation architecture is considered here. The following bullets highlight main themes of the project:

— operate a private and public consortium
— build scaleable, distributed multimedia information management systems
— use advanced, standards-based technologies
— proceed as a consensus project (U.S. DLI-2 is competitive)

The reference model reflects modern multi-tier distributed systems architectures. It features messaging middleware, agent technology, multimedia databases, mobile agents, and CORBA distributed object management. The project is practical, and the plan calls for a prototype system in the next two years.

## 4.5. Future of Digital Systems

Advanced, mission-specific digital library systems are driving certain public institutions and commercial enterprises forward. These systems are usually part of a business process reengineering effort caused by rapid changes in the nature of information creation, consumption, and distribution technologies that affect core business functions and create new business opportunities. In these cases, architecture and systems are driven by business processes.

Individually, technology companies are doing exploratory work on components for integration into current systems, but also looking forward to new computing paradigms that imply fundamental changes in systems, particularly with respect to information access and distribution. In these cases, it is clear that the interest is in providing advanced core technologies that support many information technology market segments.

Libraries and museums, whose approach to information management in many ways inspires the technologies we saw, are split between those that are doing interesting, but limited demonstration or exploratory projects, and those that are aggressive "early adopters" with comprehensive visions and commitments to change the ways information is acquired, managed, and utilized in their environments. The library and museum sector featured many digitization projects, and offered numerous insights into the capture and cataloging subcomponents of an overall digital library system.

## References

Mitchell, A. M. & Surratt, B. E. *Cataloging and organizing digital resources: a how-to-do-it manual for librarians*. New York: Neal-Schuman Publishers. 2005.

Prudlo, M. E-archiving: an overview of some repository management software tools. *Ariadne*, 43. 2005.

Rhyno, A. *Using open source systems for digital libraries*. Westport, CT: Libraries Unlimited. 2004.

Rydberg-Cox, J. A. *Digital libraries and the challenges of digital humanities*. Oxford: Chandos Publishing. 2005.

Tedd, L. A. & Large, A. *Digital libraries: principles and practice in a global environment*. Germany: K.G. Saur. 2005.

Tennant, R. *Managing the digital library*. New York: Reed Press. 2004.

Theng, Y. L. & Foo, S., eds. *Design and usability of digital libraries: case studies in the Asia-Pacific*. Hershey, PA: Idea Group Publishing. 2004.

# 5

# Digital Library Tools

New technology is changing the world. The library has the opportunity to be at the forefront of that change through the development and use of technology. Three related tasks for library involvement in the 1990's are:

1. To upgrade existing services by making use of technology.
2. To plan and develop new services and products which make use of technology.
3. To study library users, anticipating and meeting their changing information needs.

To remain viable and competitive into the next millennium, the library must both meet the needs of users and maintain a favorable position relative to other information providers.

The key to the evolution of the library for the information age is not to introduce technology on the basis of technological criteria alone. It is necessary to consider the goals of the library and its users and then assess the appropriateness and utility of a given technology for achieving those goals.

The digital electronic library is not limited to books and periodicals. Services now offered by commercial information and entertainment industries are indicative of the information- intensive environment in which libraries operate and the changing needs and desires of their users.

The successful library of the twenty-first century will extend beyond the doors of one building. It will provide immediate access to a wide variety of print and electronic information resources when users need them.

Many libraries are already engaged in making use of technology to upgrade facilities, increase productivity, and provide better service to users. They offer, for example:

— Online catalog access via modem or computer network
— Access to periodical indexes, full text databases, and other data sets through the catalog or CD-ROM systems
— Coordination of other libraries' holdings records and bibliographic utilities in order to extend available resources and facilitate their exchange
— Management information systems (MIS) for improved library management and planning

As the digital electronic library emerges, it will become increasingly attuned to the information needs of its users. Electronic resources will supplement traditional print resources, and the library will be a center for access to new information services and products. Some areas of study and development for the near future include:

— Development of technology for management and communication:
  — email for internal and patron use
  — access to Bitnet/Internet mailboxes and other networking tools currently available only to academics or some corporations
— Development of technology for question answering and information retrieval
  — expert systems for reference questions
  — email access to specialists, with cooperation among libraries to maximize the expertise available to users
  — gateways to commercial information providers
  — systems to help users to choose the best information resource for their needs
— Investigation of the impact of technology on users
  — ongoing study of the impact of technology on users; assessment of technology effectiveness

- competition with commercial information services and the entertainment industry for some information services, such as public access to a wide range of commercial databases, or electronic "shopping"
- training of users for new technology
- rejection of technology for technology's sake, but openness to changes which better meet the needs of users

The upgrade of existing services and implementation of new services can not be accomplished without some difficulty. Of primary concern is insuring that technological solutions really meet the needs of users. It is also important to maintain reasonable cost, and reasonable payoff, for these investments. The library has the opportunity to be a leader of innovation for information resources. The digital electronic library of the future is not just a place to get a book or ask a reference question. It is a vital part of the information society.

## 5.1. Digital Storage Media

It is difficult to preserve all the different storage media, whether paper, tapes, video or discs, partly because knowledge about their durability is relatively limited. To this should be added the fact that the old media require some kind of playing device to access their contents, and these devices are disappearing from the market because there is less and less demand for them and spare parts cannot be found. Digitalisation of print, images and sound provides new opportunities for preservation and storage, but the durability of the digitised media is also an unknown quantity. It is, however, possible to provide access to the contents of documents in archives via digitalisation, thus avoiding the wear and tear on and possible damage to the original document. The digital media are really rather new, and no general regulations and standards for their use as preservation media have yet been established.

One of the first uses of computerisation was for the compilation of library catalogues. At first computers were used as a part of the printing process, and later they entered into the process of designing online catalogues. Large indexes and abstract publications have followed a similar path, going from print, to print via computer, to online and to CD-ROM. Computer technology has also led to the development of search tools such as citation indexes and concordances which are produced automatically.

A number of search processes, such as Boolean operators, have been developed and refined over the last few years. They are very expensive, as are the connect-time prices for the databases. For many libraries the prices are prohibitive and one of the ways to solve the problem is to write contracts between the vendors and all the libraries in a country or with large groups of non-commercial institutions. Such types of negotiations, which also cover vendors of electronic periodicals and other products, will be of growing importance to the information services institutions in the future.

The data storage capacity of computers has made it possible to store not only the bibliographic data on a publication, but the full text of the publication itself. Older, originally printed or even handwritten texts, are scanned and digitised, thereby making the works of great authors available to all. The texts can be read page by page or, by searching with a combination of words, certain parts can be selected. One of the major problems for the information services institutions in relation to full text documents, sound recordings and images is the complexity of copyright issues. In most countries, copyright regulations have developed over the centuries, and the use of printed material by libraries is adequately regulated for all parties. However, as far as the digital media are concerned, there are no such fixed practical arrangements, not only because of the short time they have been in existence, but also because of the difficulties of protecting against unlawful copying. Huge sums of money are involved in this area and private copying is very easy and fairly cheap as the technique is rather simple.

## 5.2. Use of ICTs

The use of computers is revolutionising working processes in libraries and archives, and the network of computers known as the internet, is a revolution of similar importance. It is now possible to retrieve information independently of time zones and geographical location, and to obtain the most uptodate information, because the printing and editing processes are either no longer necessary or have been considerably reduced. The system of e-mail provides a communication facility which, to a great extent, replaces the traditional mail and fax systems formerly used by institutions, thus saving time for the user.

The world wide web (WWW) can be regarded as a huge reference base, with all types of information available, either as metadata or full text, sound and images. Issues related to the illegal use of information technologies, more particularly the internet. The world wide web, which is one part of the internet, is useful in many daily activities involving the transmitting of information which in the past could be found only in print or by teletext. There are many kinds of useful sources of information for education and research on the internet. Such activities can be said to have laid the foundations for the worldwide electronic information and communication networks. Individual institutions also have the opportunity to create their own Websites to inform users about their services and to guide them through the organisation. Different Websites are linked together so that one entry or access point will lead on to several others. Libraries and their catalogues can also be accessed via the internet. The most recent *Online Public Access Catalogues (OPAC)* Directory, published in 1998, which is a guide to catalogues on the internet, contains 1,434 entries worldwide, but 888 are from the United States and most of the remainder from Australia, Canada, New Zealand and Western Europe. Developing countries and Eastern European countries have few or no entries.

The formation in the guide was collected in the spring of 1996, and since then the number of libraries with internet-accessible OPACs has grown considerably in Western Europe and Canada, Denmark, for example, had 11 entries in the 1998 guide, all of them university libraries. At the end of that year, there were more than 125 libraries with OPACs in Denmark, and among them, 75 public libraries.

The internet has made new activities possible. Electronic conferences or informal discussion groups can be arranged with limited or open access, and surfing on the net has become the equivalent of zapping on the television or browsing through the shelves in the library. The internet uses sensitive and vulnerable techniques, so there are many possibilities for malfunctioning to occur. This is particularly threatening for institutions serving a great number of users or involved in large and expensive programmes, such as mass digitisation, but can also have catastrophic consequences in small institutions.

The traffic on the internet and the number of Websites are growing exponentially and this leads to problems with queuing and unacceptable answering times. For the library and archive professions, there are other aspects of the world wide web which give rise to problems. The central issue with all electronic documents is that of authenticity. Is there any certainty on the internet that the document has in fact been produced by the author/ organisation that claims to have done so?

The second problem is that of searching in large quantities of data, because a search based on one or a few keywords easily leads to several thousand addresses. The search can be refined by using the tools developed for this purpose, such as Boolean operators, language or geographical limitations, provenance, etc. Problems will remain, however, because the internet is, from this point of view, completely anarchic. Large parts of it are unedited and there are no general rules about the use of vocabulary. Searching in the areas of education and research may result in a large number of opinion papers with no academic quality control whatsoever. Published material in print and other media have usually been through an academic, professional and economic selection process, but this is not true of individual home-made 'information' products.

Much development work needs to be carried out by the information profession to address the concept of selectivity. This, however, raises the problem of censorship versus confusion and uselessness.

The vision of gathering all human knowledge together in one place is very old and has existed in many civilisations: one example is the library of ancient Alexandria, and another the great encyclopaedic enterprises in the Arabic, Chinese and European civilisations. The aim is to achieve a total overview of the recorded knowledge, as with the Universal Decimal Classification system, or by means of one large computer. Recently and due to the growth of the internet, this vision has manifested itself once again in the form of the library without walls, or the virtual library.

The assumption is that everybody will obtain instant access to all recorded information in the world through the nearest library. This phenomenon has been described in several ways, and the term 'electronic library' has often been used. Unfortunately, this expression could equally well mean a large database or further developments in library automation, or applications of hypertext on the world wide web. The preferred term within the profession is the digital library, which is not just a name for a collection of digitised media. First of all, the term refers to a library, which is not necessarily in a particular building, but a systematic organisation where various professional operations, performed by a professional staff and directed towards specific user groups, are carried out. The collection or parts of it might be digitised and access to electronic and other networks provided.

One of the most important items in the digital library is metadata, which describe the contents and attributes of the library collection. They are important to the process of searching among millions of documents. The most prominent example here is the so-called 'Dublin Core' which defines 15 core elements to be used by authors as well as intermediaries. Another problem is naming, which means strings of characters that uniquely define digital objects and therefore form a part of the documents' metadata.

A system of naming must be permanent, and this means that a name cannot be bound up with a specific location. The creation of such a naming or identifier system is organisational, not technical, and different systems have been suggested. Examples are Persistent User Requirement Languages (PURLs) developed by the Online Computer Library Centre (OCLC), where a server looks up the corresponding Uniform Resource Location (URL) in a database; the Uniform Resource Name (URN) developed by the Internet Engineering Task Force (IETF) but still not in operation; and the Digital Object Identifier system (DOI) developed by the Association of American Publishers and the Corporation for National Research Initiatives. They all provide methods by which digital objects can be identified and accessed. Issues concerning the management of the intellectual property right have given impetus to the development of these systems.

National bibliographics are the cornerstones of the library system and they are facing many problems with electronic documents. Such documents do not have a permanent existence, and a hyper link may lead to an empty address. In principle, a similar problem can occur with printed material, when a card catalogue refers to a document which has been lost or stolen. But the problem takes on a completely new dimension on the web because of the large number of hyperlinks and the very transient nature of web pages. A recent pilot project in Sweden aims at testing methods of collecting, preserving and providing access to online electronic documents in a way that allows them to be regarded as published. This is done by taking a snapshot of the relevant Hypertext Markup Language (HTML) pages, but concerns only static electronic documents. The internet is not the virtual library, but constitutes an important part of it. In the library environment a slogan during recent years has been 'from collection to connection'. This is certainly a very precise description of the development, but the vision of the virtual or the digital library must include collection as well as connection.

The main reason for defining an information services sector is that there are several similarities in the tasks of the institutions therein and in the work of their staff. Archives preserve documents for future use; these items range from a unique rare manuscript to samples of mass documents such as census forms and tax reports. To this end, statistical sampling methods have been developed so that the number of items preserved is sufficient for various research purposes.

The intellectual, technical and administrative work and the classification and filing of documents have merged so that this profession has extended its range and expanded its systematic approaches. The person carrying out this work is usually called a records manager. Libraries, for their part, are collectors of printed material and have developed systems for retrieval through catalogues and classification systems. Library work also includes selection, when purchasing or weeding out. With a growing focus on users, networks such as union catalogues and inter-library loan systems have been developed. Such systems have been further developed by the use of ICTs. The third group, information service enterprises, has its roots in the documentation movement from the beginning of this century, and services to decisionmakers in business and industry are their main task. They use basically the same tools as libraries, but are highly focused on speed in the delivery of information; the use of ICTs responds very well to their needs.

All types of personnel in the three groups perform similar tasks in the management of their institution or enterprise. The common characteristic of the three areas, their institutions and their professionals, is that they are acting as intermediaries between documents (printed or electronic) and users. The ICTs have blurred the borderlines between the different types of documents. Computers are used for administrative purposes, and electronic networks have become more extensive, so that other types of institutions such as museums are also performing similar activities. This leads to professional specialists being replaced by generalists capable of mastering the ICTs, or by new professionals such as designers of home-pages and webmasters, who combine different specialities, which may include both aesthetic and information training.

A general trend in the development of relevant education for the sector is to put more emphasis on the ICTs, first of all on their use, but in several educational institutions on programming and technical skills as well. Computers are used in education and research in all fields, and students through their e-mail addresses and websites become adept in the regular use of technology and the opportunities it provides. Bibliography courses used to focus on printed bibliographies, supplemented with online databases. Now the situation has been reversed. Professional education also puts the emphasis on theory and methodology rather than practical skills, because developments are so rapid that the reality will change between the beginning and the end of an educational programme. Methodological knowledge for its part has longer durability and produces a more versatile workforce.

User friendliness is an important aspect of the ICTs, but there is still a strong need for user-education in libraries. Users must improve their skills in the digital systems and the different OPACSs should be designed not only for the professionals but also for ordinary users, whether they visit the library or have electronic access from their home or workplace. The changes in professional work and in the educational programmes are illustrated by the labels and titles used. For example, librarianship has changed to library science and further to library and or information science to information systems and information management, and those seeking employment in this area include webmasters and web designers. A number of new jobs have been created in the private and public sector for professionals who are capable of mastering ICT use. Moreover, their traditional background with its systematic approach is an advantage. Software developers, designers of information systems for all types of enterprises and organisations, consultants on internet issues, specialists in teaching and training and in marketing and sales, who work in the information institutions, are all a far cry from the traditional archivist or librarian.

The general trend is very much in favour of the information professions, but of course economic recession, whether local or more widespread, can call into question such optimistic future perspectives. It is nevertheless clear that the rapid development of ICTs will require the information professionals, like professionals in many other fields of activities, to commit themselves to lifelong education and require educational institutions and professional associations to develop adequate programmes and facilities.

The growth in the use of ICTs has some built in paradoxes. On the one hand, access to information and communication is becoming easier, and PCs are better, faster and cheaper. These factors may be considered as a global trend in democratisation. On the other hand, the development of technology, software and data processing requires more and more capital investment, and this is leading to global monopolies among producers and vendors. Another paradox stemming from the enhanced access to ICTs is the emergence of a new type of illiterates, those who have not grown up with the technology and are therefore at a disadvantage on the employment market. From this point of view, the use of a PC may be compared with the mastery of a foreign language which requires regular practice. Libraries can play an important role in fighting this form of illiteracy by giving all users access to PCs and to the networks. In some Western-European countries, there is an ongoing discussion about whether public libraries should give free access to the internet to all users.

The development of ICTs has taken place principally in the capitalist world and within the framework of capitalist economies. In this context, one driving force is the substitution of relatively expensive labour by machines, leading to reductions in the costs of production and services. However, developments are so rapid that there is a general lack of qualified personnel. This gives qualified groups of professionals opportunities for very good salaries and working conditions. As the ICTs spread to other parts of the world, such as Eastern Europe and developing countries, there will also be a lack of professionals in these regions and the situation may well get worse, if market forces tempt qualified personal to move to Western Europe and North America. Another issue here is that American English may achieve a more dominating position in international communication.

The quality of information raises the problem of retrieving relevant and accurate information among the millions of documents available on the internet. Some years ago, large databases were already nicknamed GIGO-systems ('garbage in/garbage out') and the problem has become more acute with the linking of all databases. This is one of the main issues which the information professionals of the future will have to tackle. The changeability of electronic documents presents the profession with further difficulties. Authencity must be defined if solutions to the problems of filing, retrieval and intellectual property rights are to be found. Librarians and software agents do work delegated to them by a user; both apply some expertise to the user's problem or need; and both work in the background, completing tasks for the user's information needs. Librarians are more than technicians. They are, it seems, information therapists who analyse problems as well as find answers.

## 5.3. Information Filtering

Information filtering is a process in which a filtering agent reads every document in an information stream and compares it to a set of interest profiles. If the document matches a profile, the filter sends it to the appropriate user's inbox or stores it somewhere for the user. The rest of the documents are filtered out. Librarians filtering information in three key ways: first, the act of selecting a database or databases. This choice established the constraints on the results and defined the search space, including the depth and breadth of the search. The second way is the act of choosing search terms and operators. Finally, when he/she eliminated false drops (noise) from the results, he/she is filtering the results the end user would see. Using his/her knowledge of the context of the information need and the profile he/she had constructed of the user, he/she will be able to identify applicable results for the physician, relevant to the specific context of this particular information need.

## 5.4. Information Packaging

Librarians do more than connect people to raw information: they use their expertise to help clients make sense of information. Librarians usually arrange search results and other information products into customised sets for their clients. Librarians can be seen as distributed, cooperative agents. They inform and negotiate with each other; cooperation is built into the fabric of library work. It is not too far-fetched to say that there is no such thing as a librarian who works truly alone: one-person libraries certainly exist, but that lone librarian works within a library community. Indeed, there is a real international community of librarians. For example, a librarian can connect to a library system called WorldCat and tell a client, within a couple of minutes, which libraries in the world own a certain book. Further, he/ she can, with a few key strokes, send a request to any one of those libraries asking to borrow that book for the client.

Librarians rely on each other in other activities: many librarians practise cooperative collection development. No one medical library, for instance, can afford to subscribe to all published medical journals. When considering a purchase, acquisitions staff check to see if that title is owned by a nearby library with whom they have a cooperative arrangement. Libraries communicate and share information to an amazing degree. Librarians are great users of internet mailing lists; some of the highest volume lists are those run by and for librarians. They are communicating all the time: via e-mail, phone, fax, and in person. By the very nature of work, they are collaborative creatures who communicate extensively and constantly. They distribute information, share documents, strategies, and innovations with each other. A single library can even be seen as a distributed system of agents: the reference librarian fields this inquiry, passes that one to the acquisitions staff; the systems librarian consults the clinical librarian. Each librarian acts autonomously with the frequently used option of consulting another librarian-agent. Within the library field, librarians efficiently share specialised knowledge and skills.

## 5.5. Digital Library Agents

Both human and software agents work in the background; much of the work of human library agents is invisible by design. Human agents make a point of making their jobs look easy. In a sense, that is part of the service they provide.Both human and software agents begin to achieve a goal or solve a problem by building a representation of the problem state. Software agents create this representation using knowledge representation techniques such as first order logic and predicate logic. Agents are goal-driven: they seek to solve a specific problem, fill a specific need. Context is all-important to both agents; objectives and rewards are situation-dependent. Each information act is meaningless if not carried out in relation to some specific goal. Both human and software agents possess certain domain information. Agents accomplish their work using some variation of a profile of the user. Agents seek to minimise work by load balancing and the efficient allocation of temporal, financial, and computational resources.

The work of both human and software agents is of an iterative nature. Much back and forth takes place in checking results. Both have as their goals efficiency and optimality. The mechanical agent uses artificial intelligence techniques to aim at optimally achieving its goal. Librarians aim for optimality by striving for relevant results obtained speedily and cost-efficiently. Both agents work in uncertain worlds. Their environments are dynamic and the agents themselves affect the information state. Human and software agents face many of the same challenges, concerns, and goals.

Intelligent software programmes all face the brittleness problem: how well do they function at a task outside their limited domain? They may excel at chess but flail when queried for obvious information. Librarians are rarely brittle: in fact, so agile at handling and finding way through information spaces that become far too modest. Flexibility from client request to client request is often staggering.

User acceptance of an agent is a very individual thing based on personal preferences, skill levels, and previous experience with an agent. Users have varying skill levels. Many prefer to delegate most of their information search tasks to a librarian; some prefer to search themselves. Some users will never feel comfortable with the results a software agent provides; other users prefer to deal with computers over people. Some users overestimate technological abilities and some users are Luddites who miss the wooden card catalouge with its paper entries. Some users need the human touch, preferring to brainstorm with a librarian than to deal with a literal computer programme. Once a person has a good experience with a librarian agent or with a software agent, that user is more likely to use the agent again in the future.

A good librarian is more competent than a software agent at this point in time, hands-down. A really good librarian has to develop by experience and by training, just as software agents do, but the development time for a human agent is quicker than for a software agent. Librarians are cheaper to install, so to speak. Hire one, give him or her a year or so to get up to speed, and you have got a professional agent who will provide clients with relevant information. Once installed, though, librarians are also much more expensive to keep and are slower in their work than software agents. The artificial intelligence community is working to make software agents more agile and more competent. It is just a matter of time before intelligence software agents are turn-key installations able to competently perform lower-level reference (and other) library tasks.

A reasonable information future will include human librarians and intelligent software agents. Since a real general artificial intelligence is not yet within sight, a collaborative future makes the most sense. Software agents can automate some of the more tedious and repetitive library tasks and librarians can be freed to do what they do best; guide clients through the maze to the best information for that client's particular need. Rather than seeing human agents and software agents as in competition, as vying for the same place in world, the wiser course is to leverage the strengths of each, deliberately designing work practices and institutional arrangements that reflect and exploit the possibility of collaboration between human and software agents.

Librarians and intelligent software agents must work together to efficiently balance workloads in the most optimal way for a particular user and in that particular user's specific context. Librarians need to resist feeling defensive about jobs and value and keep focus on which technologies and which methods make the most sense for clients.

Librarians are becoming more important in this information-centric universe. Intelligent agents will act as catalysts to enhance the role of librarians as the next century dawns, heralding a renaissance in information science and librarianship. Librarians are already fulfilling new roles as content providers, search strategists, digital cataloguers, and information mechanics. These roles will only grow, and new opportunities will flourish, with the development of truly 'intelligent agents' that build upon the experience of librarians and information professionals.

Faced with both new opportunities and new temptations, universities and their libraries will need an effective combination of internal clarity concerning what matters most and the right kind of external support if they are to retain the perspective of the poet; if they are to continue to stand, with Cavafy, "at a slight angle to the universe".

In the beginning of the 1970's, libraries' started to use the internet, however, access was mainly for basic database searching in large systems such as OCLC, RLIN, BRS and DIALOG. During the early years of internet use, the database searching was mainly restricted to the reference and interlibrary loan librarians. With the growth of the internet and the addition of more diverse electronic resources, the capacity for searching the internet also increased. In the years between 1980 and 1990, the number of new internet databases grew nearly 25 per cent per year. Between 1985 and 1990, the number of full-text data bases grew by more than 50 per cent each year.

According to Malinconico, the computerised systems libraries used as recently as the 1980's maintained an obvious and continuous relationship with traditional library functions such as bibliographic searching and online public access catalogues or OPAC's. It is also interesting to note that the internet was mainly utilised for its communication functions or e-mail systems.

Librarians viewed the internet as their "electronic Rolodex" because it enabled them to communicate with colleagues around the world in a convenient, timely, nondisruptive, and inexpensive manner. With the expansion of databases and their overall use by librarians, the traditional services and roles of the librarian were beginning to be called into question.

Recent dramatic advances in computer networking and the accelerated growth of information retrieval technology have brought about the beginnings of an evolutionary leap in resource sharing that is profoundly impacting the library landscape. Literature in the early 1990's discussed the growing prevalence of digital or electronic resource sharing and the beginnings of what are now call virtual libraries. With internet access, librarians and an increasing number of clients were able to access these resources remotely. Underlying models and ideas of the traditional library as a repository of information resources were beginning to be replaced by the idea of remote, geographically unconstrained access. Since 1993, the internet has experienced unprecedented growth. In July 1993, there were a total of 1.8 million network hosts. That number has increased to 6.6 million hosts in 1995. There were an estimated 56 million worldwide internet users in 1995 with a projected increase to 200 million users by 1999.

With the growth of internet resources and users, the library functions and roles concerning internet use and the digitisation of libraries and their resources also continues to evolve. Use of the internet and telecommunications technology is becoming a prevalent aspect of libraries. According to Schneider, a 1994 survey of public libraries found that more than 93 per cent of libraries surveyed were connected to the internet. Use of the internet and other network resources is changing the traditional library functions.

In the early 1980s and 1990s, the internet was used mainly for communications, database searching, and bibliographic access, today the internet's modalities are changing traditional functions of library professionals such as the information transfer process and the perceived nature of information itself. Use of the internet has changed or augmented all aspects of the information transfer process.

Now, researchers or business people are able to search the internet's collection of electronic resources. Furthermore, they are able to use e-mail or teleconferencing to exchange information with others in almost real-time collaborative group think-tank sessions. Diffusion of their research findings can also be accomplished in the same manner, as opposed to face-to-face meetings or conferences. Internet use has also indirectly affected the other aspects of the information transfer process.

For example the organisation, storage, and preservation of information has been both simplified and complicated. The internet provides a medium in which to organise and store the vast new amounts of information available. New technologies such as hypertext and html have organised information in hopefully searchable formats. Powerful search engines have been created to assist users in sifting through the information.

The internet is also a medium for the preservation and storage of information. In the past, libraries were seen as the main storage facility of information. As society becomes increasingly more digital and more information resides on the internet, the focus on storage and preservation is shifting. For example, some academic libraries are now faced with the problem of whether or not to purchase serials that can be just as easily accessed online. Preservation of these same media also becomes an issue of economics, not the just in case preservation ideology of the past paradigm. Co-joined to the function of preservation is the destruction of information. Since the internet can be seen as a medium for preserving information, the process of destruction of information also is affected.

Along with the changes to the information transfer process, society's definition of the nature of information is also changing. In the past information was considered to be mainly oral and textual. However, because of changing information technology, information now is thought of as multimedia—as graphical, voice or sound, and the visual combination of all elements in video. It is no longer feasible to think of information as static words on a page.

One school of thought believes information has become fragmented and disembodied as a result of the above formats, which may also serve to change the meaning behind the information. Therefore, there is no longer accessing the "whole fabric of information, rather the bits of data, sound bites, and images torn from it".

The second school of thought, however, views hypertext as part of a new dynamic knowledge/thought/technology paradigm which pairs librarianship with the use of computer technology in order to expand capacities for storing, retrieving, representing, and manipulating information. Gapen first proposed the idea behind this new way of thinking in 1988. She described a new knowledge/thought system in which the human brain will complement computer software. This new collaboration will allow rapid storage and transfer of information, but also new and different ways of processing and representing information. Gapen sees hypertext and hyperlinks, such as those now utilised by the internet, as the first step in the creation of new interconnected resource sharing and cooperation between 'hypersystems.'

Students or researchers are relying more and more on computerised databases or internet databases to search and retrieve information. However, the problem with internet digital publishing is that the validity or accuracy of digital information is seen as a given, with little consideration to source or authority. Since information on the internet can be created by anyone, there is little or no editorial or peer review process. As a result of this preconceived notion of accuracy, internet authors can easily distort or manipulate information to suit their purposes. Users want rapid dissemination of information, so the burden of 'weeding' for quality control is placed upon the shoulders of the information consumers.

Learning to use the internet requires a major time commitment, both for the librarian themselves and in training library users to utilise it more effectively. Interesting enough, librarians view using the internet as remaining on the cutting edge of their profession. They have begun to equate the internet with their perception of their profession, as have library clients. According to Woodward, 'the internet is slow and circuitous'. While in some cases the internet may provide the best, fastest, and most cost-efficient way to attain the needed information, users can get buried or lost in the endless menus, and dead-end links, and end up with useless or inaccurate information. Search engines or information sifting methods are still fairly basic—users are really accessing an excess of information. Schuman believes are really experiencing an information-glut or an access to excess. The mere fact that there is more data available does not mean that people either want it or can use it meaningfully.

## References

Andrews, J. & Law, D. G. *Digital libraries: policy, planning and practice*. Aldershot, Hants, England; Burlington, VT: Ashgate. 2004.

Bishop, A. P., Van House, N. A. & Buttenfield, B. P;, eds. *Digital library use: social practice in design and evaluation*. Cambridge, MA: MIT Press. 2003.

Brogan, M. L. *A survey of digital library aggregation services. Washington,* D.C.:; Digital Library Federation, Council on Library and Information Resources. 2003.

Chapman, S. *Techniques for creating sustainable digital collections.* Chicago: ALA TechSource. 2004.

Chowdhury, G. G. & Chowdhury, S. *Introduction to digital libraries.* London: Facets Publishing. 2003.

Hickey, T. B. 2003. *Web services for digital libraries.* European Library Automation Group, ELAG 2003: Cross language applications and the Web, 27th Library systems seminar, Bern (Switzerland) 2-4 April 2003.

# 6

# Digital Preservation

Preservation is the act of physically and intellectually protecting and technically stabilising the transmission of the content and context of electronic records across space and time, in order to produce copies of those records that people can reasonably judge to be authentic. To accomplish this, the preservation system requires natural and juridical people, institutions, applications, infrastructure, and procedures."

What is 'Preservation'? Most collectors know that organising and storing physical collectibles is likely to provide more assurance of retrieval than simply throwing items on a coffee table. This is the equivalent of depositing an electronic paper in an IR rather than simply uploading it to a personal server and Web page. The organisation of the IR together with the commitment of the sponsoring institution will provide greater assurance than a server with unknown support looking forward.

Simple storage is hardly a complete solution, however. In the long term, even physical materials suffer some degradation. The equivalent process of degradation for digital materials is typically caused by format obsolescence due to changes in software applications technology, often regarded as a rapid process in comparison with degradation of physical materials and can be ameliorated by specialised technical processes such as format migration. In both cases, the extended risks to physical and digital materials might be most cost-effectively tackled by specialist preservation services. For information materials like books and journals, these services have traditionally been offered by libraries and archives, and such organisations might be well positioned to serve digital sources too.

Digital preservation thus covers a wide range of activities, from storage to transformation, depending on the nature of the resources and the source, and the range of preservation services could be equally wide. Since such services are not yet widely practised or available, a useful starting point is to consider what is known about the target content in IRs.

## 6.1. Evolution of Institutional Repositories

It is helpful to consider what IRs are, what they do and where the idea comes from, because this is a relatively recent development.

An IR provides access to the content and materials produced by members of that institution, typically a university or other educational establishment. The impetus for IRs was boosted by the Open Archives Initiative (OAI) in 1999, not to be confused in preservation terms with the Open Archival Information System. Institutionally based, or more typically departmental, 'archives' were known before this, especially in areas such as computer science and economics that were served by the Networked Computer Science Technical Reference Library and Research Papers in Economics, respectively. OAI introduced the Protocol for Metadata Harvesting (OAI-PMH) to provide common services that could operate over more general, independent sites. Search is the most obvious example of such a service. OAI-PMH enables compliant sites to be *interoperable*, thus making institutional, rather than only disciplinary, repositories visible and viable. For the first time institutions such as universities have the ability to capture, store and disseminate copies of the published work of their own researchers. The significance of this cannot be underestimated.

OAI was aimed initially at eprint archives, and although the protocol was soon applied to other digital library content, the first software to support it was EPrints, developed at Southampton University. EPrints is software for building IRs that capture and provide open access to an institution's research outputs and publications, which are deposited directly by authors in principle using the version they created, a process known as 'self-archiving'. One of the consequences of this approach is that IRs incur low cost per item deposited, in turn creating the conditions for open access: immediate and permanently free access to published research papers. As such, where digital preservation might generally be concerned with preserving access, for IRs it is concerned with preserving open access, which has cost implications.

EPrints software first appeared in 2000, and an OAI-PMH 1.0-compliant version was announced on the same day this breakthrough version of the protocol was unveiled in January 2001. This application to IRs was reinforced with the emergence of DSpace software the following year, and other IR software applications have followed since.

Growth in the number of IRs has accelerated since 2002 and, despite some lag in time, there has been corresponding growth in the volume of content in IRs. According to data recorded by a wider registry of OAI-compliant repositories, OAIster, there was a 25% growth in the number of such repositories (up to 726), and a 59% increase in the number of records in those repositories (up to 9,931,910) between December 31, 2005 and the same date in 2006.

The fundamental requirements of repositories were characterised by Heery and Anderson:

- Content is deposited in a repository, whether by the content creator, owner or third party.
- The repository architecture manages content as well as metadata.
- The repository offers a minimum set of basic services, e.g., put, get, search, and access control.
- The repository must be sustainable and trusted, well-supported and well-managed.

IRs are additionally characterised by the institution, and the type of content it requires and permits to be deposited, and for what purpose, most commonly research outputs for open access.

This description of what IRs are and what they represent is not to say that the role and target content of IRs won't evolve legitimately and in an informed way to serve institutional needs and research purposes, as suggested by Dempsey. Other types of content, such as research data sets, theses, reports and multimedia can be deposited and managed within EPrints-based IRs.

Taking the age profile of most repositories into account, the need for preservation is perhaps less critical than for older digital content sources, but other factors such as growth and diversity point towards a more urgent need to plan for preservation by the more content-rich repositories.

## 6.2. Automated Data Management

Since one of the main reasons for the implementation of an Information repository is to reduce the maintenance workload placed on IT staff by traditional data storage systems, information repositories are automated. Automation is accomplished via polices that can process data based on time, events, data age, and data content. Policies manage the following:

— File system space management

— Irrelevant data elimination (mp3, games, etc.)

— Secondary storage resource management

Because information repositories are intended to reduce IT staff workload, they are designed to be easy to deploy and offer configuration flexibility, virtually limitless extensibility, redundancy, and reliable failover.

Information repositories feature robust, client based data search and recovery capabilities that, based on permissions, enable end users to search the information repository, view information repository contents, including data on off-line media, and recover individual files or multiple files to either their original network computer or another network computer.

## 6.3. Digital Preservation Programmes

Digital preservation is used to describe the processes involved in maintaining information and other kinds of heritage that exist in a digital form. In these Guidelines, it does not refer to the use of digital imaging or capture techniques to make copies of non-digital items, even if that is done for preservation purposes. Of course, digital copying, may well produce digital heritage materials needing to be preserved. Digital materials is generally used here as a preferred term covering items of digital heritage at a general level. In some places, digital object or digital resource have also been used. The terms have been used interchangeably and generically: they do not imply a particular kind of item unless that is clearly stated. Preservation programme is used to refer to any set of coherent arrangements aimed at preserving digital materials.

More commonly used terms such as digital archive and digital repository have been avoided because of their potential ambiguities: archive has different meanings for the records management community and the ICT community, whereas both archive and repository may imply a single storage site - not an appropriate implication where very distributed arrangements may be in place

Of course, the term programme also comes with some baggage. It should be understood to cover all the aspects of preservation responsibility, including policy and strategy as well as implementation. Presentation, re-presentation are used to describe the processes of providing access to digital materials. The second term has been consistently (and idiosyncratically) hyphenised to emphasise the understanding that digital preservation seeks to re-present what was previously presented.

Not all digital materials need to be kept, only those that are judged to have ongoing value: these form the digital heritage. For those materials that warrant keeping, continuity of survival and accessibility is critical. The chances of recovering lost access to large amounts of data are very slim. Continuity requires sustained, direct action (called digital preservation) rather than passive 'benign neglect.'

Digital materials cannot be said to be preserved if access is lost. The purpose of preservation is to maintain the ability to present the essential elements of authentic digital materials. Digital preservation must address threats to all layers of the digital object: physical, logical, conceptual and essential.

Digital preservation will only happen if organisations and individuals accept responsibility for it. The starting point for action is a decision about responsibility. Everyone does not have to do everything; everything does not have to be done all at once. Comprehensive and reliable preservation programmes are highly desirable, but they may not be achievable in all circumstances of need.

Where necessary, it is usually better for non-comprehensive and non-reliable action to be taken than for no action at all. Small steps are usually better than no steps.

Currently, preservation efforts have to work against the prevailing trend of digital technology and how it is developed and used. Digital materials are very often created without long-term preservation intentions in mind. Working with producers to influence the standards and practices they use, and to increase their awareness of preservation needs, are important investments.

Preservation programmes must clarify their legal right to collect, copy, name, modify, preserve and provide access to the digital materials for which they take responsibility. Digital heritage materials must be moved to a safe place where they can be controlled, protected and managed for preservation.

Digital heritage materials must be uniquely identified, and described using appropriate metadata for resource discovery, management and preservation. 18. Taking the right action later depends on adequate documentation. It is easier to document the characteristics of digital resources close to their source than it is to build that documentation later. Preservation programmes should use standardised metadata schemas as they become available, for interoperability between programmes.

The links between digital objects and their metadata must be securely maintained, and the metadata must be preserved. Authenticity is a critical issue where digital objects are used as evidence. It may also be important for other kinds of digital heritage. Data that underlies digital objects must be safely stored and managed if there is to be any chance of re-presenting authentic objects to users.

Digital preservation programmes are subjected to increased authenticity concerns because they so frequently have to use processes that involve change. Authenticity is best protected by measures that ensure the integrity of data is not compromised, and by documentation that maintains the clear identity of the material. Data protection is built on the principles of system security and redundancy.

For preservation programmes, redundancy must include securely stored backups designed around the long-term maintenance of data rather than a cycle of overwriting old data with new. The goal of maintaining accessibility is to find cost-effective ways of guaranteeing access whenever it is needed, both in the short-term and the long-term. Standards are an important foundation for digital preservation, but many programmes must find ways to preserve access to poorly standardised materials, in an environment of changing standards.

Preservation action should not be delayed until a single 'digital preservation standard' appears. Digital data is always dependent on some combination of software and hardware tools for access, but the degree of dependency on specific tools determines the range of preservation options. It is reasonable for programmes to choose multiple strategies for preserving access, especially to diverse collections.

They should consider the potential benefits of maintaining the original data streams of materials as well as any modified versions, as an insurance against the failure of still uncertain strategies. Strategies for preserving accessibility do not stand alone: they are supported by other responsibilities, and many strategies can be combined to good effect. Preservation programmes are often required to judge acceptable and unacceptable levels of loss, in terms of items, elements, and user needs.

Preservation programmes require good management that consists largely of generic management skills combined with enough knowledge of digital preservation issues to make good decisions at the right time. Digital preservation incorporates the assessment and management of risks programmes are usually faced with more material and more issues than they can cope with, so they must set priorities.

The costs of preservation programmes are hard to estimate because they encompass so much uncertainty, including evolving techniques, changing technologies and very long timeframes. Costs may well be lower per unit of information than for non-digital materials, but the amount of information to be managed in digital form is very large so total costs are also likely to remain high, including set-up costs and significant recurrent costs.

Preservation programmes may start as pilot projects but they eventually need to establish sustainable business models. While suitable service providers may be found to carry out some functions, ultimately responsible for achieving preservation objectives rests with preservation programmes, and with those who oversee and resource them. Working collaboratively is often a cost effective way to build preservation programmes with wide coverage, mutual support and the required expertise.

## 6.4. Digital Heritage

Digital heritage is made up of computer-based materials of enduring value that should be kept for future generations. Digital heritage emanates from different communities, industries, sectors and regions. Not all digital materials are of enduring value, but those that are require active preservation approaches if continuity of digital heritage is to be maintained. Heritage is explained in UNESCO documents as "our legacy from the past, what we live with today, and what we pass on to future generations." A heritage is something that is, or should be, passed from generation to generation because it is valued. The idea of cultural heritage is a familiar one: those sites, objects and intangible things that have cultural, historical, aesthetic, archaeological, scientific, ethnological or anthropological value to groups and individuals.

According to the Draft Charter for the Preservation of Digital Heritage:

> Resources of human knowledge or expression, whether cultural, educational, scientific and administrative, or embracing technical, legal, medical and other kinds of information, are increasingly created digitally, or converted into digital form from existing analogue resources.

Where resources are "born digital", there is no other format but the digital original. Digital materials include texts, databases, still and moving images, audio, graphics, software, and web pages, among a wide and growing range of formats. They are frequently ephemeral, and require purposeful production, maintenance and management to be retained. Many of these resources have lasting value and significance, and therefore constitute a heritage that should be protected and preserved for current and future generations. This heritage may exist in any language, in any part of the world, and in any area of human knowledge or expression. Using computers and related tools, humans are creating and sharing digital resources - information, creative expression, ideas, and knowledge encoded for computer processing - that they value and want to share with others over time as well as across space. This is evidence of a digital heritage. It is a heritage made of many parts, sharing many common characteristics, and subject to many common threats.

For example, UNESCO defines a world heritage made up of globally outstanding sites of cultural and natural value that should be preserved; many national and state legislatures also define their own national, regional or state heritage. However, heritage value may also be based on what is important at a group or community level. Heritage materials can exist well beyond the limits suggested by national legislation or international conventions. Anything that is considered important enough to be passed to the future can be considered to have heritage value of some kind.

This digital heritage is likely to become more important and more widespread over time. Increasingly, individuals, organisations and communities are using digital technologies to document and express what they value and what they want to pass on to future generations. New forms of expression and communication have emerged that did not exist previously. The Internet is one vast example of this phenomenon. It is also likely that the development of tools to support greater multi-lingual and multi-script use of the Internet will lead to further rapid growth in digital heritage in parts of the world that are currently disadvantaged by the predominant use of English on the Internet. Making sure this burgeoning digital heritage remains available is thus a global issue relevant to all countries and communities.

### 6.4.1. Types of Digital Heritage

Over time, new types of digital heritage can be expected to emerge: we have already seen the enabling power of the technology in forms as diverse as word processing, email, websites, relational databases, computer models and simulations, digital audio and video, space imagery and computer games. Electronic publications, being information that is made available for wide readership. Publications are distributed in various ways including online via the World Wide

Web, or on portable carriers such as CDs, DVDs, floppy disks and various electronic book devices.

Some publications manage to combine both online and portable carrier access to different parts of the publication. As well as their means of distribution, digital publications may be classified by genres, some familiar from traditional publishing formats like monographs and serials, and others less easily defined like websites and e-zines. Some publications are released as complete items, but others evolve over time, their creators taking advantage of the interactive potential of the Internet.

Print publishing continues to grow, but increasingly publications are appearing in digital versions, increasingly in digital-only versions. Both commercial and non-commercial publishers produce digital publications, as do millions of other people who would not see themselves as publishers at all. 'Semi-published' materials such as pre-print papers and theses held in e-print and other archives available for restricted use within specific communities such as universities and scholarly societies

Organisational and personal records of activity, transactions, correspondence, etc. A very large part of the world's business and government records now exist in electronic record keeping systems. Email, messages to discussion lists and bulletin boards, web diaries, 'blogs' and 'cams' - dynamic, informal interactions enabled by digital technology - may also include important digital records amongst a tidal wave of data.

Electronic 'manuscripts' such as drafts of works and personal correspondence. Entertainment products from the film, music, broadcasting and games industries, both commercial and non-commercial. Digitally generated artworks and documentary photographs. Digital copies of images, sound, text and three-dimensional objects from non-digital originals.

Many of these materials exist only in a digital form (even if carried on a physical carrier of some kind). With no equivalent non-digital version, their content is especially vulnerable to the influences that threaten digital materials. There are also rapidly growing collections of digital copies. Having originally been generated from non-digital sources, these might appear to be less vulnerable, but many of them are the only surviving version of originals that have since been damaged, lost or dispersed.

### 6.4.2. Continuity of Digital Heritage

Continuity of the digital heritage is profoundly important. Increasingly this is a heritage that documents the actions of governments, the results of scientific research, the debate of ideas, the aspirations and imagination of communities, the histories of the current and coming world. If these are not to be lost or distorted, continuity is required: continuity of production, continuity of survival, and continuity of access. This must be achieved in the face of many threats:

— The carriers used to store these digital materials are usually unstable and deteriorate within a few years or decades at most

— Use of digital materials depends on means of access that work in particular ways

The Internet is an interesting scenario in which many of these threats are played out. In assessing the risks associated with the Internet, it is necessary to distinguish between two overlapping but different concerns. One concern is to look at the Internet as a whole. There is no central agency that can decide what happens to material made available through the Internet. Typically, users connect with a kaleidoscope of information for which no single creator, publisher, or any other agency is responsible.

A different viewpoint is to look at individual resources published through the Internet. These may also be quite unstable, but their instability reflects the decisions and actions of their owners in deleting, changing, moving, or renaming them. The loss of materials in this environment is attributable to how they are managed at a local level, exposed to many of the same threats that other kinds of digital materials experience.

While it is largely beyond the power of Internet users to control whether information remains available, it is very much within the power of those owning and managing digital objects and sites. If they are committed to maintaining access, it is generally within their power to do so. However, the Internet does present some special risks. For example:

— There is a strong novelty factor, so some publishers choose to change things frequently - sometimes the way information looks, sometimes also the content

— Many Internet resources are a virtual composite drawn from a number of sources, which may not be stored together anywhere.

## 6.5. Digital Preservation Strategies

Digital preservation consists of the processes aimed at ensuring the continued accessibility of digital materials. To do this involves finding ways to re-present what was originally presented to users by a combination of software and hardware tools acting on data. To achieve this requires digital objects to be understood and managed at four levels: as physical phenomena; as logical encodings; as conceptual objects that have meaning to humans; and as sets of essential elements that must be preserved in order to offer future users the essence of the object.

Digital preservation can be seen as all those processes aimed at ensuring the continuity of digital heritage materials for as long as they are needed. The most significant threats to digital continuity concern loss of the means of access. Digital materials cannot be said to be preserved if the means of access have been lost and access becomes impossible. The purpose of preserving digital materials is to maintain accessibility: the ability to access their essential, authentic message or purpose.

There is an underlying similarity in the way digital objects are accessed in the present, and how they will be accessed in any future use. In both cases, access can be seen as a performance. Digital objects are made accessible by applying software and hardware tools to data in order to create a presentation or performance that has meaning to a user. It may be the presentation of a word processing document, or a piece of recorded audio, or a Web page, or results from a database query, or any other kind of digital object depending on the way the data is encoded and on the actions the tools are programmed to perform.

Digital preservation must work in the same way, somehow re-presenting what are judged to be the essential elements of the original performance when required at some later time. Conceptualised in this way, digital preservation can be seen as straightforward. Indeed, copying data from carrier to carrier, and providing the right tools to recreate the intended performance will preserve continuity of access to most digital objects.

However, this simple model encompasses great complexities: it may be hard to define the performance that must be re-presented; it is usually difficult to work out what tools are needed once the original ones have been lost; the tools themselves typically rely on other tools that also may have been superseded; and it may be difficult to find tools that will create the required performance in a reliable, cost-effective and timely way, especially in the context of many thousands, millions or more of digital objects.

Despite such underlying complexities, the performance model helps in recognising what digital preservation programmes must aim for: the best means of re-presenting what users needs to access. Preservation programmes must deal with digital objects in four guises:

— As physical objects, consisting of 'inscriptions' (usually binary states of 'on-ness' or 'off-ness') on carrier media such as computer disks or tapes.

— As logical objects consisting of computer readable code, whose existence at any particular time depends on the physical inscriptions but is not tied to any particular carrier

— As conceptual objects that have meaning to humans, unlike the logical or physical objects that encode them at any particular time.

— As bundles of essential elements that embody the message, purpose, or features for which the material was chosen for preservation.

This multi-layered nature of digital objects has profound implications for digital preservation. Preservation means different things for each layer. Preservation programmes for non-digital heritage have traditionally worried about preserving the physical object as the embodiment of the object's meaning. However, individual physical manifestations of a digital object are almost inevitably lost, one after another, because the media used for physical storage are typically unstable and liable to short-term deterioration.

Preservation requires a succession of data transfers from one physical carrier to another. Despite this shift in focus from the physical object to a conceptual object inherent in digital preservation, it must never be forgotten that digital objects cannot survive without some kind of appropriate physical form.

The logical encoding normally has a much longer life than any particular physical inscription, but it is by no means sacrosanct. As the layers of technology used for access - hardware such as computer processors, disk drives and peripheral equipment, and many layers of software such as operating systems, specific applications, and presentation tools - become obsolete, it may be necessary to change the logical encoding so that it can present the same conceptual object using different technology.

The conceptual object is the ultimate focus of preservation concern; as noted above, it is at this level that digital objects convey meaning to human users. However, for most digital objects there is a further layer that must be considered. Many objects consist of several elements, some of which are more important than others in carrying the object's essential message. Preservation programmes have to decide which sub-set of elements should be preserved for re-presentation to users.

Digital preservation involves choosing and implementing an evolving range of strategies to achieve the kind of accessibility discussed above, addressing the preservation needs of the different layers of digital objects. The strategies include:

— Working with producers (creators and distributors) to apply standards that will prolong the effective life of the available means of access and reduce the range of unknown problems that must be managed
— Recognising that it is not practical to try to preserve everything, selecting what material should be preserved
— Placing the material in a safe place
— Controlling material, using structured metadata and other documentation to facilitate access and to support all preservation process
— Protecting the integrity and identity of data
— Choosing appropriate means of providing access in the face of technological change

— Managing preservation programmes to achieve their goals in cost-effective, timely, holistic, proactive and accountable ways.

Preservation programmes have certain responsibilities and functions that have been defined, at least at a conceptual level. Comprehensive programmes must take control of appropriate digital materials and ensure they remain understandable and usable as authentic copies.

This generally involves taking the materials, properly prepared, along with associated documentation or metadata, into an archival digital storage system of some kind, where they can be managed to deal with the threats of data loss an technological change. The characteristics or attributes of programmes that can be relied upon to deliver ongoing digital preservation have also been described, in terms of responsibility, viability, sustainability, technical suitability, security, and accountability.

Digital information objects are generally not understandable or re-presentable by themselves: users need help to use them. Preservation depends on maintaining digital objects and any information and tools that would be needed in order to access and understand them. Together, these can be considered to form an information package that must be managed either as a single object or as a virtual package.

Preservation programmes must identify a safe place where digital materials can be stored and managed. Because the concept of the preservation programme allows for distributed arrangements and shared responsibilities, it is quite conceivable that while some programmes will create their own repositories, others may decide to look for a suitable 'safe place' operated and managed by someone else.

The processes of receiving, preparing and transferring digital materials into the archival system are usually referred to as ingest. Preparing material for entry into the archival information system is critical to the way the whole system is managed. It involves a number of important steps that may determine how easy or difficult it is to maintain the archived information packages in the system. These steps include:

— Applying collection policies and selection criteria to assess whether material is in scope so that it can be sought, or accepted if submitted

— Clarifying or negotiating rights issues with rights owners
— Checking the quality of the submitted information package, including its completeness, the functionality of its component parts, its authenticity, and whether it contains unwanted material such as viruses
— Labelling the material with unique identifiers
— Assessing the elements that must be maintained, and assigning preservation objectives
— Setting retention and review periods for the material, if appropriate
— Checking and if necessary upgrading the documentation that describes the material, including the technical and preservation metadata
— Assessing the file format(s) and deciding if they need to be changed to comply with the Programme's policy on what formats it will manage
— If necessary, changing the file formats to comply with the policy
— Adjusting the documentation to reflect any changes.

Once the digital object and its metadata have been prepared and associated with each other to form an information package, they are saved to the archival storage system. A preservation programme must provide archival storage that maintains, protects and verifies the integrity of the stored information packages, both the digital object and the metadata, whether stored as a single data stream or as separate but linked data streams.

To achieve this, the storage function must include practices that protect the data stream from unintended change, damage or loss: this will usually require regular copying of the data stream to fresh media, and when necessary copying to new media types. Storage practices must also include checking that the data stream has not been corrupted; system security; backup regimes that place copies at remote sites; and disaster recovery plans that address contingencies such as complete loss of the system's operating infrastructure.

Obviously, this requires technical capabilities to provide a suitably secure and reliable storage service. Such a capability can be achieved with modest equipment so long as the equipment and the whole system are well managed. The more material there is, and the more diverse and complex it is, the more sophisticated the storage system needs to be.

For most digital materials, preserving accessibility requires more than the data protection offered in the Archival Storage function. Only material being kept for very short periods could be stored without further attention to the means of providing access. The purpose of the Preservation Planning function is to monitor threats to accessibility, and to specify action to pre-empt or respond to them. The relevant threats mostly relate to changes in the technology that underlies access, so this function looks for such changes and takes action to maintain accessibility despite these changes.

## 6.6. Managing Digital Preservation

### 6.6.1. Managing Information Packages

Managing information packages in the archive generates its own data about what material is stored, what can be accessed, and about the management of the archive. This data must be managed to support use of the archive, and to support its effective administration. This function provides a user interface to the archive, allowing users to discover what is held, to request material and if appropriate to receive copies. For many archives, access will be subject to restrictions for some or all potential users. The Access function may well require mechanisms to control access. The preservation programme must find ways to advocate good practices among producers, aimed at facilitating preservation of the material for which the programme will be responsible.

There is also a need to understand who the likely users of the material will be, so that preservation and access arrangements can be tailored to their needs and expectations. The overall operation of the programme must be managed. In part this responsibility involves the development of policy frameworks and standards covering all areas of operations; in part it involves the ongoing supply of appropriate resources and infrastructure including suitable technical systems; and in part management processes such as monitoring and reporting on the programme's operations.

Reference Model for Open Archival Information Systems (OAIS), released in 2002 as a draft international standard by the International Standards Organisation. The OAIS Reference Model is the most successful attempt to define both a conceptual model for managing digital materials of enduring value, and a vocabulary with which to discuss it. Anyone contemplating a responsibility for managing digital materials should seek to understand the concepts articulated in the Reference Model itself.

The Reference Model is a high level conceptual framework that can be used as a reference point for those designing, using and evaluating real implementations. It is important to realise that it is not an implementation specification: it does not provide a set of instructions on how to preserve digital information. Its value lies in explaining what is required at a highly conceptual level, regardless of the means chosen to achieve it.

The reliability and trustworthiness of digital preservation programmes are very important issues to many stakeholders. Producers, users, investors and the broad community have a strong interest in ensuring that digital heritage materials are managed by arrangements that can be trusted. Those potentially responsible for the programmes also have an interest in assessing what they can offer and the risks of accepting responsibility.

Preservation programmes offering long-term reliability are expected to have the following characteristics:

— *Responsibility*: a fundamental commitment to preservation of the digital materials in question · Organisational viability, including the prospect of an ongoing mandate; a legal status as an organisation that would support an ongoing preservation role; and a demonstrated ability to put together the resources, infrastructure and work teams that could manage the complexity of digital preservation

— *Financial sustainability*: a likely prospect of the organisation being able to continue to provide the required resources well into the future, with a sustainable business model to support its digital preservation mandate

— *Technological and procedural suitability*: the use of appropriate systems and procedures to do what is required to manage and preserve digital resources

— *System security of a very high order:* Procedural accountability, with clear allocation of responsibilities and mechanisms for reporting and assessing performance.

Arrangements that are able to demonstrate these attributes should be trustworthy. Development of trust may be a matter of demonstrating these characteristics over time. In the long term, certification programmes will probably be needed but at the time of writing no certification programmes for digital preservation arrangements have appeared. It remains very much the responsibility of those proposing digital preservation programmes to show why their arrangements should be trusted, and very much the responsibility of other stakeholders to determine that any arrangements on offer can provide an acceptable level of reliability.

### 6.6.2. Preservation Responsibility

Responsibility is a crucial issue in the preservation of digital heritage. The starting point for action is a decision about responsibility. Because the cost implications for an organisation can be significant, and because the requirements may be complex and uncertain, it is no small thing to accept a responsible role. The purpose of such arrangements is to provide a good prospect of preservation continuing beyond their own involvement, should that become necessary. Fail-safe arrangements extend along a continuum, from a commitment to find someone else to take over responsibility before discarding digital materials, through to legally mandated arrangements for one agency to take over the management of data held by another agency if it fails to meet its preservation responsibilities. Responsibility for initiating and maintaining succession plans obviously lies with whomever is managing the material, but there may be other players who should accept some responsibility.

In facing the daunting challenges of preservation responsibility, it may help to consider some pragmatic principles:

— *Someone has to take responsibility*: if no one does, the chances of any particular materials surviving are very small

— *Everyone does not have to do everything*: responsibility can be shared. As these guidelines indicate, there are more than enough responsibilities for one preservation Programme. Many tasks, such as deciding what should be preserved, are best managed in partnership with others. If there is no one suitable to share responsibilities, preservation programmes should make realistic judgments about the responsibilities they can carry alone

— *Everything does not have to be done at once*: developing all the components of a large-scale, comprehensive preservation programme takes time. It is good to approach the task with a sense of urgency, but it may also be necessary to look for ways of buying time. This might require prioritising the issues that need to be addressed, or the material that needs attention. It may involve looking for easily managed materials ('low hanging fruit'). Some problems must be addressed without delay; some can be addressed in stages; and some can wait

— *Responsibility does not have to be forever*: there is definitely a place for time-limited contributions to an overall preservation programme, so long as the time limits are explicitly understood

— *Limited responsibility should not mean causing harm*: preservation programmes may need to take steps before all problems are solved and all techniques settled, but they must also try to minimise the harm of making later preservation efforts more difficult

— *Someone must take a leading role*: even when responsibility is shared, progress usually depends on at least one partner accepting the responsibility to lead.

Some people believe that new institutions will be needed to take on the task of preserving digital heritage. Presumably these agencies would offer specialist expertise and facilities dedicated to digital materials, and possibly dedicated to preservation rather than a wider range of functions which existing collecting institutions perform, like arranging and interpreting materials and promoting their use.

Many data archives fit into such a field already, as they exist solely to manage and preserve digital materials. They often have the paradoxical advantages of being able to focus on a limited range of materials and management tasks, while being able to offer services to a wider range of data-producing communities.

Just as it is too early to judge the long-term role of libraries, archives and museums, it is too early to attempt a definitive list of others who may play an important role. Universities and other institutes of research and learning have a natural interest in ensuring ongoing access to certain kinds of digital materials, and may have both the long-term viability and the technical infrastructure to play a preservation role · Publishers and creators of digital content have a range of interests in ongoing management and accessibility.

In many cases this extends beyond immediate commercial considerations to a longer-term investment in the exchange of ideas and the intellectual and cultural capital that ongoing accessibility encourages. Some publishers and creators may be willing and able to provide the infrastructure needed to maintain digital heritage materials in which they have an interest.

When preservation programmes have decided what kind of responsibility they will take, it is very important that they declare their intentions. This makes it easier for others to work with them, reduces the likelihood of effort being unnecessarily duplicated, and provides a clearer picture of what material is likely to survive and what is not.

### 6.6.3. Managing Digital Preservation Programmes

Preservation programmes require good management, often drawing on generic management skills such as tailoring programmes to the priorities and circumstances of the case, and making the right decisions at the right time. Digital preservation programmes present some particular management issues associated with their developing nature, the range of stakeholders, and the long-term impacts of current decisions.

Like all programmes, preservation programmes need to be managed in a coherent way. Digital preservation management should not be seen as a mysterious art: it draws on good general management skills, allied with enough subject knowledge and understanding of technical issues to see realistic possibilities and to make good decisions. The discussion that follows focuses on those issues specifically relevant to digital preservation.

Good management often comes down to knowing what decisions have to be made and making them at the right time. The important decisions do not have to be made all at once, but eventually they will be required on issues including:

— Whether to get involved in preserving digital materials at all
— The mission of the programme

Preservation programmes must seek to understand and respond to threats that would jeopardise ongoing accessibility and other aspects of the programme's mission. A risk management approach provides an appropriate basis for deciding what risks warrant attention, and for planning action that will lower the level of risk. There are many suitable risk management models available. Risk analysis, even undertaken informally, helps in a number of ways:

***6.6.3.1. Recognising:***

— The most pressing threats (such as web publications disappearing; media failure of magnetic carriers; impending replacement of equipment or software; a change in government agency arrangements that will threaten record keeping systems)
— Threats that may not require immediate action (such as the eventual obsolescence of a standardised, ubiquitous file format such as TIFF, the impact of which should be manageable when a replacement standard appears) - Threats over which the programme may have no influence (such as the business imperatives of producers)
— Threats that are so pressing but so intractable that the programme may decide to withdraw from responsibility (such as a refusal by rights owners to allow any form of access or preservation copying at any future time).

***6.6.3.2. Deciding:***

— Where to allocate resources
— What steps to take as a priority
— When action may be needed
— What supporting action is needed to address priority risks.
— Planning ahead
— Justifying decisions.

Risk assessment is especially helpful if it is extended beyond the immediately apparent risks to include:

— The risks associated with the action that is proposed to deal with the threat. For example, the programme may not have the required skills, resources, permissions, etc. This in turn might lead to action that is a prerequisite for dealing with the priority threat

— The causes of the original threat. For example, web publishers may not be aware of steps they could take; producers may be using standards incorrectly; or producers may be at risk of business failure. This analysis might lead to action that addresses the causes, such as education campaigns, the development of standards in conjunction with producers, or development of indicators of impending business failure including signs that web sits are not being maintained or personal knowledge that projects are coming to a close.

A broad range of stakeholders have an interest in digital heritage materials and how they are managed. They may include those creating or distributing the materials, those who need to use them now or in the future, and those who cite the materials, assuming that they will remain available. Some stakeholders may be hidden but play a very influential role behind the scenes, such as hardware and software manufacturers, providers of funds, and bodies authorised to control access to certain materials.

Some stakeholders may be of direct interest to the preservation programme itself, such as potential collaborative partners, standards bodies, and researchers developing new digital preservation methods. Preservation programmes must recognise those who have an interest in their objectives or who could exert an influence on them. Risk assessment is likely to indicate which stakeholders will be most important, as well as suggesting the kind of relationship the programme needs to develop with them.

Because the windows of opportunity for preservation are much narrower than for non-digital heritage, preservation programmes may have to be much more active in pursuing relationships with producers of heritage materials. They may also have to look for ways of influencing the 'hidden' stakeholders whose decisions may have a critical impact. Reliable preservation programmes must be sustained over long periods, so they require business models that guarantee adequate resources will continue to be available.

Unfortunately, such guarantees are rare in the real world. Most programmes have to survive with less certainty. Especially in the initial stages, sustainability presents a dilemma: programmes must eventually have it, but they often cannot tell what resources will be needed to fulfil their responsibilities, nor what resources may become available once a successful programme has been established.

Programme managers have the challenge of finding long-term business models, but they may also have to find short-term funding arrangements, and recognise the appropriate time to switch from one to the other. (In fact, some managers may find they can only build a long-term programme on the back of a series of short-term funding arrangements.) Some of the business models commonly considered for preservation programmes include:

— General community funding, often through taxes or the allocation of grants from special sources such as lottery funds
— Funding by a specific community with an interest in the programme, such as a local community project, or an industry peak body levying members
— Central funding by a parent organisation as a normal cost of business, such as a university library or a business archive
— Payments by users of the material
— Payments by producers who deposit material with the programme.
— Sponsorship or philanthropic assistance
— Cross subsidisation by other activities within an organisation

Standards and practices in digital preservation are evolving rapidly (though perhaps not as rapidly as they are needed), and programme managers must find ways to keep their knowledge up to date. There are a number of international initiatives dedicated to just such a purpose, including the journals, websites and subject gateways included in the Reading List. Despite some overlap, these initiatives complement each other; they offer excellent ways of keeping abreast of developments.

There also appears to be an opportunity to explore solidarity relationships between programmes with different levels of experience and expertise. Most existing programmes are willing to share information and ideas but often find themselves overwhelmed with requests. Formal information sharing arrangements may ease that burden while offering real benefits to those developing new programmes.

Digital preservation programmes often start as experiments and projects with a speculative mission and an uncertain future. They can be easily dismissed as important but bothersome add-ons to already overstretched organisations. It often takes some time for a definite set of workflows to emerge and for the programme to take shape.

Availability of resources is always a critical constraint. It is important to tailor the ambitions of the programme to a reasonably realistic idea of what can be achieved: it may not be possible to do everything! It is difficult to estimate the long-term costs of digital preservation. While unsatisfactory from a planning point of view, it may be necessary to estimate expected costs over a short- to medium-term period, such as five years, and to use the knowledge gained in that timeframe to inform more accurate estimates of long-term costs.

However, there is always likely to be a problem in estimating the costs of long-term actions that are still unclear, such as migration costs. Some costs do become much easier to predict following a few years' experience in collecting material, preparing it for storage, and protecting it. Some cost assumptions can be reasonably made:

— Development costs are likely to be high, depending on how ambitious the programme is from the start. Systems design is a necessary investment in the long run but it can be a significant set up cost

— There are obvious recurrent costs associated with staff, accommodation, energy supplies, network use, telecommunications costs, storage media such as disks and tapes, and consumables. Although often funded as capital expenditure, equipment and software should be seen as recurrent costs because they will have to be replaced on a regular basis

— The staff costs of working with producers can be high because of the need to address new issues with each change in technology. The costs of negotiating rights may vary depending on the complexity of rights ownership and on whether or not rights need to be purchased

— The costs of identifying and selecting materials for preservation are likely to be low per unit, but there may be many units. A nonselective approach may reduce costs, although adding to long-term preservation costs overall, as more material must be stored, processed, preserved and organised for access. Human judgments about selection are expensive where labour costs are high; automating decisions may reduce costs if the high set-up costs can be spread over a large amount of material, and if it is feasible to automate what are often complex human judgments

— The costs of collecting or transferring materials are likely to be low per unit but large programmes may generate significant transfer costs overall. This may incorporate high transmission costs where automated gathering searches and downloads large amounts of data. The cost of quality control checking is likely to be high unless it can be automated

— Converting material to a restricted range of standard formats may be inexpensive if the conversion is easy, but expensive if individual handcrafting or correction is needed. However, there may be considerable long-term cost benefits in being able to deal with a restricted range of formats

— The costs of describing material and adding metadata are likely to be high because of the amount of information to be recorded, and the difficulty of finding it in some cases. Costs could be greatly reduced by producers using more standardised structures and creating good metadata and documentation themselves. For heavily standardised formats such as those widely used for archival versions of images and audio, costs will be reduced by automated gathering of metadata from files and during production processes

— Costs associated with storage are theoretically low and decreasing, but in total they reflect the amount of data to be stored, which may be large. Estimates of storage and processing costs should take account of backups and multiple versions of material. The cost of regularly copying data to new media is generally discounted by regular increases in storage densities

— The costs of providing means of access - such as analysing data structures, writing new code for migration, writing or finding emulators, quality checking, and so on -may be high or low, depending on how difficult the process turns out to be. For example, if a conversion software tool can be developed that works automatically for millions of similar files, the unit costs may be extremely low, although the total cost of computer time could still be significant. On the other hand, strategies that must be managed item by item will be very expensive

— Computer costs to store and serve large numbers of access copies, or to generate them on request, should not be ignored. These would generally not be counted as preservation costs, but preservation programmes may still have to bear them as part of their business function.

Where the material is very similar and well organised, and where the preservation tasks are straightforward, it may be possible to automate most processes and reduce staffing requirements to a minimum. On the other hand, where repeated human intervention is needed, the programme will need staff who are adequately equipped to provide it. It is very hard to automate processes that require subjective judgments, although not impossible.

Even highly automated programmes, however, will eventually need staff to deal with changes in the operating environment and with the need to replace systems.

Programme managers need to have:

— Good problem solving skills, and an ability to deal with complex problems for which there may be no current long-term answers

— A pro-active approach that considers short-term, medium-term and long-term issues

— Adequate awareness of the relevant technical, preservation, corporate, legal and political aspects

— An ability to think critically, but also to receive new ideas and to adapt to change

— Collaborative abilities and in interest in sharing information and looking for ways to work with others.

Preservation programmes require sophisticated systems and tools, although small programmes dealing with largely un-automated processes and with carriers that can be stored on shelves may be able to get by using quite modest computer equipment that is already available. Where services have been contracted from an outside supplier, the programme itself may not need to provide much of the technological infrastructure.

The systems and tools likely to be required include those for:

— Storing and managing the collection material
— Storing and managing metadata
— Managing the transfer of material to the collection, possibly including gathering
— Managing information about rights and managing access in accord with rights
— Storing and managing accessibility tools such as original software, plug-ins, conversion and emulation programmes
— Searching by users
— Making appropriate copies available for users
— Managing many of the processes described in these guidelines, especially those that generate management information, copy material from one place or format to another, or require automated process checking.

Procurement of appropriate systems is a significant task, requiring special attention to specifications and the evaluation of options. Some existing programmes are willing to share information on the specifications they have used and their experience in procuring suitable systems.

## 6.7. Standards of Preservation

Standards lie behind almost everything that computers do, so they form a crucial foundation to the creation and use of digital materials. However, they have not yet been great enablers of preservation. They can be expected to make several important contributions if they are well chosen and well used. Those contributions can be seen in:

— The creation of digital materials that should be relatively straightforward to preserve. Some file formats (themselves standardised) have proven to be so widely useful that they have been adopted by creator communities as a best practice, raising the prospect that they will continue to be used for a long time. Examples include the Tagged Interchange File Format (TIFF) for images, and the Structured General Markup Language (SGML) family of formats including HTML and XML, for structured documents

— Where such widely adopted formats are based on open source, non-proprietary specifications (as is the case with TIFF and SGML), it should be relatively easy to find or develop tools when they are needed to provide ongoing access across changes in technologies

— Agreed approaches to a number of preservation processes, including the recording of metadata, migration processes, data protection and item identification. Standards are still evolving in these areas

— Defining the responsibilities and functions of certain kinds of preservation programmes. The outstanding example of this to date is the Reference Model for an Open Archival Information System (OAIS), accepted by the International Standards Organisation in 2002.

Standards should not be seen as a preservation panacea. Even where they exist, they are subject to change, versioning and non-standard use by producers. Many format standards are in fact proprietary specifications that may not be publicly available, so it may be impossible to know whether tools for future access will be available. While increased standardisation of processes can only help preservation programmes, it is important not to wait for a single 'digital preservation standard' to emerge before taking sensible preservation action.

There are many different models that have been used as organisational structures to manage digital preservation. Some possibilities include:

— Setting up a single separate digital preservation unit to look after all aspects

— A series of specialist units looking after different aspects

— A matrix of people working in different areas, responsible to an overall programme manager

— Mainstreaming of the work through existing work areas so that it becomes part of the normal work integrated with other operations
— Embedding the programme in a particular existing work area such as IT, preservation, collection development, or collection management sections.

These different models tend to produce different emphases, reflecting various levels of comfort with IT tools, collecting objectives, preservation thinking, etc. Any model can be made to work effectively, so long as it draws on the perspectives and skills that are needed and has strong management support.

Preservation programmes should be guided by a policy framework that says what the programme is trying to do and how it will try to achieve it. In a field of such complexity and evolving understandings, a policy document needs to provide clear, long-term direction as well as regularly reviewed guidance. In implementing policy and developing action plans, it is almost always necessary to decide what issues, actions and materials should be given priority for attention, and to understand what work is critical before other work can be attempted.

There may be alternative paths for achieving the preservation commitments of the programme. Organisations should consider whether they will get a better result from doing the work in-house, or by contracting with someone else to do it, or by a combination of approaches. Many processes such as storage and documentation may be amenable to contracting, which may offer access to specialised expertise and facilities that would not be available otherwise.

In many cases, programmes may not be able to afford the initial investments involved in setting up and maintaining infrastructure, so paying for someone else to provide services may be attractive. Contracting may present some potential risks, including:

— Creating a distance between programme objectives and service provision
— The possibility of being locked into the service provider's services because the cost of seeking alternatives is greater than the cost of continuing
— Less control over what happens on a day-to-day basis

- — Higher costs (they may also be lower) than in-house arrangements over the long term ·
- — Fewer learning opportunities that might suggest better ways of doing things.

The succ...: of contracting may depend on the programme manager's ability to define what is needed; finding a reliable supplier who can offer the services required at a suitable price; being able to negotiate a suitable contract with adequate safeguards; and skills in managing the contract. In working with service providers, preservation managers must ensure they:

- — Understand their business and what they need to achieve
- — Communicate their needs
- — Rigorously assess the capabilities, motivations, and understandings of potential suppliers
- — Prepare and negotiate an appropriate contract
- — Ensure communication channels are open so that any problems that be reported early
- — Monitor performance closely and evaluate arrangements regularly. Ensure there are responsible exit strategies and succession plans in place for when arrangements come to an end.

There are good technological, economic and political reasons for preservation programmes to cooperate. Decisions about collaboration should be based on assessment of the benefits expected and the costs involved. There are a number of possibilities regarding where to look for partners, what the focus of the relationship should be, and structural frameworks that would be suitable. Successful cooperation is usually the result of careful attention to these choices, and to putting in the effort required to manage the collaboration in practice.

### 6.7.1. Perspectives of Management

Digital heritage and collaboration go together very well. The technology of digital materials supports collaboration: such materials are easy to duplicate, and many are designed for networked access, so remote management is not difficult. It is also expensive - often too expensive - to set up the whole infrastructure of digital preservation for every preservation programme, so there is a strong incentive to look for ways of sharing facilities.

There may even be a political imperative to work cooperatively: the community may reasonably expect that programmes will collaborate to ensure as much digital heritage as possible can be preserved, as coherently as possible.

Organisational priorities can be sidetracked by problems in the collaborative relationship itself, taking attention away from the real mission of preserving digital materials. In the face of such potential costs and difficulties, it is important to identify the benefits that any collaboration is meant to deliver. Benefits driving a cooperative effort could include:

— Access to a wider range of expertise
— Shared development costs
— Access to tools and systems that might otherwise be unavailable
— Shared learning opportunities
— Increased coverage of preserved materials
— Better planning to reduce wasted effort
— Encouragement for other influential stakeholders to take preservation seriously
— Shared influence on agreements with producers
— Shared influence on research and development of standards and practices
— Attraction of resources and other support for well-coordinated programmes at a regional, national or sectoral level.

The benefits of collaboration usually do not happen by accident, but result from careful attention to choices. Programmes need to consider their potential partners, ways of working together, structural models, and the steps involved in making the proposed collaboration work. Potential partners are likely to be others working in the same sector. Examples could include a consortium of university libraries, or networks of data archives, or government agencies agreeing to use the same application software, or a group of recording studios sharing storage facilities for masters.

It may be possible to join an existing collaboration, or to form new partnerships. However, there may also be benefits to be gained from looking beyond sectoral boundaries, especially as digital technologies and users expectations are increasingly blurring the edges between sectors. For example, a number of libraries, archives, research institutes, data archives and producers in a regional area may consider joining forces to develop a local programme that meets all their needs.

There may also be opportunities for formal cooperative arrangements between preservation programmes and interested stakeholders including groups of producers, industry peak bodies, user groups, IT industry groups, or government bodies interested in fostering good practice. There are many ways that preservation programmes can work together, depending on the benefits they want to achieve and what each partner has to offer. They include:

— *Shared standards*: agreements to do things in the same ways, either with a view to interoperability between programmes, or simply based on a shared understanding of what practices will best support preservation objectives

— *Information sharing*: agreements to share information either at a general level or on specific issues, such as procurement specifications or research results

— *Speaking with a common voice*: agreements to develop and present a common message in advocacy campaigns, or in publicity aimed at raising the profile of digital heritage preservation

— *Division of labour*: agreements to work together at an operational level, taking preservation steps in a coordinated way, with responsibilities either carried out in parallel or divided between programmes

— *Shared resources*: agreements to share resources such as systems, staff or funds to work on a common programme.

It is usually necessary to decide what digital materials are worth keeping, as has been the case with non-digital materials. Many of the same approaches - selection based on criteria embodied in collection development policies, and good knowledge of the materials and their context - are fundamental for digital heritage selection. Preservation programmes also need to define the elements or characteristics of the materials they select that give them value, so that those elements can be maintained.

Deciding what should be preserved, by whom, and for how long, have been fundamental decisions in managing all kinds of tangible heritage. Such decisions are necessary because there are usually more things - more information, more records, more publications, more data than we have the means to keep. Every choice to preserve is at the expense of something else.

The selection of digital heritage is conceptually the same as selection of non-digital materials. Any existing programme with well-established procedures for assessing and selecting material for preservation will already have policies, skills and tools that can help in selecting digital materials, even though they may need some adjustment. However, digital materials do present some new challenges that programme managers must take into account in making the best selection decisions they can.

- There is often a large amount of material to be assessed
- The means of producing and disseminating digital materials are widely available, so their quality is often inconsistent
- At the same time, there may be pressure to preserve the entire traffic carried by new communication channels such as the World Wide Web, regardless of quality
- Timing of selection is usually critical, as digital materials quickly de-select themselves by becoming unusable. It may not be possible to wait for evidence of enduring value to emerge before making selection decisions
- Some digital objects may be hard to pin down. New genres may not fit into existing classifications; some digital resources consist of linked or overlapping parts; many also exist in parallel versions.
- Even when external boundaries have been defined, it may be hard to tell which elements need to be maintained if the digital object is to fulfil its essential purpose
- It may even be difficult to tell where digital materials come from, making it hard to decide who is responsible for their preservation

and with whom to negotiate the rights required by preservation programmes.

There are dangers in assuming that current value assessments are a completely reliable guide to future values. For example, remote sensing data collected in previous decades has become unexpectedly important for assessing environmental change. This experience suggests it is probably better to err on the side of collecting more material rather than less, if the preservation programme can manage it.

Where digital materials can only be understood by reference to a set of rules such as a record keeping system, database or data generation system, or other contextual information, selection processes must identify the documentation that will also need to be preserved. Producers of digital materials may have a significant role to play in selecting what should be preserved. They are often well placed to understand why digital objects were brought into being, their essential 'message', and the relationships between objects and their context. If that information is not captured from the producer it may be too difficult to reconstruct it later.

Both comprehensive and selective approaches are supported by strong arguments. Advocates of a comprehensive approach argue that any information may turn out to have long-term value, and that the costs of detailed selection are greater than the costs of collecting and storing everything. Advocates of a more selective approach argue that it allows them to create collections of high value resources, with some assurance of technical quality and an opportunity to negotiate access rights with producers.

There may well be a place for both approaches, as they are likely to produce quite different collections of digital heritage that are valued for different purposes. To minimise the risk of important materials being missed, and to avoid unnecessary duplication of effort, it may be necessary to seek agreements with other potential collecting and preservation agencies about respective roles and responsibilities.

Selection policies may have to decide whether to select whole items and whole collections, or samples only. It is generally preferable to preserve whole items to retain their integrity, but it may be necessary to restrict collecting to representative samples as a way of at least evidencing the existence of some kinds of materials. Selection policy may also have to consider whether the re-use of material constitutes a new item that should also be preserved.

Rights issues may influence selection decisions. Preservation programmes often select materials that are still subject to rights, but generally would not select material if rights were so restrictive that arrangements for giving access at some future stage cannot be negotiated. If the material can never be made available for use, or if necessary preservation steps cannot be taken, there is little point in selecting it as heritage material.

Managing selection also requires the development of criteria for appraisal. Where the amount of material is so large that it is not feasible to assess items individually, it may be necessary to establish classes of material that can be assessed on the basis of representative samples. Preservation programmes often act as agents for other stakeholders: they take preservation action on behalf of someone who wants material kept for a reason.

The 'someone else' may be as broad and many-faceted as 'the nation' or 'the general community', who may mandate a programme to collect and preserve a very broad range of materials; or it may be as narrow as the members of an organisation or researchers working in a particular discipline who want their own research output preserved for later use.

The needs of the 'community' - however defined - for whom the material is being kept will drive many decisions, from what material is selected, to the kind and level of documentation that is recorded, to the level of concern with authenticity, to the strategies that are used. For example, some programmes must offer users the option of interrogating old data to produce new results, whereas others have a brief to present material in a read-only form to that it cannot be changed or manipulated.

Some programmes may even have to ensure users can run old simulations, play old computer games, or view digital art in ways that reproduce the original experience rather than a speeded up experience that later technologies may provide. Defining the essential elements or characteristics (also referred to as significant properties by some programmes) is not conceptually difficult, as the examples above illustrate. In some circumstances - such as clearly defined and constrained user expectations, and easily characterised materials that are all similar - defining and encoding the essential elements should be straightforward.

For instance, a programme may decide that users of a large collection of electronic mail messages only need to see elements that can be characterised as 'content information', such as the name and address of the sender, subject, date and time, recipients, and the message, in a standardised structure with only the most simple of formatting. A government archive with this approach could expect to apply this essential elements template to very large numbers of email records.

On the other hand, some materials are much more difficult to characterise, and expectations about how they will be re-presented for use, especially to an open-ended community of potential users, may be so hard to define in advance that it becomes almost impossible. Approaches to this issue are developing as more people encounter the problems of describing, storing and planning to re-present digital objects in growing collections over long periods of time.

Preservation programmes with few resources must still make decisions about the materials for which they accept responsibility. Because the costs of preservation are related to the amount of material to be managed, such programmes may need to be highly selective, limiting their ambitions to a small amount of highly valued material. Preservation costs are also related to the range of problems and formats that need to be managed, so it may also make sense to severely limit the kinds of materials selected to a very few formats.

Collecting agreements with other programmes may shift some of the burden of selecting materials. While these would normally be negotiated with other preservation programmes, there may be potential for agreements with producers that would lead them to make decisions about what should be collected and preserved. The preservation programme would still need to take some responsibility for quality control, as well as articulating the criteria by which material should be chosen.

Digital heritage is often created without consideration of ongoing use and accessibility. However, there are definitely standards and practices that producers can use that either help or hinder preservation. Programme managers need to look for ways of exerting a positive influence from as early in the digital heritage life cycle as possible. This often requires a willingness to work with producers.

Digital materials are created by producers who are not necessarily concerned with long-term availability: creation of 'digital heritage' may not be part of their intention. Even those hoping to make something of enduring value may not have the knowledge or the means to do so, or be constrained by other impediments in their working environment. Without some kind of intervention, it is unlikely that digital heritage materials will automatically be made in ways that will minimise costs and remove barriers to preservation. Many practices in fact make preservation much harder.

Preservation efforts that wait until problems start to appear are likely to be more costly, more difficult, and less effective than efforts that start early. Organisations that have both heritage-creating and heritage-preserving functions have learnt from experience that care invested from the start in the use of standards, documentation, good file management and other practices, pays dividends later in lower preservation and maintenance costs, as well as more easily accessed, re-used and managed collections.

While all preservation programmes do not have the same opportunities to influence production practices, all programmes should seek to influence the way materials are created, and managed, from as early in their life cycle as possible. It is important to recognise that creators of digital materials work in different environments and are likely to be quite diverse in many ways: how they approach their work, their size of operations, the organisational and technical support at their disposal, and their interest in long-term access issues.

For example, scientists collecting data are likely to have an overriding interest in how accurately and securely their data is protected; how well any proposed formats and standards fit with their working needs; the convenience of transfer arrangements; and maintenance of moral rights and access controls over their data. On the other hand, commercial publishers of CD-ROM packages are likely to be more interested in controls on unauthorised copying; the costs and risks associated with providing 'unprotected' versions to a preservation programme; the potential re-use of their content; and their licence obligations to software owners whose products they have used.

There are many ways in which those responsible for preserving digital heritage may approach working with those who create and disseminate it. Preservation programmes should proactively promote awareness of their own role. It may be advantageous to identify particular groups of producers and work with them, addressing specific issues, rather than trying to resolve everyone's concerns at a generic level. At a broader industry level, it may be helpful to develop a code of practice that sets out agreed understandings about roles and responsibilities, and defines the scope and terms of ongoing cooperation.

Many sectors have active industry groups that provide forums for discussing issues. As well as offering opportunities for dialogue with industry leaders, such forums may help in establishing new norms of thinking that incorporate a longer term perspective. It is important for preservation programmes to offer positive encouragement and feedback for the steps producers are willing to take, and to provide a level of accountability for the way preservation programmes deal with their materials.

In many situations, working with producers means a real input by the preservation programme, not just the producer. Possible areas of input may include:

— Providing written guidelines and specifications
— Providing training for staff
— Help in designing systems and workflows
— Exchange of information and working tips
— Succession arrangements for material in a producer-managed preservation programme.

Specifications and best practice guidance Guidance on good practice is likely to include advice on the following:

— *Organisational issues that will make it easier to manage digital materials:* Project planning, emphasising system design prior to the creation of any records or publications
— *Choice of carrier*: Producers should be encouraged to use 'industrial strength' products that will survive long enough for the data to be transferred to other carriers, either by the producer or on transfer to the preservation programme

— *Choice of appropriate file formats and data standards*: Unless there are very good reasons to do otherwise, creators should be encouraged to use very widely adopted, well-standardised file formats that fit their purposes. Generally speaking, data in simpler formats using open source, non-proprietary software are easier to preserve (although some proprietary applications achieve such widespread use that they may be accepted as an industry standard, especially if their specifications are openly published).

Online materials published for public access should be readable by commonly used browsers. Structuring documents in a standard, easily recognised and durable format such as XML (Extensible Markup Language) should be considered for material of enduring value

— *Validation of formats*: It is not enough simply to choose a standard format and then to use it in non-standard ways: formats should be implemented in compliance with their standard and if necessary validated to remove any idiosyncrasies likely to complicate preservation.

— *File names should be consistent and unambiguous*: Online files should be managed for persistent access through the use of a persistent identifier and resolver service, or re-direct messages if files are moved. A number of PI schemes are in use internationally in different sectors, although none are in universal use. The DOI (Digital Object Identifier) scheme used by commercial publishers to manage rights has the widest acceptance.

Creators should create good quality metadata for the resources they create, using a widely accepted schema such as MARC, the Dublin Core metadata elements or one of its many sector-based enhancements. The metadata will help users find and use their resources. Metadata should also be recorded that describes the technical nature of the digital objects, what is required to access them, and any changes in these details over their life cycle: this information will be needed in managing them. The metadata can be either embedded in the resources or stored in a linked metadata file

— *File management*: Preservation master files should be stored and managed separately from dissemination copies. Database management procedures should ensure that data is not overwritten before it is captured

— *System security*: Files and systems should be fully protected from damage or loss by adopting best practice security measures and by appropriate backup arrangements even for short-term storage

— *Authenticity*: All files should be identified and their provenance and history documented to provide continuous evidence of authenticity

— *Training*: Staff, contractors and others coming into contact with the digital materials should be guided by appropriate procedures and manuals, and be adequately trained, motivated and equipped to use them

— If access or copying barriers are considered necessary to protect intellectual property, they may well make preservation impossible. Arrangements will be needed to allow preservation processes such as copying to take place.

Initial steps in maintaining access may include keeping all the software required for access, as well as any specialised hardware. This will not be an effective long-term strategy but may well be necessary in the short term. There may be a need to evaluate digital materials, decide how long they should be kept and by whom, in accordance with an approved policy such as an archival disposal authority.

Digital preservation programmes with few resources may find they are unable to spare any resources to work with producers. However, it may be possible to make a worthwhile investment in reducing future costs by taking limited, targeted actions aimed at influencing the material they have to manage.

## References

Gopal Krishan, *Digital Libraries in Electronic Information Era*, Authorspress, New Delhi, 2000.

Johnson, C.A., "Retrospective Conversion of Three Library Collections", *Information Technology and Libraries*, 1982.

Kahle, B., *Archiving the Internet*, Paper submitted to Scientific American for March 1997 issue, 1997.

Kantor, P.B., *Objective Performance Measures for Academic and Research Libraries*, Washington, DC: Association of Research Libraries, 1984.

Malwad N. M., *et al* (ed.), *Digital Libraries: Dynamics storehouse of digitised information*, New Delhi, New Age International, 1996.

Raitt, David, (ed.), *Libraries for the New Millennium: Implication for Managers*, London, Library Association Publishing, 1987.

Sproull, L., and S. Kiesler, *Connections: New Ways of Working in the Networked Organisation*, MIT Press, Cambridge, MA, 1991.

# 7

# Metadata Management

The rapid changes in the means of information access occasioned by the emergence of the World Wide Web have spawned an upheaval in the means of describing and managing information resources. Metadata is a primary tool in this work, and an important link in the value chain of knowledge economies. Yet there is much confusion about how metadata should be integrated into information systems.

## 7.1. Principles of Metadata

The paragraphs in this section provide a guiding framework for the development of practical solutions for semantic and machine interoperability in any domain using any set of metadata standards.

### 7.1.1. Modularity

Metadata modularity is a key organizing principle for environments characterized by vastly diverse sources of content, styles of content management, and approaches to resource description. It allows designers of metadata schemas to create new assemblies based on established metadata schemas and benefit from observed best practice, rather than reinventing elements anew.

In a modular metadata world, data elements from different schemas as well as vocabularies and other building blocks can be combined in a syntactically and semantically interoperable way. Thus, application designers should be able to benefit from significant re-usability as they gather existing modules of metadata and 'snap' them together much as individual Lego™ blocks can be assembled into larger structures. The appeal of the Lego™ metaphor has partly to do with the underlying engineering and design that sustains 'interoperability' across many years of evolution, and partly from the variety of 'semantics' reflected in the various themes of Lego™ sets.

Children think nothing of mixing cowboy themes and pirate themes and undersea exploration themes. While the 'semantics' of such combinations may not always be obvious to adults, children don't seem to be bothered by such incongruities. Similar flexibility should be achievable in the metadata architecture of the Web, allowing application designers to mix a variety of semantic modules within a common syntactic foundation, even though the designers of the modules might not have anticipated a given combination. For example, a discovery metadata module and an instructional management metadata module, expressed in a common syntactic idiom such as XML, should be able to be combined in a compound schema that embodies the functionality of each constituent. In this way, modular sets can be assembled to meet the specific requirements of a given application, meeting domain-specific and local requirements without unduly sacrificing cross-domain interoperability.

The notion of namespaces is a fundamental part of the infrastructure of the Web (and particularly XML [NAMES]), though the concept predates the Web and is familiar to most. Simply put, a namespace is a formal collection of terms managed according to a policy or algorithm. For example, the base protocol of the Web is HTTP, which is a namespace that guarantees that a given URI is globally unique. LCSH (Library of Congress Subject Headings) is a namespace managed by the U.S. Library of Congress according to rules governing the assignment of subject headings to intellectual artifacts. Any metadata element set is a namespace bounded by the rules and conventions determined by its maintenance agency.

The technicalities of declaring and managing namespaces in an XML environment are beyond the present discussion, but the idea is a critical part of the infrastructure necessary for deploying modular metadata systems on the Web. Namespace declarations allow the metadata schema designer to define the context for a particular term, thereby assuring that the term has a unique definition within the bounds of the declared namespace. Thus, the declaration of various namespaces within a block of metadata allows the elements within that metadata to be identified as belonging to one or another element set.

Expressed as natural language, such a declaration might read:

— The Dublin Core metadata element set is defined at a Web location specified by a URI; all Dublin Core elements within the scope of this namespace declaration can be recognized by the prefix *dc:*.

— The IEEE-LOM metadata element set is defined at a Web location specified by a URI; all IEEE-LOM elements within the scope of this namespace declaration can be recognized by the prefix *lom:*.

Using this infrastructure, metadata system designers can select elements from suitable existing metadata element sets, taking advantage of the investment of existing communities of expertise, and thereby avoid reinventing well-established metadata sets for each new deployment domain.

### 7.1.2. Extensibility

Metadata systems must allow for extensions so that particular needs of a given application can be accommodated. Some metadata elements are likely to be found in most metadata schemas (the concept of *creator* or *identifier* of an information resource, for example). Others will be specific to particular applications or domains (*degree of cloud cover,* for example, in remote sensing data).

Metadata architectures must easily accommodate the notion of a base schema with additional elements that tailor a given application to local needs or domain-specific needs without unduly compromising the interoperability provided by the base schema. Another application encountering such extensions should be able to ignore such extensions while making use of any elements understood by both.

### 7.1.3. Refinement

Application domains will differ according to the degree of detail that is necessary or desirable. The design of metadata standards should allow schema designers to choose a level of detail appropriate to a given application. Populating databases with metadata is costly, so there are strong economic incentives to create metadata with sufficient detail to meet the functional requirements of an application, but not more.

There are two notions of refinement to consider. The first is the addition of qualifiers that refine or make more specific the meaning of an element. *Illustrator, author, composer,* or *sculptor* are all examples of particular types of the more general term, creator. *Date of creation, date of modification,* and *date of acceptance* are all narrower senses of a date attribute. Such refinements might be useful or even essential in a given metadata application, but for general interoperability purposes, the values of such elements can be thought of as subtypes of a broader element.

A second variety of refinement involves the specification of particular schemes or value sets that define the range of values for a given element. Thus, identifying that a metadata value has been selected from a controlled vocabulary or has been constructed according to a particular algorithm may make it much more useful, especially for automated processing. In this way, semantic interoperability across applications can be increased, by relying on a common value set.

The encoding of dates and times is an example of the use of an encoding standard to remove ambiguity from the expression of a metadata value. The string *03/06/02* is interpreted as *March 6, 2002* in North America and *June 3, 2002* in Europe and Australia. By using an encoding standard such as the W3C date and time format, a date can be encoded in an unambiguous manner (*2002-03-06*). Specifying the encoding format in the metadata allows unambiguous machine processing as well as improving human comprehension.

The use of controlled vocabularies is another important approach to refinement that improves the precision for descriptions and leverages the substantial intellectual investment made by many domains to improve subject access to resources. The Dewey Decimal Classification System, for example, affords a multilingual classification system long used in traditional library environments that can be applied to electronic resources as well. There are hundreds of domain-specific thesauri and classification systems, as well, that can be imported into the Web metadata architecture to support subject descriptions. Specifying the use of a particular vocabulary in a given collection of metadata will allow applications to provide more coherent search and browsing facilities. Even in cases where an application is not designed to take advantage of a classification scheme or thesaurus, users may still benefit from the inherent coherence that such a scheme affords.

### 7.1.4. Multilingualism

It is essential to adopt metadata architectures that respect linguistic and cultural diversity. The Web as a global information system is important in that it affords unprecedented access to resources of global scope. However, unless such resources can be made available to users in their native languages, in appropriate character sets, and with metadata appropriate to management of the resources, the Web will fail to achieve its potential as a global information system.

Standards typically deal with these issues through the complementary processes of *internationalization* and *localization:* the former process relates to the creation of "neutral" standards, whereas the latter refers to the adaptation of such a neutral standard to a local context.

It is important to note that these two processes can sometimes work at cross-purposes. While global resource discovery is best served by internationalization (common conventions of practice, languages, and character sets), the needs of any given community may be better served by supporting local conventions. One of the challenges for a global metadata architecture is to assure that the underlying infrastructure can support either strategy equally well, or a mix of the two. Thus, a given application will reflect design choices based on an understanding of this balance and its implications.

A basic starting point in promoting a global metadata architecture is to translate relevant specification and standards documents into a variety of languages. DCMI maintains a list of translations of its basic documents. Likewise, the European workshop on Learning Technologies is maintaining translations of the LOM specification.

Another essential dimension is to include provisions in the metadata for the description of lingual and other cultural aspects of a resource. For example, metadata can describe the language and character set of the resource. The metadata may identify alternative versions of resources, in different languages, as well as the origin of the translations.

On a somewhat more technical level, it is important for global adoption of the standards that both the specifications and the ways these specifications are encoded are as "culturally neutral" as possible. As an example, it would be inappropriate to define the value space of a data element such as educational context in a way that is specific to one national system.

Multilingualism is one aspect of the broader issue of multiculturalism, which includes, for instance:

— The way in which dates are represented in different calendars,
— The direction in which text is displayed and read,
— Cultural connotations of certain icons and pictograms,
— Standards of practice (name order, collation standards, leading article standards).

Clearly, many of these aspects go beyond the immediate context of metadata. However, as mentioned above, it is important that metadata can describe the relevant characteristics, and that it can do so in ways that respect cultural and language differences.

## 7.2. Practicalities of Metadata

The metadata principles as set out above, lead, at a minimum, to the following practicalities. These practicalities represent aspects of the emerging ecology of metadata creation and management on the Internet.

### 7.2.1. Application Profiles

No single metadata element set will accommodate the functional requirements of all applications, and as the Web dissolves access boundaries, it becomes increasingly important to be able to also cross discovery boundaries. Application profiles will facilitate this by allowing designers to 'mix and match' schemas as appropriate.

An application profile is an assemblage of metadata elements selected from one or more metadata schemas and combined in a compound schema. Application profiles provide the means to express principles of modularity and extensibility. The purpose of an application profile is to adapt or combine existing schemas into a package that is tailored to the functional requirements of a particular application, while retaining interoperability with the original base schemas. Part of such an adaptation may include the elaboration of local metadata elements that have importance in a given community or organization, but which are not expected to be important in a wider context.

One of the benefits of this approach is that communities of practice are able to focus on standardizing community-specific metadata in ways that can be preserved in the larger metadata architectures of the Web. It will be possible to snap together such community-specific modules to form more complex metadata structures that will conform to the standards of the community while preserving cross-community interoperability.

Application Profiles achieve this modularity through a number of mechanisms:

— *Cardinality enforcement:* Cardinality refers to constraints on the appearance of an element. Is it optional? Mandatory? Conditional? The status of some data elements can be made more stringent in a given context. For instance, an optional data element can be made mandatory in a particular application profile. A typical example would be an element that specifies the human language of a resource: such an element can be made mandatory in a multi-lingual community. Along the same lines, an application may make the status of an optional element conditional, or a conditional element mandatory. As an application profile must operate within the interoperability constraints defined by the standard, it cannot relax the status of data elements.

— *Value Space Restriction*: For some data elements, the value space can be made more restrictive than in the standard. This mechanism can apply when the standard is very loose about the values for a data element. A typical example is the restriction of values about people involved in the life cycle of a resource to references into a registry of people and organizations (e.g., as an LDAP service). The same mechanism can also apply when the standard is already quite explicit about the value space, when the context of use allows for further restrictions. A typical example can restrict reference to the human language of a resource (typically an extensive list, as defined in ISO 639) to those languages that are relevant in a particular community.

— *Relationship and dependency specification:* An application profile can define interrelationships between data elements and their value spaces. For instance, the presence of one data element may impose the requirement that another element be present. Similarly, an application profile can restrict the value set of a data element, based on the value of another data element.

— *Declaration of namespaces*: Application profiles support the use of multiple namespaces, such that designers may choose elements appropriate to their needs from various different element sets. Schema designers may also add local elements through the use of a locally defined namespace.

Namespace declarations are the XML infrastructure that allows the construction of mixed metadata sets within an application profile. A schema designer can invoke several such declarations to include elements from existing schemas that can be combined in a modular way to form a compound schema that meets the functional requirements of an application without destroying the possibility of interoperability with existing schemas that also use these elements in other combinations. The main goal of application profiles is to increase the "semantic interoperability" of the resulting metadata instances within a community of practice, by going beyond the universal consensus of a single standard, without compromising the basic interoperability that the standard enables across the boundaries of these communities.

### 7.2.2. Syntax and Semantics

Semantics is about meaning; syntax is about form. Agreements about both are necessary for two communities to share metadata. Two communities may agree about the meaning of the term title or creator or identifier, but until they have a shared convention for identifying and encoding values, they cannot easily exchange their metadata.

It is important, however, to keep syntax and semantics separate as far as possible. The rapid changes of the first decade of the Web illustrate this well. We have witnessed several versions of HTML, the emergence of XML, and the development of derivative technologies that include at this time both XML Schemas and RDF Schemas. The lack of stability in the structured markup realm emphasizes the necessity of maintaining independence between the semantics of metadata elements and their syntactic representation. However, as more information is 'born digital', one expects metadata facilities to be an intrinsic part of the creation and management of the resources, so issues of syntax cannot be ignored even though we are in general more concerned with the meaning of metadata statements rather than how they are exchanged.

At this writing it is not possible to predict which, if any, of the various metadata encoding schemes will prevail. A few observations are appropriate, however.

HTML-encoded metadata accounts for the majority of metadata embedded within Web resources (and hence available for harvesting). This approach has the great virtue of simplicity (no additional systems are necessary—Web infrastructure provides the system in the form of HTML markup and http protocols), but it limits the structural richness of the metadata assertions that can be made.

XML markup, while still a small part of the total markup on the Web, is the idiom of choice for the encoding and exchange of structured data. The XML namespace facility provides structural capabilities that HTML lacks, making it easier to achieve the principles of modularity and extensibility. The XML Schema specification defines a schema language that allows for the specification of application profiles that will increase the prospects for interoperability.

The Resource Description Framework (RDF) promises an architecture for Web metadata and has been advanced as the primary enabling infrastructure of the Semantic Web activity in the W3C. Designed to support the reuse and exchange of vocabularies, RDF is an additional layer on top of XML that is intended to simplify the reuse of vocabulary terms across namespaces. Most RDF deployment to date has been experimental, though there are significant applications emerging in the world of commerce (Adobe's deployment of their XMP standard which is based on RDF).

The IEEE Learning Object Metadata standard provides an example of how this critical need for independence between the semantics of metadata and their syntactical representation can be addressed. LOM will be what is known as a "multi-part standard" where the semantic data model is an independent standard and then each syntactical representation is an independent standard developed as a specific "binding" of the LOM Data Model standard. DCMI also provides recommendations on encoding of Dublin Core metadata in alternative encoding idioms.

Finally, it should be noted that there is a third requirement beyond syntax and semantics for interoperability: content vocabularies. This may be as open and unconstrained as a shared natural language (English, Dutch, German...). The use of a specific controlled vocabulary or namespace will further narrow the scope and increase the precision of a description, as discussed elsewhere in this paper.

### 7.2.3. Association Models

There are various ways to associate metadata with resources:

*Embedded metadata* resides within the markup of the resource. This implies that the metadata is created at the time that the resource is created, often by the author. Experts differ concerning whether author-created metadata is best or whether it is better to have trained practitioners evaluate and describe resources. As a practical matter, resource description expertise is a scarce and costly commodity, and thus any investment by authors in the description of their intellectual products is likely to be of value.Embedded metadata can also be harvested, and the presumptive increase in visibility that might result is an incentive for creators to assign metadata.

*Associated metadata* is maintained in files tightly coupled to the resources they describe. Such metadata may or may not be harvestable. The advantage of associated metadata derives from the relative ease of managing the metadata without altering the content of the resource itself, but this benefit is purchased at the cost of simplicity, necessitating the co-management of resource files and metadata files.

*Third-Party metadata* is maintained in a separate repository by an organization that may or may not have direct control over or access to the content of the resource. Typically such metadata is maintained in a database that is not accessible to harvesters, though the emerging Open Archives Initiative Metadata Harvesting Protocol proposes a system that encourages the disclosure of metadata repositories among federated OAI servers.

Syntax issues and association models are often confused. Many assume HTML based metadata is equivalent to embedded metadata, and that other representations are necessarily other types. Any of these three syntactic idioms can easily be embedded within the markup of an electronic resource or managed as a separate entity.

A given information resource will often have multiple metadata records reflecting the various purposes and perspectives of the organizations that create and manage them. A resource may be created with embedded metadata supplied by the author. A separate record might be created by the issuing organization (an academic department or publisher, for example) and stored in a separate database. A third party (perhaps a library) might create yet another version of metadata, either from scratch or derived from a previous record. In most cases these records will not be managed in a coordinated way, and differences may arise among them that may cause ambiguity or confusion. This may be less than ideal, but must be expected in an environment where various organizations may choose to manage resource descriptions with different objectives.

### 7.2.4. Identifying and Naming Metadata Elements

The global scope of the Web URI namespace means that each data element in an element set can be represented by a globally addressable name (its URI). Invariant global identifiers make machine processing of metadata across languages and applications far easier, but may impose unnatural constraints in a given context. Identifiers such as URIs are not convenient as labels to be read by people, especially when such labels are in a language or character set other than the natural language of a given application. People prefer to read simple strings that have meaning in their own language. Particular tools and applications can use different presentation labels within their systems to make the labels more understandable and useful in a given linguistic, cultural, or domain context.

### 7.2.5. Metadata Registries

Metadata registries represent an important topic of digital library research at this time. As the number of metadata and application profile schemas designed to meet the needs of particular discourse and practice communities increases, the importance of the management and disclosure roles of registries will similarly increase. The expectation is that registries will provide the means to identify and refer to established schemas and application profiles, potentially including the means for machine mapping among different schemas. In addition, it is expected that such registries will contain, or link to, important controlled vocabularies from which the values of metadata fields can be selected.

Such registries will assume the characteristics of an electronic dictionary, available for consultation by:

— Application designers, who will be able to consult registries to identify existing metadata schemas and schema components that might meet their needs or to identify extensions to those schema that other application designers have developed to meet a given local need.

— Creators and managers of metadata, who can consult a registry to ascertain the definition or usage statements concerning an element or the available or preferred candidate value sets to be used to populate particular elements.

— Applications, which can resolve URIs associated with a schema, an element, or a value set in order to compare or evaluate elements or their values in a set of metadata.

— End users, who might consult a registry to better understand definitions or context of metadata terms, and thereby improve their search or processing effectiveness.

Thus, registries will provide the means to manage and disclose metadata schema declarations, application profile declarations, and value space declarations. As any given metadata schema or application profile evolves, registries will maintain the relationships among that schema's various versions in order to promote semantic and machine interoperability over time.

The DCMI Registry Working Group is exploring some of these issues through the explication of functional requirements for a multilingual DCMI metadata registry and vocabulary management system. Initial prototypes for this system can be accessed at.

It is likely that registries will vary in the depth of their functionality with some being simple links to schema declarations while others may be richly functional databases. Some registries will be managed by namespace authorities and will hold the canonical copies of schema and value space declarations while other registries will harvest those declarations from such authoritative sources and thereby make them available in a more distributed manner.

### 7.2.6. Completeness of Description

There is a strong inclination on the part of creators of metadata to 'fill in all the blanks.' If an element is available, people want to use it in a description. Applications should be designed to make evident that not every available element is necessarily appropriate for every resource type. Similarly, applications should provide assistance where possible in selection of an appropriate value for a particular element. To the extent that metadata creation facilities are built into content creation applications, the application can identify values for some elements more reliably than the user.

Ultimately, the richness of metadata descriptions will be determined by policies and best practices designated by the agency creating the metadata, and those policies and practices will be guided by the functional requirements of services or applications. Some of the tradeoffs for systems and searchers:

1. Detailed metadata descriptions:
   — may improve searching precision

— require higher investment in creation of metadata
— make it more difficult to promote consistency in creation of metadata

2. Simple descriptions:
— are easier and less costly to generate
— may result in more false results, or more effort on the part of searchers to identify most relevant results
— improve probability of cross-disciplinary interoperability

### 7.2.7. Mandatory Versus Optional Elements

Designing metadata standards for a global, cross-disciplinary information environment requires a high degree of flexibility. An element that is essential in one domain may not even be sensible in another, hence few, if any, elements in a general metadata set should be thought of as mandatory.

On the other hand, it is entirely reasonable within a given application or even an application domain, to require particular elements. Thus, communities of practice should be encouraged to further specify standards of practice for a given metadata standard that will encourage uniformity of descriptions within a given domain. This can be done in the form of an application profile as described earlier, and shared with others within a community of practice in order to promote convergence and thereby increase interoperability.

### 7.2.8. Subjective and Objective Metadata

Metadata is broadly defined as structured data about data. However, the process of creating metadata can involve both subjective and objective input. Some metadata is clearly objective: assertions of fact about authorship, date of creation, version, and other attributes are generally able to be determined in an objective way. This objective metadata can also be machine generated in most instances, such as the "properties" metadata generated when creating a file in a word processor or spreadsheet application.Other metadata may be subjective, either because such elements are subject to differing points of view (assignment of keywords, summarization of content in an abstract), or because they are specifically intended to represent a subjective evaluation (a review of a book or a presentation). Even more formal metadata elements become subjective when used within a cultural or domain context that is subject to local interpretation. For example, a pedagogical characteristic that is dependent on a particular educational philosophy may be important within a given context, but will have no meaning outside that context. The requirement for metadata design is, as far as possible, to make that context explicit so that applications can more easily recognize when a given element is constrained by such context as opposed to being more broadly applicable.

### 7.2.9. Automated Generation of Metadata

Most resource discovery metadata prior to the Web was created by humans in the labor-intensive activity of library cataloging. Cataloging metadata remains the most successful standard for resource discovery of books and periodicals, but it is costly to create and impractical for many materials available on the Internet.

Web search engines harvest and index a significant portion of the Internet and provide low cost index access to it, generally in an advertiser-supported model. Such indexing can be thought of as a kind of metadata, and for many information needs, it provides a surprisingly cost effective solution to resource discovery.

Between these two extremes lies a broad range of metadata creation that can be automated to some degree, and which can be expected to grow in importance as advances in such areas as natural language processing, data mining, profile and pattern recognition algorithms become more effective.

Content creation applications (word processors, electronic paper such as PDF, and Website creation tools) often have facilities for author-supplied attributes or automated capture of attributes that can simplify the creation of metadata. As these facilities grow more sophisticated, it will be easier and more natural to combine application-supplied metadata (e.g., creation dates, tagged structural elements, file formats and related information), creator-supplied metadata (keywords, authors, affiliations, for example) and inference-based metadata (classification metadata based on automated classification algorithms, for example). Combining attributes from these approaches will increase the quality and reduce the cost of metadata descriptions.

## 7.3. Metadata Preservation

Controlling what happens to digital materials is a key preservation step. In most cases this requires the safe transfer of data and documentation to the care of a preservation programme, where they are given unique identification, and described using various kinds of metadata. Metadata enables digital materials to be found and, crucially from a preservation point of view, to be managed and re-presented accurately.

Although preservation metadata standards are still developing, programmes must describe the technical characteristics, provenance and preservation objectives of the digital materials in their care. In most cases this requires the transfer of data into the care of a responsible preservation agency. The transfer process itself is not without risks as it provides opportunities for data to be lost, changed, misidentified, or divorced from the context that gives it meaning. Because the producers of digital materials generally have some rights in the materials they produce, transfer raises a number of legal and moral rights issues. Once digital materials have been transferred, they must be controlled and organised in effective and efficient ways. This generally includes requirements that materials can be easily located, accessed, used, managed and preserved, in accord with permissions.

Transfer and control are long-established practices in managing non-digital heritage. When applied to digital materials, these processes must be modified. An appropriate legal basis for transfer is required. It must address concerns over the ease with which materials can be re-used, as well as the need to copy data for its preservation. Transfer must affected without loss of data, often using quite different methods from those used for transfer of non-digital materials. The transfer of accompanying documentation is particularly critical for digital data that may not be understandable without it.

Most transfer strategies are variations of two basic concepts: producers pushing digital materials to the preservation programme, or the preservation programme pulling materials from the producer.

Programme managers must decide which approach will be most suitable for the materials being transferred and for the workflows of the parties involved.

Many programmes impose controls at the point of transfer on the formats of the material they receive. The purpose of this is to simplify preservation by reducing the variations that have to be managed in storing the material and in keeping it accessible. Not all programmes are able to restrict the formats they accept, but they should seek to verify that formats have been used in a standard way.

Digital files must be given suitable file identifiers so they can be retrieved. Each file within a storage system must be identified with a unique file name so that it cannot be confused with any other file. It is also most important for preservation programmes to ensure that the materials they keep can be reliably found, whatever their location. The Universal Resource Locator (URL) used to identify Web-based resources, for example, does not allow users to find material once it has been moved. Thus, items can be effectively lost even though it may still exist and be well protected.

Overcoming this problem requires some form of persistent identification, built around an identifier and a means of resolving or linking to the file in its current location. There are a number of schemes proposed or in place including the Digital Object Identifier (DOI) used by publishers, and various schemes being investigated by libraries and archives, but none has yet found universal acceptance.

Preservation programmes use metadata - structured information about data resources - to describe the digital materials in their care. Preservation programmes generate large amounts of information about way material is created, transferred and used; about rights and who is authorised to do what; and other management processes. Preservation metadata describes the means of providing access, along with those elements of resource management metadata required to manage preservation processes. It is critical for any preservation programme; its careful design and management is especially important for large collections that must be processed with as much automation as possible.

Metadata is itself an information resource that must be managed and preserved, along with the material that it describes. Individually developed metadata schemes can be successful in describing collections of digital materials, but there are increasingly good reasons to use a standardised approach in line with other widely adopted schemes:

— To reduce the considerable costs of developing individual schemes

— To take advantage of available software tools that automatically recognise and record standard metadata elements from digital materials, greatly reducing the cost of metadata capture

— To allow preservation programmes to share information, making their collections visible and searchable to a much wider audience

— To allow collection materials to be moved from one repository to another without the need for wholesale rewriting of metadata

— To encourage the standardisation of preservation processes that are described and controlled by the metadata.

The reproducibility of digital materials means that transfer no longer requires removal of the material from one site in order to move it to another. Perfectly authentic copies can be transferred for preservation while 'live' copies remain with the creator · The timing of transfer may be critical. Even though material may have been selected for preservation, selection of itself does nothing to slow down processes like media deterioration or obsolescence of technology.

There is no standard way of effecting the physical transfer of digital materials. Data can be transferred on a wide range of physical carriers such as various forms of diskettes, CDs, tapes, cartridges, and disk drives; or through communication networks using means such as email attachments, file transfer protocol (FTP), and downloading from Web sites. The choice of transfer media depends on the needs of the parties involved.

Whatever means are chosen, the data must remain secure. Some transfer environments may present particular risks for specific media; for example, physical carriers may be easily lost or stolen, while communication networks may be unreliable and it may be safer to hand deliver a physical carrier. The transfer medium must allow the data to be loaded and retrieved. When both sender and receiver use the same technologies, transfer should be relatively straightforward. When technologies are mismatched, one or both parties will need to bear the cost of using different technologies.

Preservation programmes may have facilities to handle a wide range of media, or their.facilities may be more restricted. Physical carriers require specific hardware which preservation agencies may not be able to provide. In such cases they will need to decide whether it is reasonable to require transfers via specific media that they can process, or to invest in facilities to handle a wider range of media.

On the other hand, preservation programmes relying on deposit may find that transfers depend on production factors beyond their control, including changes in personnel, changes in priority, or declining levels of interest, all leading to inconsistent transfers. Pull approaches place more control in the hands of the preservation programme regarding timing and content of transfers. Some producers consider this an infringement of their rights and either block the software used to copy their files or demand rights agreements, so the control offered by pull approaches is not absolute.

Digital objects can have a number of identifiers variously used for local control, for system-wide identification, and for global access, (just as a book on a library shelf can be identified by its title, a classification number, a shelf location, an accession number, a record number in the catalogue database, an International Series Book Number, and so on). Persistent identification of some kind is needed so that items can be found even if they are moved in a storage system. Any links embedded within objects will only continue to work if linked to persistent identifiers.

It has already been noted that metadata must be not only recorded, but also looked after. There are a number of elements to this:

— *Structuring*: Organising metadata into a standardised document structure such as an XML template should make it easier to preserve

— *Linking*: The links between metadata records and the digital objects they describe must be maintained. There is much debate about the best place to store metadata to achieve this. While some metadata must be attached so that software tools can automatically process the material, there is disagreement on whether full metadata records should be stored separately, attached to, or even become part of, the objects they describe.

Separate storage allows metadata to be accessed and updated without needing to extract the linked digital objects from storage - a great advantage. On the other hand, many programme managers worry about the potential for the essential link between object and record to be disrupted over long periods of time. Managers should assess the risks they operate with and decide which approach is more suitable

— *Quality control*: Ensuring the trustworthiness of metadata records is a high priority. Quality control measures are needed whenever metadata records are created or changed

— *Protection*: The integrity of metadata records must be ensured, requiring the same preservation attention as the objects they describe.

Once the digital material has been transferred and any necessary control and description work undertaken, it must be prepared for entry into a storage system, ensuring the various part of the information package (including the content and any metadata) are linked, and a data stream created that can be safely stored on the storage media in use and can found by the appropriate file searching programmes. The package is then saved to storage.

Preservation metadata is structured information about a digital object, which:

— Identifies the material for which a preservation programme has responsibility

— Communicates what is needed to maintain and protect data

— Communicates what is needed to re-present the intended object (or its defined essential elements) to a user when needed, regardless of changes in storage and access technologies

— Records the history and the effects of what happens to the object

— Documents the identity and integrity of the object as a basis for authenticity

— Allows a user and the preservation programme to understand the context of the object in storage and in use.

Arrangements for recording preservation metadata must accommodate the fact that the same basic content (or conceptual object) may exist in many manifestations during its life. Some of these manifestations will co-exist as digital objects, while others may follow each other in a series of separate or overlapping generations.

Some preservation programmes reflect this by creating a record for a single version identified as a Preservation Master, documenting variants and changes as part of the history of that object. Other programmes create a record for each manifestation requiring preservation action, ensuring the relationships between manifestations are explicit in their metadata records. The information required for preservation metadata is often divided into two classes:

— Content information, consisting mainly of details about the technical nature of the object which tells the system how to re-present the data as specific data types and formats. As access technologies change, this re-presentation metadata also needs to be updated

— Preservation description information, consisting of other information needed for long-term management and use of the object, including identifiers and bibliographic details, information on ownership and rights, provenance, history, context including relationships to other objects, and validation information, Obviously, some of this metadata may refer to other information objects such as software tools and format specifications that must also be managed.

The interdependent nature of digital materials means that programmes often have to manage networks of linked objects and their metadata. There are still no accepted standards for preservation metadata schemas for universal use, so programmes may have to choose between accepting (and possibly adapting) one of a number of models being used by others, or designing their own schema (either as a complete solution or as a minimal interim one until a standard emerges).

### 7.3.1. Legal Rights for Management

There are a range of right and expectations held by stakeholders, which preservation programmes must be aware of and, if necessary, include in their management planning. Many of these rights have legal implications, including intellectual property rights and privacy rights. Because preservation programmes must copy digital materials to preserve them, and because most programmes aim to provide some level of access, active rights management approaches are needed.

Digital heritage materials are subject to a range of rights and expectations, some of which have legal force. Many, such as copyright, result from the intellectual property invested in the material. However, there may be other rights and expectations that also need to be taken into account. The range of rights and expectations that preservation programmes may encounter and have to manage typically includes:

- Intellectual property rights of producers including copyright, which may exist in various layers associated with different aspects of the material; the right to set conditions of access and use; and the creator's moral right to be recognised
- Legislated rights of certain institutions to collect, preserve and provide access to some materials. The rights and expectations of privacy, confidentiality and authorisation of use associated with some subjects of materials such as organisational records, oral history recordings, personal data and private communications.

Preservation involves many processes where rights issues are relevant. In order to achieve continuity of digital heritage, preservation programmes must:

- Obtain and hold material, usually involving making copies
- Make further copies for preservation purposes
- If necessary, bypass devices used by producers to limit access and prevent copying
- Decide what materials and what aspects of materials should be preserved
- Add metadata
- Modify file structures and file names if necessary
- Use whatever means are available at the time to preserve accessibility
- Provide managed access for authorised users.

Preservation programmes must be aware of the legal frameworks in which they operate, including their legal rights, constraints and obligations. This may require reference to specific legal advice from a competent source. Even with good intentions to preserve important heritage materials, preservation programmes are responsible for seeking ways to achieve their mission without infringing the legitimate rights of others.

Preservation programmes must decide on the extent to which they should engage in advocacy on rights issues, presenting arguments for legislation that would make it easier for a wide range of digital materials to be preserved. At a minimum, preservation programmes should ensure that interested parties are aware of the rights required for effective preservation action.

There may be a number of frameworks which allow preservation programmes to assume the right to collect and preserve specific digital materials. The most common include:

— Legal deposit or records management legislation
— Organisational rules governing corporate information
— Contractual requirements to deposit data
— Conditions of grants, awards, employment, or membership of organisations
— Rights inherited by one organisation from another
— Negotiated or purchased licence agreements
— Rights implied by voluntary submission of material to a preservation programme
— Some preservation agencies capture and store materials such as publicly available, free access Web sites without seeking prior approval. Some do this on the assertion of 'fair use' for material in the public domain; others rely on an 'opt out' option whereby rights owners are generally invited to express an objection.

It is the responsibility of the preservation programme to determine, on the basis of competent legal advice, whether any of these or other approaches is applicable, and what is required as an adequate legal defence.

Each situation requires its own set of arrangements, but preservation programmes should consider the need to take some common steps including:

- Determining the legal situation regarding rights specified by legislation, existing organisational rules, or licence agreements
- Identifying the rights that will be needed to carry out a preservation responsibility
- Identifying relevant rights owners, and other stakeholders with an influential interest in what rights are negotiated
- Preparing a clear explanation of what is needed and how it will be managed
- Approaching rights owners and negotiating a rights regime that is mutually acceptable
- Recording rights management responsibilities in metadata that is clearly and securely associated with the relevant materials.
- Ensuring the responsibilities are understood by staff
- Having secure systems, procedures and tools in place to control access and copying, and to monitor compliance
- If necessary, isolating preservation actions from other kinds of access and use
- Ensuring users understand their legal rights and obligations
- Regularly evaluating systems and procedures to ensure they do what they are supposed to do
- Monitoring any triggers for a change in rights, such as the passing of a specified period of time.

The level of access that preservation programmes should seek will depend on their mission: it may be appropriate for some digital heritage materials to be subject to very limited access for privacy, security, or other reasons, whereas it seems reasonable to expect that published materials would be available for ongoing access through a well-managed preservation programme. Some possibilities that may be attractive in negotiating access conditions include:

- Geographical restrictions, such as limiting access to onsite users
- Restrictions on the ability to copy, such as use of a stand alone computer without access to external networks or disk drives
- Restrictions on the number of users who can access the material at any one time

— Time thresholds allowing unrestricted access after a reasonable period for commercial exploitation
— Mutually agreeable triggers for a transfer of access rights, such as when the material is no longer available from a publisher's site
— Restricting access to authorised users who are required to meet specified conditions.

When rights have been negotiated, they must be managed as a core business responsibility of the preservation programme. Preservation programmes can expect to deal with large amounts of material, so the use of standard licence agreements covering classes of material will avoid the need to negotiate and manage rights item by item. System tools to manage rights are available and can be expected to continue to evolve. Such tools record access conditions applying to individual items, record and filter requests for use, and report on usage.

In choosing rights management tools, it is important to decide what tools are appropriate to support a balanced approach to rights management. It should be made easy for users to contact rights owners to negotiate their own permissions, such as the right to copy, where it is the user's responsibility to do so. Making authorised access as easy as possible may act as a disincentive to unauthorised access and use. Encouraging creators to use open source software should help reduce complications and costs involved in negotiating rights with proprietary software developers.

Rights issues have the potential to add greatly to the costs of preservation programmes, so all programmes have an interest in finding efficiencies and in avoiding exposure to litigation. programmes with few resources may particularly need to look for standard agreements that reduce the costs of negotiating rights approvals. They may also have to accept that rights management is a limiting factor on the size of their operations.

### 7.3.1. Data Protection

Data protection is a fundamental of all preservation programmes. For many programmes, authenticity is also critically important. Authenticity relates to the ongoing integrity of data, and its clear and sustained identification. Data protection strategies include allocation of responsibility, technical infrastructure, maintenance, data transfer, proper storage of data carriers, backup, system security and disaster planning. Authenticity also relies on clear documentation of the origins and history of digital materials.

Data must be stored. While it is appropriate to focus preservation attention on how best to re-present digital objects as originally intended, it must never be forgotten that the digital object has an underlying form as data. It is as data that it must be stored, managed and protected if any digital object is to be available for presentation to a user.

Heritage materials are often valued, at least in part, for their authenticity - the degree to which one can trust that they are indeed what they are thought to be. For archival records, scientific data, and many other kinds of digital materials, trust in their ongoing authenticity is critical, for without it they are of virtually no value. Authenticity derives from being able to trust both the identity of an object - that it is what it says it is, and has not been confused with some other object - and the integrity of the object - that it has not been changed in ways that change its meaning.

Maintenance of both identity and integrity implies sustained and documented links between an object as originally created and as currently presented. Evaluating, maintaining and providing evidence of continued authenticity are key responsibilities for most preservation programmes.

The nature of digital materials, and how they must be managed for preservation and access, both present challenges:

— Digital materials can be changed easily, with or without fraudulent intent, and even without any intent at all
— Changes that happen may not be obvious
— Preservation processes almost always involve making changes - transferring data from one system to another, from one carrier to another, adding or updating metadata, creating new copies that need new file names, changing the means of presentation as technologies change, and so on.

Where digital materials have value as records that offer evidence of some kind, authenticity is extremely important. Not all digital materials are made or selected to provide evidence: for example, they may reflect creative expression, the debate of ideas, or the desire to entertain and be entertained.

Even for these materials authenticity may be an issue, as the integrity of their creators' work or ideas should be protected, Ultimately, preservation programmes must decide how much to invest in ensuring that the authenticity of material in their care can be trusted, bearing in mind that object identity and data integrity are fundamental responsibilities.

Data protection must play a key role in any preservation programme, for two reasons: i) So that there is a digital object for a user to access. This is a fundamental requirement: if data is lost or seriously corrupted it may be impossible to re-present the intended digital object at all, and the preservation process must be judged to have failed ii) So that the integrity of the data can be maintained without tampering or corruption in order for users to trust the authenticity of the re-presented object.

### 7.3.2. Documentation

Documentation also plays a key role, for two reasons:

— By explaining the links between objects and by clearly distinguishing between them, it provides evidence of identity

— By showing what changes, if any, have taken place, with whose authority, and to what effect, it provides an audit trail to attest to authenticity.

Of all the responsibilities of preservation programmes, storage and data protection may be the ones for which it is easiest to find suitable third party service providers. The considerable investments required for equipment and expertise may make this an attractive alternative to managing data in-house. However, the critical nature of data protection means that the preservation programme must still accept responsibility for ensuring that any contracted services deliver the necessary levels of care and control.

Data must be stored and managed with appropriate systems and on an appropriate carrier. There are digital asset management systems or digital object storage systems available that meet the requirements of digital preservation programmes. Once requirements have been determined, they should be thoroughly discussed with potential suppliers. Different systems and carriers are suited to different needs and those chosen for preservation programmes must be fit for their purpose.

The overall system must have adequate capabilities including:

*Sufficient storage capacity*. Storage capacity can be build up over time, but the system must be able to manage the amount of data expected to be stored within its life cycle -As a fundamental capability, the system must be able to duplicate data as required without loss, and transfer data to new or 'refreshed' carriers without loss -Demonstrated reliability and technical support to deal with problems promptly -The ability to map file names into a file-naming scheme suitable for its storage architecture. Storage systems are based around named objects.

Different systems use different architectures to organise objects. This may impose constraints on how objects are named within storage; for example, disk systems may impose a hierarchical directory structure on existing file names, different from those that would be used on a tape system. The system must allow, or preferably carry out, a mapping of system-imposed file names and existing identifiers

*Error checking*. A level of automated error checking is normal in most computer storage. Because heritage materials must be kept for long periods, often with very low human usage, the system must be able to detect changes or loss of data and take appropriate action.

Technical infrastructure must also include means of storing metadata and of reliably linking metadata to stored digital objects. Large operations often find they need to set up digital object management systems that are linked to, but separate from, their digital mass storage system, in order to cope with the range of processes involved, and to allow metadata and work interfaces to be changed without having to change the mass storage.

While the cost of replacing data carriers must be considered, replacement media typically offer increased storage capacity. Unfortunately, any savings are usually offset by growth in the amount of data to be stored. The market for data storage and management systems extends well beyond preservation programmes, so there are good COTS (Commercial Off The Shelf) products available.

Using COTS technology is possibly the most easily managed, low risk and cost effective approach as technical support and upgrades are provided by vendors in a competitive marketplace. Standards are sufficiently widely used in the storage market to allow mixing and matching products from various vendors so that a number of upgrade and replacement paths are available when needed.

Storage systems rely on safe and complete replication of data, rather than enduring carriers, for data protection. Data must be copied from carrier to carrier to avoid the impact of carrier deterioration. As new kinds of carriers prove their usefulness in storage systems, data is transferred from older kinds of carriers. This must happen before any hardware or software required to retrieve the data are discarded. Planning for data transfers is a management challenge, whatever the system used.

For example, a small, low use archive storing data on shelved CDs, must keep track of the age and condition of the CDs as well as signs that CD technology will have to be replaced. More sophisticated mass storage systems generally automate decisions about regular transfer of data between carriers, but managers still need to decide when carriers should be replaced with new media, and when underlying technology has been superseded. Appropriate storage and handling conditions for carriers.

Digital data carriers must be stored in conditions that do not accelerate their rate of deterioration. The main risks for data carriers are excessive temperature and humidity which endanger the carrier; dust or other particulates which may obscure access to the data; and in the case of optically encoded material, light, which may damage the optically inscribed data. Modern data tapes are of such a high coercivity, that accidental erasure by a magnetic field does not constitute a major risk.

Magnetic data tapes may be integrated into a digital storage system. Typically this would be housed in a clean computer room with controlled temperature and relatively humidity set at 18°C, and 40% RH, a continuous influx of clean, dust-free air, with daily cleaning to prevent contamination. The conditions would fluctuate no more than 2°C and 10% RH in any given 24 hour period. Magnetic data tapes stored for optimum carrier life should be stored under more stringent conditions, at a temperature between 18°C and 10°C, with a daily tolerance of no more than 1°C, and between 30 and 40% RH with a tolerance of no more than 3%RH.

Optical carriers, such as CD-Recordable, should be stored under similar conditions, in a darkened environment due to their sensitivity to light. There are suggestions that very low temperatures (approaching or lower than 0°C), may be detrimental to the life expectancy of certain carriers, however, this has not been proven.

While storing multiple copies of the same data does offer some protection against failure, preservation programmes must also consider the risks of a disaster which damages all copies stored at the same site. Storing copies at different sites is a basic requirement; to avoid the impact of region-wide disasters such as floods, earthquakes, wildfires, and war, programmes should consider the need to store additional backup copies of important data outside their own region.

Preservation programmes may also need to adjust normal backup schedules so that preservation data, which must be kept, is refreshed (i.e. rewritten) not overwritten with new data.

Data protection is such a critical responsibility that even programmes with few resources must give it a high priority. The simplified risk analysis above may suggest areas of lower risk for some programmes. It also suggests that some risks may be reduced at the cost of reducing the level or speed of access. This may be perfectly acceptable for some collections.

Changes in software and hardware add up to a loss in the means of access to digital heritage materials. This is expected to be the core challenge for most preservation programmes. Using understandings of the relationship between digital objects and their means of access, and taking account of what has to be presented to a user in providing access, programme managers must decide on strategies that will guarantee accessibility whenever it is needed.

Strategies, which are likely to vary over time and according to needs, are still evolving. The strategies discussed are grouped into those based on investment of resources from early in the life cycle of digital materials, those with short-term and with medium- to long-term effectiveness, and some alternative 'non-digital' and 'non-preservation' strategies.

## References

Baker, Thomas. A Grammar for Dublin Core. *D-Lib Magazine,* Vol. 6 No. 10 .

Dekkers, Makx and Stuart Weibel. Dublin Core Metadata Initiative Progress Report and Workplan for 2002. *D-Lib Magazine,* Volume 8, #2 February 2002.

Duval, Erik. Metadata standards: What, who & why. *Journal of Universal Computer Science,* 7(7):591-601, July 2001. Special Issue: I-Know 01 - International Conference on Knowledge Management.

Lagoze, Carl. The Warwick Framework: A Container Architecture for Diverse Sets of Metadata. *D-Lib Magazine,* (July, 1996).

Paepcke, Andreas, Chen-Chuan K. Chang, Terry Winograd, and Hector Garcia-Molina. Interoperability for digital libraries worldwide. *Communications of the ACM,* 41(4):33-42, 1998.

Sutton, Stuart, and Jon Mason. The Dublin Core and Metadata for Educational Resources. *Proceedings: International Conference on Dublin Core and Metadata Applications 2001,* pp 25-31. (2001)

# 8

# Access to Digital Library

Conventional libraries are expensive and research libraries are particularly expensive. Even in the United States, few people can afford good access to scientific, medical, legal and scholarly information. In less affluent countries the situation is worse; even the best universities cannot afford good libraries. With the growth of the web, this situation is changing. An ever-increasing amount of high quality information is available on the web with open access. Anybody connected to the Internet has access to this information at no charge. Moreover, free services, such as the web search services, are emerging that organize this information and provide access to it. Already, many people use the web as their library.

## 8.1. Open Access

Open access is one of the marvels of the web. Vast collections of high-quality information are available for everybody to use without payment. Creating and distributing this information is expensive, yet individuals and organizations provide it freely. Here are some examples of information previously available only at considerable expense that is now available openly.

— The National Library of Medicine's PubMed service provides medical information that formerly required a subscription to Medline.

— The commercial product *Books in Print* used to be the only list of currently published books.

— Research articles in many branches of physics appear first in the arXiv archives at Los Alamos National Laboratory before being published in conventional journals.

— Cornell's Legal Information Institute provides legal information that was previously available only through expensive publications or the online services Westlaw and Lexis.

Sometimes, the open access service is not as good as the fee-based service, but often it is a genuine substitute. And these are just a few examples. With a web search engine and a little ingenuity, a user can find high-quality information about almost any topic, from Texan wildlife to international taxation. In some disciplines, all the primary materials needed to teach an advanced course or carry out research are available with open access.

This abundance was not anticipated. Early digital libraries assumed that restrictions on access were essential for high-quality information to be distributed over the Internet. This misunderstanding came from a mindset that the only incentive for creating information is to make money — royalties to authors and profits for publishers. A glance at the web today shows that this view was wrong.

Most open-access web sites do not generate revenue. They are supported by external funding, usually by the producers of the material on them. When the web provides an efficient channel to reach the desired audiences, existing budgets have been transferred from print products to the web. Marketing and promotion are obvious examples; government information is another. In many other cases, organizations have developed new budgets to publish open access information on the web. The publication of scientific research is an important example. Ten years ago, very little scientific research was available free of charge. Today, huge volumes are online with open access.

In areas such as these, the creators of the information have strong incentives to have their materials used. Their interests are best served by eliminating barriers to use. The result is that every year additional information is provided with no restrictions on access.

## 8.2. Automated Libraries

For the web to function as a library requires more than high-quality collections. Services must be provided to manage the collections and help people use them effectively. The term "automated digital library" can be used to describe a digital library where all tasks are carried out automatically, including tasks that were traditionally carried out by skilled professionals. These include selection, cataloguing and indexing, seeking for information, reference services, and so on. Each of these activities requires considerable mental activity, the type of activity that people are skilled at and computers find difficult.

Good services in automated digital libraries do not replicate the procedures of classical librarianship. Automated libraries provide users with equivalent services but rethink the way that they are delivered. The contrast between web search engines and conventional library catalogs is illuminating. Almost everything that is best about a library catalog is done badly by a web search service. On the other hand, web search services are strong in ways that catalogs are weak. It is wrong to claim that conventional catalogs or indexes are superior because of their quality control and it is equally wrong to claim that the web search services are superior because of their coverage and currency. The value to users depends on what the user wants to achieve.

Consider the choice between Google and Inspec as tools to discover information about computing. In computing, almost every significant result first appears on a web site and only later reaches the printed journals, if ever. Hence, a web search service such as Google is more up to date and its coverage is broader than Inspec, which is restricted to formally published materials. In computing, substantially the same information is often available from several sources. Google provides a direct link to an open access version. Inspec references the official version, which is usually printed or online with restricted access. By conventional criteria Inspec has much higher quality, but for many people Google's broad coverage and convenient links make it the better tool.

### 8.2.1. Brute Force Computing

Simple algorithms plus immense computing power can often outperform human intelligence. The rate of progress in computing power is described by Moore's Law, that the number of transistors on a semiconductor doubles every eighteen months. This is roughly equivalent to saying that computing power increases 100-fold in 10 years or 10,000-fold in 20 years. Few people can appreciate the implications of such dramatic change, but the future of automated digital libraries is likely to depend more on brute force computing than on sophisticated algorithms.

Here are some current examples of how this computing power is being used. Each example is the direct result of research in computer science or digital libraries.

— The web search services are the state-of-the-art in automated information discovery. Computers can index every word in a billion pages (roughly the size of the web) and search the indexes for simple patterns almost instantaneously.

— To decide how closely a document matches a query would seem to require human judgment, yet standard methods of information retrieval do remarkably well. They use the power of computers to match word patterns as a surrogate for the human ability to relate concepts. A basic method, developed by Salton at Cornell University, represents each document as a multi-dimensional vector and uses the angle between the vectors to measure the similarity between two documents.

— Evaluating the importance of documents would appear to be another task that requires human understanding, but Google's ranking algorithm, developed by Page and Brin at Stanford University, does very well and is entirely automatic. It ranks web pages by analyzing what other pages link to them.

— Citation analysis is a long-standing success story of applying computers to library information. Automatic systems are becoming capable of extracting a reference from a document and linking it to the digital object that it references. Currently, the most versatile system for reference linking is the SFX system, created by Van de Sompel and colleagues at the University of Ghent.

— ResearchIndex is a digital library of computer science materials, created entirely automatically by Lawrence and colleagues at NEC. It makes extensive use of citation analysis and reference linking.

— There are a number of projects that extract metadata from digital objects automatically. Perhaps the most remarkable is the Informedia project, led by Wactlar at Carnegie Mellon University. Informedia has the extremely ambitious goal of providing access to segments of video, such as television news, entirely automatically.

## 8.3. Digital Library Research

The development of the web as a library that is open to everybody is a powerful and welcome trend. Research in computers science and digital libraries can claim credit for much of the success. However, the web as a library presents challenges that need to be the subject of further research.

Perhaps the most worrying is quality. In conventional publishing, publishers and libraries play an important role in evaluating the quality of materials. On the Internet, with most information mounted by the creators, it is hard for users to distinguish good information sources from inaccurate, sloppy, malicious or fraudulent information. With a few minor expectations, the user is forced to make private decisions on what information to respect, based on very limited clues. Automatic linking of quality measures to online information is one of the topics that we are beginning to study in our work for the NSF's National Science Digital Library.

The next is permanence. Important information on web sites may be supported by transient organizations. Yet, increasingly, vital information exists only online. Information integrity is the subject of the Prism project, led by Lagoze at Cornell as part of the NSF's Digital Libraries Initiative, but this is a huge topic and much more work is needed. One success story in automatic preservation is the Internet Archive, directed by Brewster Kahle. Each month, a web crawler gathers every open access web page. The Internet Archive preserves these files for the future and mounts them on computers for scholarly research today. Without the work of the Internet Archive many of these materials would already have been lost.

Within the changing environment, research libraries understand more keenly than ever the new ways in which clients are seeking and using information. Libraries see an expanding base of users and, in many instances, changing service demands. There is ample evidence that when libraries make quality content available through the Web, its use increases and it reaches more people within the institution.

In addition, the user base for any individual library has expanded to include users beyond the institution. This has been achieved through more efficient resource-sharing arrangements (often statewide) as well as by targeting new user groups for digitized content and e-services.

In many cases, openly accessible digitized collections on the Web are also being used heavily by people from beyond the educational world. Despite press accounts to the contrary, research libraries report that use of the library's physical facility remains heavy, especially for collaborative learning and research activities and for access to computers and information technologies.

As a result, many libraries have moved to provide 24/5 access to the library buildings. At the same time, there is growing evidence in the data collected from ARL member libraries that the service demands of users may be changing. Many libraries see declining use of some traditional services, such as use of some print materials, circulation transactions, and reference transactions.

However, the data confirm that the demands for interlibrary borrowing and for user education are steadily increasing. These trends signal a shift in the behavior of information users that is being closely monitored. Research on the information-seeking behavior of people is growing almost as fast as the Web itself.

The Pew Internet & American Life Project creates and funds original, academic-quality research that explores the impact of the Internet on children, families, communities, the workplace, schools, health care, and civic/political life. The project aims to be an authoritative source for timely information on the Internet's growth and societal impact, through research that is scrupulously impartial.

An overwhelming number of college students reported that the Internet, rather than the library, is the primary site of their information searches. "Many students are likely to use information found on search engines and various Web sites as research materials....A great challenge for today's colleges is how to teach students search techniques that will get them to the information they want and how to evaluate it.... While few universities require college students to take courses on information seeking, many include a session on it during freshman orientation meetings.

To better understand how usage patterns are changing, the Digital Library Federation (DLF) and Council on Library and Information Resources (CLIR) commissioned Outsell, Inc., to conduct a large-scale study of over 3,000 undergraduates, graduate students, and faculty members from a wide range of academic institutions.

The results revealed that the highest percentage of resources used were print materials, which students ranked higher than library and non-library electronic sources in four out of five factors. The Internet-based sources scored high only on the factor of convenience, while print materials scored high on the factors that make a difference in the quality of research and learning: generating the information for which the student is looking, the usefulness of the material, its reliability, and the availability of assistance.

There are differences across disciplines in terms of how information is used and to what extent new technologies are being embraced; libraries are recognizing these differences as they offer new services. There are also differences in the pace of change in different institutions; institutional cultures that allow, for example, some flexibility in personnel policies and practices as well as in budgetary reallocations, are more accommodating of experimentation and change.

In this rapidly changing environment, libraries must continue monitoring trends, assessing their performance by seeking feedback from current users, and anticipating the needs of future users. To meet and anticipate these needs of the academic and research communities, libraries are collaborating as never before, forming partnerships both within and outside their own institutions, often sharing control in order to effect critical change.

While circumstances will vary from library to library, the results of the task force survey demonstrate many ways that libraries are responding to user expectations. Libraries are expanding the amount and variety of high-quality information resources that are directly available to academic and research users via the Web. They are also expanding the definition of collections to include "born-digital" content that is neither owned nor licensed by the library. The varied efforts toward this goal may be characterized as follows: changing collection development policies to emphasize the acquisition of electronic resources, engaging in digitizing and electronic publishing projects, and assuming responsibility for managing and servicing born-digital content that resides outside the domain of the library.

Even in the electronic and networked environment, the economic model continues to feature the library as the central agency on campus that buys and/or manages information resources on behalf of the institution. Libraries have shifted the focus of their collection development policies to the acquisition of more electronic content, much of it via consortia.

While aggregate data documenting the quantity of e-resources currently being made available by libraries has proven elusive, there is data on the spending trends. Over the last decade the average percentage of a research library's materials budget that is spent on electronic resources has grown from 4% to 16%. One hundred six ARL university libraries report spending more than $132 million on electronic resources in 2000-01.

The vast majority of that was spent on electronic serials and subscription services, expenditures which have increased sharply, from just $11 million in 1994-95 to more than $117 million today. To support this increased spending on electronic content, libraries have reallocated resources from the purchase of print. The extent of such reallocations will vary depending on institutional user expectations and financial circumstances.

Many libraries have adopted a policy of adding the e-version of journals when available and are showcasing titles of e-journals available to users via the Web by making this a staff priority and by applying software management tools for titles included in aggregated electronic databases. The processes for selecting, budgeting, and acquiring electronic materials are continually changing and greatly differ from those for the selection and management of print.

The print process is orderly: discrete amounts of money are allocated by discipline, the marketplace is fairly predictable, and materials are selected and ordered using established procedures. By contrast, the processes for selection and management of electronic resources are chaotic. The migration from print to electronic varies in speed and extent by discipline; electronic products are interdisciplinary and expensive, giving rise to selection by committee; projections for future funding are guesswork; and archiving and content control are problematic.

Legal and negotiation skills are now mandatory. To complicate matters, decisions are often made through a consortium. The process for acquiring electronic resources turns the traditional acquisitions and user service model topsy-turvy. In building electronic collections, libraries must also constantly respond to changing publisher behavior.

The most profound influence on a library's collection management and access strategies has been the extraordinary price increases for scholarly journals, combined with publishers' use of licensing to define the terms under which a library may make the content available and to whom. It is reasonable to speculate that these phenomena, driven by some of the larger publishers but now employed widely, make up one of the forces that prompted libraries to blend the previously distinct operations of collection management and access.

Some libraries have fully embraced initiatives stimulated or endorsed by SPARC (the Scholarly Publishing and Academic Resources Coalition) and other affordable publishing venues and are using acquisitions funds as investments in the future of scholarly communication. These libraries focus acquisitions on publications from scholarly societies and less expensive publishers, nonprofit and for-profit, that provide high-quality titles at affordable prices.

These less expensive titles tend to be the most highly ranked by faculty but labor intensive to obtain, since each publisher has only a few titles and often lacks sales and technical staff. These libraries try to consistently view collection expenditures as investments, and to seek out publishers likely to contribute to a sustainable future for scholarly information. Libraries are also supporting open access projects that experiment with alternatives to the current subscription-based funding model or the current journals-based publishing model for scholarly communication.

These approaches are seen as those of a good citizen, especially in an institution whose needs for funding include many urgent priorities in addition to library needs. These libraries are investing in initiatives that may help solve the long-term problem of high prices for journals.

## 8.4. Online Catalogs

It is clear that the role of the online catalog has changed. That catalog has become one of many databases available to users; libraries are linking to and from the catalog to integrate all of these resources. In recognition of this broader role for the library catalog, some libraries are considering modifying cataloging to favor timely access to a wider variety of formats.

One proposal called for reallocating funds that are devoted to describing books and journals to materials that are proportionately underrepresented in today's catalogs, such as films, music, photographs, and digital objects. Libraries are also reconsidering their current efforts to collect and catalog free Web resources, concluding that these labor-intensive activities can be avoided by perfecting nascent machine harvesting and cataloging techniques.

A small number of libraries and library organizations are participating in experiments funded by The Mellon Foundation to test the application of harvesting and search engine technologies. Using the recently developed OAI metadata harvesting protocol, these libraries are delivering information from the "hidden Web" not normally found by Internet search engines and from databases with retrieval formats that present special processing or presentation problems.

For example, several libraries are working with vendors to adapt existing portal software into multifunctional products with features and services desired by users in research communities. Other examples of library involvement in development of software applications are ILL management systems, instructional tutorials, management of content and services for digital libraries, and institutional repositories.

Although where information resides matters less to the user, the library as place—the physical entity—remains more important than ever and performs a host of functions vital to learning and research. Much research library space is busier than ever before. Library facilities are being reconfigured to provide space for collaborative learning and research. There are classrooms and media labs where faculty and librarians may interact in providing student learning experiences, group study spaces, and community spaces where students can meet to discuss ideas.

The transformation of library space has also become an opportunity to attract new academic collaborations such as writing studios and academic skills tutoring. Library space is now seen as learning space on an equal footing with classrooms and laboratories. Libraries are being renovated to expand e-access and foster community by providing electronic classrooms, wireless data networks, offering laptops, and expanding library hours.

Libraries are establishing spaces called "information commons" where library reference services are offered jointly with information technology support. At the same time, libraries are responding to decreasing use of in-person reference service by combining service points and shifting resources to online reference service and online tutorials. To make the best use of prime real estate, libraries are adopting new approaches to managing large print collections by using storage centers with delivery services for less frequently used materials and engaging in cooperative approaches to long-term preservation copy retention.

The branch or departmental library remains valuable but its role too is changing. While access to information and library services is far less geographically based, branch and departmental libraries still play a role in development of community and serve as sites for collaboration. Yet, in the Internet world there are opportunities to rethink the role of multiple libraries and their configuration within an institution.

One library reported establishing a program to replicate the opportunities for personalized services and contacts that characterize branch library service without the cost of creating additional branches. Some of the same opportunities for reorganization may present themselves when libraries work in collaboration with other libraries outside their institutional boundaries.

Libraries are active participants in building awareness among researchers, faculty, and students of uses of high-quality content and information technology in teaching and research. Curriculum review and changing expectations for teaching faculty present opportunities for libraries to contribute expertise and resources.

Libraries provide classrooms; training and consulting in finding and evaluating information; and assistance with creating electronic theses and dissertations, displaying and visualizing data, publishing journals on the Web, and using geographic information systems (GIS) and remote sensing. Recognizing that disciplines are adopting new technology at different rates, librarians are:

— Working with faculty to integrate information literacy skills and digital content into the course curricula
— Expanding the number of people reached by offering basic information literacy and fluency training through online tutorials
— Assisting researchers in acquiring, accessing, displaying, and visualizing spatial and numeric data by providing training in use of software and partnering with faculty to provide classroom instruction in its use
— Developing systems and instructional tools for pedagogical use of digital resources, including images
— Managing campus instructional technology initiatives
— Making Organizational Changes within the Library to Innovate and Improve Services

Libraries are embracing change—being willing to change what libraries do and how it is done—and, as a result, are reorganizing their operations and re-deploying staff to respond to the new environment. Examples of recent organizational change in ARL libraries include:

— Many libraries report having instituted an integrated approach to collection management, bringing together the activities of building, maintaining, and providing access to library resources in all formats, both in-house and remote, both acquired and locally created.
— Many libraries also report taking interdisciplinary approaches, training library staff to perform across traditional roles and to build bridges between the culture of the library and that of the faculty and information technology. An example is the creation of information commons jointly staffed by the library and

information technology, often developing services in collaboration with faculty.

— Others report organizational redesigns to achieve a system-wide view of services to coordinate communications with all library users and to deploy staff more flexibly.
— Libraries are experimenting rigorously with organizational transformation reflecting strategies for team-based decision making, learning organizations, and quality management.

## 8.5. Scholarly Communication

Libraries are assuming leadership within their institutions to advocate for enduring institution-wide knowledge management policies and programs that contribute to a robust system of scholarly communication. Some libraries are accomplishing this goal by:

— Sponsoring scholarly communication seminars to broaden faculty and graduate student awareness of trends that threaten the long-term sustainability of the current system of scholarly communication
— Advocating for institution-wide intellectual property policies that balance the rights of copyright owners and those of users and libraries in educational settings, including the development of principles that guide the licensing of electronic resources for the institution
— Promoting individual behavior and building institutional support that contributes to the long-term health and viability of scholarly communication channels, including developing infrastructure for such alternative publishing practices as publishing open access journals or creating institutional repositories

All research libraries are innovating and adapting to the changing needs of their patrons, as well as to the changing requirements of their institutions. There is no clear evidence to suggest definitive trends in change based on the size of the library collection.

There are specific types of innovation, however, that seem to be related to library or institution size. There is anecdotal evidence that library size has been influential in the development of digital library programs; libraries with more mature digital library programs tend to be libraries with larger collections and more staff members. On the other hand, smaller institutional settings may encourage innovative collaborative activities, either because of the financial necessity to join forces to make something happen or because of the potential in smaller communities for more interaction across campus units.

There is also anecdotal evidence that the institutional climate for change and the active support of groups and key individuals within the institution play a central role in the library's orientation and opportunities to innovate; to the extent that the size of the institution impacts this climate, size may be a contributing—if not driving—factor. Research libraries' ability and desire to collaborate with other research libraries, with non-university libraries, or with other organizations and industries will determine the success of many library programs.

Motivations for collaborations vary greatly and include leadership, political support, the lure of available funding, and the desire to transform the library, to move it into the digital age. An increasingly important collaboration is consortial buying of print and electronic content and services. Consortial buying and licensing for access to electronic resources have become central in every research library's arsenal of strategies for acquiring information more economically than could be accomplished by acting alone.

Many libraries find user-initiated consortial borrowing combined with rapid delivery a successful avenue for making their users' access to books as easy as access to electronic resources. There is evidence that fast delivery of books within a consortium has increased book use, especially by undergraduates. Consortia also offer accompanying services that greatly expedite the discovery and delivery of non-book content for users affiliated with libraries participating in the consortium; some consortia are centrally managing image data banks, electronic theses and dissertations, and other digital materials.

Consortial structures vary and reflect the political framework of the state or region in which they operate and the institutions they represent. In some cases, a state legislature appropriates funds centrally to support consortial activities on behalf of libraries; in others, individual libraries pay to a common fund. External funding facilitates the process of individual institutions' making the adjustments and compromises that consortia require and tends to support consortial relationships among libraries of varying sizes and characteristics.

Consortia funded solely by the participating libraries tend to be formed of libraries of similar size and characteristics. Consortia are on the front line of controversies between libraries and publishers about pricing, the terms of use defined by licenses, and publisher practices that make it difficult for a library to cost-effectively tailor its purchases from the publishers' lists or to reduce the total amount of money spent with that publisher.

The tendency of consortia to acquire or license electronic resources from the larger, commercial publishers raises concerns that content from scholarly societies or other smaller publishers will be overlooked. Research library staff are actively working with their partners in consortia to assess the benefits and challenges of consortial licensing and to influence publisher behavior in favor of scholarly communication needs.

A closely related factor to collaboration is the degree to which the organizations involved in a joint effort are willing to share control, at both the intra- and the inter-institutional levels. This sharing of control has implications for many activities such as archiving; consortial buying; expanding online resources; collaborative efforts with faculty, information technology groups, instructional technology centers; and cooperative publishing projects.

Libraries are promoting team operations to advance collaborative projects and to encourage a convergence of different organizational cultures where control is truly shared. Many research libraries are willing to establish new partnerships and share control in order to innovate.

Research libraries' ability to recognize their strengths and their willingness to leverage those strengths influences the success of library integration into the research institution. Libraries have a special kind of space on campus, space that is seen as politically neutral and representative of the intellectual commons—public-good space. This nature of space gives libraries leverage to attract and nurture collaboration with other parts of the institution.

Libraries also have human talent they may deploy for the institution. Research library staffs have a wide range of expertise that can support new approaches to meeting user and institutional needs. Many libraries are leveraging their space and human resources to the advantage of the institution, for example, in creating an information commons, establishing an institutional repository, or providing campus management of copyright clearances.

A major factor in innovation is the degree to which research libraries and their institutions are willing and able to embrace change. The willingness of the library leadership (at all levels) to change its vision of what a library is and does, and to transform library operations to reflect that vision, obviously influences innovation. However, the culture of the institution itself also influences how the library engages and supports change.

Many research libraries find themselves in the impossible position of being expected by some disciplines to implement systemic change while continuing to be responsive to the needs of other disciplines that have slower rates of adoption of new technology.19 During this period of transition, this is a major factor influencing how libraries implement change and how that change is received within the institution.

The degree to which people in the institution exhibit "interdisciplinarity" or demonstrate effectiveness in working with the various cultures of the institution—library, faculty, and information technology cultures—is another important factor in innovation. Success in collaboration depends on some degree of convergence of these cultures.

Convergence or integration of cultures is being approached in several different ways. Examples include convergence of cultures in shared space; convergence of technical and bibliographic expertise; and convergence of human capital to consolidate efforts, encourage cooperation, and provide institution-wide access to the latest equipment, software, and support as well as a wide and deep collection of high-quality content.

Experience reported in the task force survey suggests there is a need to support greater cultural integration. Some libraries pursue this goal by establishing cross-cultural task forces, developing cross-training and mentoring programs for effective performance across and outside traditional roles, adopting position classification schemes that reflect the changes required of staff, providing opportunities for staff to cross boundaries, and by giving people time to work through the process of cultural convergence.

Converting existing collections and new acquisitions from paper to electronic-only is currently inhibited by the nascent state of strategies for preserving digital content. Internationally, publishers are working with national libraries (or their proxies) for them to assume the role of the publishers' archives for digitized texts; the reliability and terms of use of these archives are still being determined.

When library, publisher, and technology communities reach consensus on how best to manage the preservation of digital resources, the transformation of library collections to largely electronic will accelerate. In this rapidly changing environment, there are many opportunities for entrepreneurial activities, which often require the financial risk of investing resources in new activities even as budget pressures tighten.

Entrepreneurship may also create new activities that bypass or challenge the standards, rules, and policies that are part of library operations. Success depends on the library's ability to reach informed judgments, usually with less than complete information, on the strategic importance of an opportunity and whether it warrants the financial and other risks that accompany change.

## 8.6. Digital Collections

Responding to user expectations for easy searching and convenient access to an expanding array of information sources, libraries are spending increasing amounts of their materials budgets on electronic resources. While up to now many libraries have actually also maintained the print, where dual versions exist, recent budget and space constraints have led many to make a choice of the format they collect.

The nascent state of strategies for preserving digital content makes some libraries reluctant to relinquish print editions. However, seeing that these preservation issues are now being addressed, and given the significant advantages of the electronic editions, many libraries have decided to collect electronic-only. Libraries are also offering printing services to meet users' expressed need for print.

As professional print-on-demand technologies become more cost effective, this option may offer, for users who require it, a way to generate high-quality bound printed editions from electronic information resources. At the same time, libraries have not abandoned print. They continue to acquire print in disciplines that are not moving as quickly into the digital world as others and in formats, such as monographs, that are still published primarily in printed form. Thus, integrating print and electronic resources and making print resources almost as easy to access as electronic content are challenges facing libraries in this hybrid environment. Portal software is being designed to enable users to search library catalogs simultaneously with both open and licensed databases to find content regardless of format, thereby building a bridge between the library's print and digital collections.

Timely, self-service resource sharing and other user-initiated services such as book renewals and book- and article-delivery are also making access to print resources much easier. In the future more information will be created, stored, delivered, and preserved digitally, but print—because of its physicality, flexibility, perceived reliability, ease of reading and sharing—will be used for reading and editing for some time to come. Even as print retains importance, the library's physical space has increasing value for other activities, especially collaborative learning and research.

Thus, to free up prime real estate, libraries are moving lesser-used print collections to storage centers (with rapid delivery service) and are exploring cooperative approaches to long-term preservation copy retention. For now, research libraries' print collections continue to play a critical role for users even as that role and how users gain access to the material are changing.

Given the rapidly changing environment, however, libraries are carefully monitoring the information-seeking and reading habits of their users to see how their use of print and digital resources changes or does not change over time. Institutional repositories—digital collections capturing and preserving the intellectual output of a single or multi-university community—provide a compelling response to two strategic issues facing academic institutions. Such repositories:

— Provide a critical component in reforming the system of scholarly communication--a component that expands access to research, reasserts control over scholarship by the academy, increases competition and reduces the monopoly power of journals, and brings economic relief and heightened relevance to the institutions and libraries that support them; and

— Have the potential to serve as tangible indicators of a university's quality and to demonstrate the scientific, societal, and economic relevance of its research activities, thus increasing the institution's visibility, status, and public value.

Institutional repositories represent the logical convergence of faculty-driven self-archiving initiatives, library dissatisfaction with the monopolistic effects of the traditional and still-pervasive journal publishing system, and the availability of digital networks and publishing technologies. This convergence manifests itself in several ways:

— *Attitudinally*: Institutional repositories build on a growing grassroots faculty practice of posting research online, most often on personal web sites, but also on departmental sites or in disciplinary repositories.

— *Economically*: While the variety of institutional contexts and potential implementations make it difficult to project institutional repository development and operational costs with any precision, the evidence so far suggests that the resources required would represent but a fraction of the journal costs that libraries now incur and over which they have little control.

— *Technically*: Digital publishing technologies, ever-expanding global networking, and enabling interoperability protocols and metadata standards are coalescing to provide practical technical solutions that can be implemented now.

The rationale for universities and colleges implementing institutional repositories rests on two interrelated propositions: one that supports a broad, pan-institutional effort and another that offers direct and immediate benefits to each institution that implements a repository.

While institutional repositories centralize, preserve, and make accessible an institution's intellectual capital, at the same time they will form part of a global system of distributed, interoperable repositories that provides the foundation for a new disaggregated model of scholarly publishing. This model unbundles the principal functions of scholarly communication, thus presenting the potential to realize market efficiencies previously hidden by the vertically integrated publishing model that now characterizes academic journal publishing.

Altering the structure of the scholarly publishing model will be neither simple nor immediate. The stakes are high for all the well-entrenched participants in the system--faculty, librarians, and publishers--and the inertia of the traditional publishing paradigm is immense. In the near-term, large journal publishers have both the power and the incentive to maintain the status quo: the prestigious journals they control appear integral to the very structure of academic professional advancement.

However, digital publishing and networking technologies, harnessed by an increasingly dissatisfied library market—as well as by authors themselves--are now driving fundamental changes to this publishing model at an accelerating pace. And new communications paradigms, especially when constructed by the scholars themselves, can eliminate seemingly insurmountable publisher advantages in relatively short order. Institutional repositories, by capturing, preserving, and disseminating a university's collective intellectual capital, serve as meaningful indicators of an institution's academic quality.

Under the current system of scholarly communication, much of the intellectual output and value of an institution's intellectual property is diffused through thousands of scholarly journals. While faculty publication in these journals reflects positively on the host university, an institutional repository concentrates the intellectual product created by a university's researchers, making it easier to demonstrate its scientific, social and financial value. Thus, institutional repositories complement existing metrics for gauging institutional productivity and prestige.

The current system of scholarly communication limits, rather han expands, the readership and availability of most scholarly research (while also obscuring its institutional origins). Rounds of journal price increases and subsequent subscription cancellations act to reduce the audience further. The role of alternative scholarly publishing models, such as institutional repositories, in breaking the monopolies of publishers and increasing the awareness of university intellectual output grows increasingly clear. Further, institutional repositories can serve this function whether they are implemented on individual campuses or in collaborative consortial projects.

## 8.7. Institutional Repositories

Stated broadly, a digital institutional repository can be any collection of digital material hosted, owned or controlled, or disseminated by a college or university, irrespective of purpose or provenance. A particular type of institutional repository—a digital archive of the intellectual product created by the faculty, research staff, and students of an institution and accessible to end users both within and outside of the institution, with few if any barriers to access.

In other words, the content of an institutional repository is:

— Institutionally defined;

— Scholarly;

— Cumulative and perpetual; and

— Open and interoperable.

Institutional repositories can assume many forms and serve a variety of purposes. Indeed, the technical and administrative infrastructures developed by academic institutions for existing digital library initiatives might often be modified or repurposed to serve the requirements of an institutional repository. The institutional repository might form a component of a more comprehensive institutional initiative, one encompassing virtually all of an institution's digital assets.

In contrast to discipline-specific repositories and subject-oriented or thematic digital libraries, institutional repositories capture the original research and other intellectual property generated by an institution's constituent population active in many fields. Defined in this way, institutional repositories represent an historical and tangible embodiment of the intellectual life and output of an institution. And, to the extent that institutional affiliation itself serves as the primary qualitative filter, this repository becomes a significant indicator of the institution's academic quality.

Depending on the university, an institutional repository may complement or compete with the role served by the university archives. University archives often serve two purposes: 1) to manage administrative records to satisfy legally mandated retention requirements, and 2) to preserve materials pertaining to the institution's history and to the activities and achievements of its officers, faculty, staff, students, and alumni. Compared to institutional repositories, which aim to preserve the entire intellectual output of the institution, university archivists exercise broad discretion in determining which papers and other digital objects to collect and store.

Developing institutional repositories does not require that each institution act entirely on its own. For many colleges and universities, existing state or regional institutional or library consortia will provide a logical infrastructure for implementing institutional repositories via collective development. Such cooperation could deliver economies of scale and help institutions avoid the needless replication of technical systems. Indeed, consortia might well prove the fastest path to proliferating institutional repositories and attaining a critical mass of open access content.

Depending on the goals established by each institution, an institutional repository could contain any work product generated by the institution's students, faculty, non-faculty researchers, and staff. This material might include student electronic portfolios, classroom teaching materials, the institution's annual reports, video recordings, computer programs, data sets, photographs, and art works—virtually any digital material that the institution wishes to preserve.

This content may include pre-prints and other works-in-progress, peer-reviewed articles, monographs, enduring teaching materials, data sets and other ancillary research material, conference papers, electronic theses and dissertations, and gray literature. To control and manage the accession of this content requires appropriate policies and mechanisms, including content management and document version control systems. The repository policy framework and technical infrastructure must provide institutional managers the flexibility to control who can contribute, approve, access, and update the digital content coming from a variety of institutional communities and interest groups (including academic departments, libraries, research centers and labs, and individual authors).

Several of the institutional repository infrastructure systems currently being developed have the technical capacity to embargo or sequester access to submissions until the content has been approved by a designated reviewer. The nature and extent of this review will reflect the policies and needs of each individual institution, possibly of each participating institutional community.

Essential to the institutional repository's role both within the university and within the larger structure of scholarly communication is that the content collected is both cumulative and maintained in perpetuity. This has two implications. First, whatever the content submission criteria for a repository, items once submitted cannot be withdrawn--except in presumably rare cases involving allegations of libel, plagiarism, copyright infringement, or "bad science." This removal would be the functional equivalent of revoking the registration initially granted to the contribution on accession into the repository. This does not necessarily mean that all content will be universally accessible in perpetuity.

Institutions must develop criteria and policies--and implement rights management systems--for allowing access to a repository's content, both inside the institution and from outside, that balance the goal of the broadest available access with the reality of encouraging faculty participation. The cumulative nature of institutional repositories also implies that the repository's infrastructure is scaleable. While initial processing and storage requirements might prove modest, institutional repository systems must be able to accommodate thousands of submissions per year, and eventually must be able to preserve millions of digital objects and many terabytes of data.

Second, institutional repositories aim to preserve and make accessible digital content on a long-term basis. Digital preservation and long-term access are inextricably linked: each being largely meaningless without the other. Providing long-term access to digital objects in the repository requires considerable planning and resource commitments. The institution needs to balance the desire to accept the farrago of file formats popular with various disciplines, in order to simplify content submission and encourage faculty participation, with the complications that migrating some of those formats or media might present as new standards evolve.

While it is possible for an institution to dictate digital formatting standards for students—in the submission of electronic theses and dissertations, for example—prescribing such formats for faculty, for both attitudinal and practical reasons, proves far more problematic. The goals motivating an institution to create and maintain a digital repository—whether pan-institutional, as a component in the changing structure of scholarly communication, or institution-centric--require that users beyond the institution's community gain access to the content.

For the repository to provide access to the broader research community, users outside the university must be able to find and retrieve information from the repository. Therefore, institutional repository systems must be able to support interoperability in order to provide access via multiple search engines and other discovery tools. An institution does not necessarily need to implement searching and indexing functionality to satisfy this demand: it could simply maintain and expose metadata, allowing other services to harvest and search the content. This simplicity lowers the barrier to repository operation for many institutions, as it only requires a file system to hold the content and the ability to create and share metadata with external systems. Given the disparate publishing practices amongst academic disciplines, an institution's content accession and access policies need to accommodate legitimate researcher concerns about access to pre-publication material deposited in the repository.

Institutional repositories typically do not permit content to be removed once submitted. However, a variety of legitimate circumstances might require an institution to limit access to particular content to a specific set of users. These circumstances might include copyright restrictions, policies established by a particular research community, embargoes that an institution's Sponsored Programs Office might require to keep the institution in compliance with the terms of sponsor contracts, and even monetary access fees for certain data.

## 8.8. Open Access Management

The advent of the Internet, the World Wide Web, and digital technologies has revolutionized scholarly communication. Creative applications of these technologies are leading to innovations in the conduct of research as well as in the conveyance of ideas to readers. And the growing availability and application of these technologies has dramatically altered how readers may discover, gain access to, and use information.

As positive and liberating as these developments are for many researchers, authors, and readers, they have also accelerated the commodification of information and drives by some content industries to make their channels of information distribution more secure. As a result,.changes are taking place in copyright, license/contract, and related laws that govern the management and use of intellectual property.

For the most part, the changes result in more limited access and more restrictive uses for copyrighted material. It is no surprise then that, as the laws change to secure content for publishers, there is a negative impact on those in the educational and research communities where the creation, dissemination, and use of intellectual property is expected and, in fact, forms the very core of learning and research.

Historically, the library and academic communities looked to copyright law as the policy framework for balancing competing interests of creators, publishers, and users of copyrighted works. To achieve its constitutional purpose to promote the progress of science and the useful arts, copyright law provides a copyright owner with a private monopoly to reproduce, distribute, perform, display, and revise a work, while simultaneously providing exceptions for the special circumstances of education and libraries.

This balance has been significantly eroded as copyright and other laws have been revised to apply in the digital and networked environment. Changes in the laws have come from many directions but are largely driven by players who are part of a large and diverse commercial marketplace seeking changes in the legal framework in order to maximize their profits from e-commerce in publishing and entertainment.

The rules promoted by these players to govern a sizeable, general marketplace of users do not lend themselves well to the educational and research communities because, with a few notable exceptions, they do not provide for the special qualities and needs of education and scholarship. Even in licensing, where libraries have made some progress in negotiating broad uses for their communities, efforts to legitimize mass-market licenses could eliminate fair use and erode the willingness of providers to negotiate at all.

In the U.S. and Canada as well as other parts of the world, the library community has been actively engaged in policy debates as laws have been revised, consistently advocating the need to retain a balance among the interests of creators, owners, and users. Our involvement has been significant but these efforts have not been able to stop the economic and political forces of the marketplace that now so clearly dominate society.

It is critical that library community advocacy activities be sustained so there is no further erosion of the balance of interests among creators, copyright owners, and users. At the same time, it is essential for the community to step back, assess the current reality, and consider additional strategies for achieving our commitment to "promote equitable access to and effective use of recorded knowledge in support of teaching, research, scholarship, and community service."

The current environment clearly favors commercial interests and thus mitigates against effective use of intellectual property for purposes of education and research. After many years of the library community's struggle to retain the balance in copyright law, scientists and scholars have cast a new light on the debate. Researchers have come to depend on new technologies for rapid peer-to-peer communications and sophisticated searching and manipulation of data. They have begun to insist that publishers support articles with large datasets, image files, and simulations. And, as the original authors, they are demanding open, easy access to the literature as soon after publication as possible.

Some publishers have been resistant to open access, fearing loss of revenues and loss of control over their content. To date, librarians have exhibited mixed responses to open-access initiatives. Some librarians, like their scientific and scholarly colleagues, see open access as an opportunity to exploit technology more fully in support of research and teaching; others express concern, particularly with the Public Library of Science, that some libraries will cancel journal subscriptions thereby motivating publishers to raise subscription prices and increasing the overall cost of access. Now is the time for librarians to fully embrace the goal of open access, and join with scholars, scientists, and their institutions in working toward this goal.

### 8.8.1. Open Archives Initiative (OA)

The goal of the OAI is to contribute in a concrete manner to the transformation of scholarly communication. The proposed vehicle for this transformation is the definition of technical and supporting organizational aspects of an open scholarly publication framework on which both free and commercial layers can be established. The origins of the Open Archives initiative lie in the growing number of electronic preprint (eprint) archives. While several of these began as informal vehicles for the dissemination of preliminary results and non-peer reviewed "gray literature", a number of them have evolved into an essential medium for sharing research results among the colleagues in a field.

These archives demonstrate a shift in the traditional scholarly communication model, which has relied on formally published scholarly journals. T' ɔ is a growing consensus that the scholarly journal system is facing significant challenges:

— The explosive growth of the Internet has given scholars almost universal access to a communication medium that facilitates immediate sharing of results.
— The rapidity of advances in most scholarly fields has made the slow turn-around of the traditional publishing model an impediment to collegial sharing.
— The full transfer of rights from author to publisher often acts as an impediment to the scholarly author whose main concern is the widest dissemination of results.
— The current implementation of peer-review-an essential feature of scholarly communication-is too rigid and sometimes acts to suppress new ideas, favor articles from prestigious institutions, and cause undue publication delays.

— The imbalance between skyrocketing subscription prices and shrinking or, at best, stable library budgets is creating an economic crisis for research libraries.

The e-print archives exemplify a more equitable and efficient model for disseminating research results. An important challenge is to increase the impact of the e-print archives by layering on top of them services-such as peer review-deemed essential to scholarly communication. This is the focus of the Open Archives initiative.

The aim of the archive initiatives described above is to try to create a more effective scholarly communication mechanism that addresses problems that exist in the established system. The approaches that are taken by individual archives differ in a number of ways. Some initiatives build on a centralized model, others on a distributed departmental, or by extension, institutional model. Some deal with gray literature only, others incorporate metadata of peer-reviewed papers or try to establish some form of peer-review outside of the established system. Some deal with metadata only, others with both metadata and full content. Yet all share the attribute of offering scholars a vehicle to conveniently and immediately disseminate research results to peers. The reason for launching the Open Archives initiative is the belief that interoperability among archives is key to increasing their impact and establishing them as viable alternatives to the existing scholarly communication model.

The Open Archives initiative has been set up to create a forum to discuss and solve matters of interoperability between author self-archiving solutions (also commonly referred to as e-print systems), as a way to promote their global acceptance. Interoperability is a broad term, touching many diverse aspects of archive initiatives, including their metadata formats, their underlying architecture, their openness to the creation of third-party digital library services, their integration with the established mechanism of scholarly communication, their usability in a cross-disciplinary context, their ability to contribute to a collective metrics system for usage and citation, etc.

Interoperability among archives offers substantial benefits to the scholars that use them. An important attribute of the traditional research library as an information provider is its role as a common entry point for a variety of information resources, not necessarily divided along disciplinary or institutional boundaries. The move from physical to digital sources should not be accompanied by the breakup of this entry point into a collection of fragmented archives.

An increasing number of scholars move fluidly in their research across domain boundaries; the technology for delivering digital information should facilitate rather than hinder such fluidity. Mechanisms for interoperability offer the potential for discovery tools and virtual collections that extend across the contents of multiple archives. Interoperability is also beneficial to the archive and service provider. Rather than having to provide an entire suite of services for its users, individual archives can instead establish a welldefined interface on which external providers can build enhanced services.

A variety of such services can be envisioned, including those that facilitate discovery, linking, and reviewing. An intriguing and essential set of services would be those that provide metrics to assist in the evaluation of the impact of certain scholarship and aid in tenure review and promotion decisions. Although interoperability has been a watchword for a variety of efforts in digital libraries and networked information, the actual meaning of it and the implementation thereof has often proven elusive.

In UK, the Santa Fe Convention presents a technical and organizational framework designed to facilitate the discovery of content stored in distributed e-print archives. It makes easy-toimplement technical recommendations for archives that-when implemented-will allow data from e-print archives to become widely available via its inclusion in a variety of end-user services such as search engines, recommendation services and systems for interlinking documents. In addition, the convention introduces an organizational framework for making information available about archives that adhere to the technical recommendations of the convention-the data providers-and about trusted parties that build end-user services for data originating from such archives-the service providers. As such it provides a communication mechanism between providers of data and providers of services and creates a community of open archives.

The Santa Fe Convention builds on on a number of definitions and concepts that are essential for its understanding. The Convention considers the following to be crucial components of an e-print archive:

— A submission mechanism;
— A long-term storage system;
— A management policy with regard to submission of documents and their preservation;
— An open machine interface, that enables third parties to collect data from the archive.

The last item is crucial for enabling third parties to create services that support the discovery, presentation and analysis of data in the archive. Most e-print archives will also provide native end-user services. However, facilitating the broad dissemination of archive data through third party services is a crucial feature of an e-print archive. Therefore, the open interface is a key part of the Santa Fe Convention.

The convention uses the notion of a record in an archive. Some archives may store metadata that describes full content without storing the full content itself. In this case, the metadata is a record. Other archives may also store full content. However, the convention assumes that if full content is stored, there will always be associated metadata stored in the archive as well as a mechanism to tie metadata and content together. In this case the combination of metadata and full content is a record.

### 8.8.2. Open Archives Metadata Set (OAMS)

The Open Archives Metadata Set (OAMS) is a collection of nine metadata elements intended to facilitate coarse granularity resource discovery among the records in distributed and dissimilar archives. The semantics of this set have purposely been kept simple in the interest of easy creation and widest applicability. There is no provision for qualification or extension of the nine elements. The expectation is that individual archives will maintain metadata with more expressive semantics and the Open Archives Dienst Subset provides the mechanism for retrieval of this richer metadata.

### 8.8.3. Open Archives Dienst Subset

The Open Archives Dienst Subset is a set of protocol requests that are delivered via HTTP. This protocol is a subset of the full Dienst protocol. The protocol requests in the subset provide the following functionality:

— List the full identifiers for records stored in an archive. An optional argument permits the client to specify that the list should only include records added after a specific date. Another optional argument allows the client to specify that the records should be accompanied by the metadata associated with the identifier.
— Return the metadata for a specific record in a requested format.
— Return the list of metadata formats supported by an archive.
— Return the list of metadata formats available for a specific record.
— Return the structure of the partitions by which an archive is organized.

Santa Fe Convention also introduces an organizational framework to facilitate its implementation and to establish a communication mechanism between data providers and service providers. An understanding of this framework can be obtained from an exploration of the core document of the Santa Fe Convention that gives a step by step approach for making an e-print archive or a service comply with the Santa Fe Convention.

The requirement to have a shared, basic metadata set to facilitate interoperability across communities was reconfirmed. Also the notion of parallel metadata sets that serve specific needs of communities and archives was reconfirmed.

The shared metadata set developed during the original Santa Fe meeting-the OAMS-was deemed inappropriate for cross-community use due to some e-print specific aspects. Instead, the Dublin Core Element Set was selected as the common metadata set. This selection leverages years of work in the Dublin Core Metadata Initiative in developing cross-community consensus.

Initial steps were taken to encourage the development of community-specific harvestable metadata sets. Representatives of the e-print community at the meeting decided to propose a metadata set targeted at the e-print community under the name EPMS by the beginning of 2001. Representatives of the research library community proposed a similar effort and calls for proposals from other communities (e.g., the museum community, Open Language

Archives) will be issued.To distinguish between metadata specific to harvesting functionality and other metadata (both shared and community specific), a carrier syntax in XML was developed. This syntax transports packages of specific sets (e.g., Dublin Core, EPMS) within a contextual wrapper that contains metadata specific to the harvesting interactions between data and service providers.

The concept of unique identifiers within an OAI namespace has been maintained. Its implementation has been revised for compliance with general URI principles and to allow for the building of resolution mechanisms and services across OAI-compliant archives.

### 8.8.4. OAI Harvesting Protocol

At the heart of the technical agreements of the OAI is the metadata harvesting protocol, which provides a simple interface to transfer metadata from a data provider to a service provider. The original specifications for this interface in the Santa Fe Convention were a subset of the more expressive Dienst protocol (called the Open Archives Dienst Subset). This protocol contains the following service requests:

- *Identify* - returns a self-description of the archive, containing information submitted at time of registration and other administrative information;
- *ListMetadataFormats* - returns a list of identifiers of metadata formats that are offered by the archive in general or for a particular record;
- *ListSets* - returns a structured list of sets (formally called partitions) within which records may be located;
- *ListRecords* - returns a list of record identifiers, and optionally metadata, within a specified range of dates and/or a specified Set. Flow control is achieved by the use of server-generated continuation tokens;
- *GetRecord* - returns the metadata associated with an identifier.

These service requests and their parameters are encoded into standard HTTP URIs. Responses to the requests are XML documents. This allows for simple implementation using CGI scripts or similar technology for data providers while service providers can exploit the proliferation of XML parsers to ease the harvesting of data.

### 8.8.5. Dienst System

The word "Dienst" refers to a number of things:

— A conceptual architecture for distributed digital libraries.

— A protocol for service communication in that architecture.

— A software system that implements that protocol.

Conceptually, Dienst is a system for configuring a set of individual services running on distributed servers to cooperate in providing the services of a digital library. The open architecture of the Dienst system - exposure of the functionality through an defined protocol - makes it possible to combine Dienst services in flexible ways and augment the existing services with other mediator services, which build on the functionality of the existing services.

The Dienst system originated with the Computer Science Technical Reports Project, a DARPA-funded collaboration to establish a digital library of computer science technical reports. Broadly speaking, there are three ways that Dienst is used:

1. Organizations that wish to join an existing digital library built using Dienst.
2. Organizations that wish to create a new distributed digital library with Dienst.
3. Organizations that wish to undertake research in digital libraries using an existing Dienst digital library or by experimenting with the software.

The modular nature of the software encourages researchers who wish explore mechanisms for enhancing existing services or using the interfaces to existing services to built other services. Notice: While the software has been built and tested according to conventional software engineering standards, we stress that it is research software. Organizations wishing to use it for mission critical applications should consider a thorough review of the architecture, protocol, and software for robustness and security.

The distributed Dienst software is configured to handle textual resources (documents) in a variety of formats. However, the Dienst architecture includes a sophisticated document model that accommodates a wide variety of digital resources. Using the Dienst software for these other resources will require some programming. The Dienst protocol and software is copyrighted but is available for free and can be used and redistributed for non-commercial uses. The Dienst protocol and software is used in a variety of existing digital libraries and projects.

In short, the Open Archives Initiative is providing a framework for the extensive interoperability of archives of scholarly research literature (and potentially other digital materials too). For this initiative to become a widespread reality, the participation of large numbers of individuals and institutions is required. In order to be able to participate, what institutions need is working, interoperable, configurable software that is freely available and easy to set up. It is this need that the EPrints software was developed to fulfill.

EPrints is a feature-rich open archive software system that is as simple to install as any normal application. It runs right "out of the box" with a comprehensive default setup that should serve most people's needs. However, it has also been designed to make it extensively and flexibly re-configurable for customized needs; almost any aspect of the archive's operation can be adapted to suit a particular requirement. This means that the archive can be used by institutions, individuals, journals or any other organization wishing to interoperate with Open Archive services.

## References

Bailey, C.W., 'Public-Access Computer Systems', *Information Technology and Libraries*, 12, March 1993.

Bawden, D., *User-oriented Evaluation of Information Systems and Services*, Aldershot: Gower, 1990.

Conway, Paul , *Preservation in the Digital World,* Washington, D.C.: Commission on Preservation and Access, 1996.

Hulser, Richard P., Digital Library: Condent Preservation in a Digital World, *DESIDOC Bulletin of Information Technology*, 17 (6), 1997.

Kelleher, J., E. Sommerlad, and E. Stern, *Evalution of the Electronic Libraries Programmes: Guidelines for e-Lib Project Evaluation*, London: Tavistock Institute, 1996.

Lynn, M.S., "Digital Preservation and Access", *Collection Management* 22, nos. 1998.

Ma, Y. *A., Semiotic Analysis of Icons on the World Wide Web*, Paper presented at the Annual Conference of the International Visual Literacy Association, Chicago, 1995, (ERIC Document Reproduction Service, ED 391481).

Moy, Naomi, *CyberSpace Reference Library: the Virtual Reference Collection*. Carson, CA: CA State University at Dominguez Hills, 1997.

Philip, H. Young, "Visions of Academic Workplace in a Brave New Future", *Library and Future: Essays on Library in the Twenty-First Century*, New York, Haworth Press, 1993.

# 9

# Digital Library Service Framework

Much progress has been made in aligning library services with changing (and increasingly digital and networked) research and learning environments. At times, however, this progress has been uneven, fragmented, and reactive. As libraries continue to engage with an ever-shifting information landscape, it is apparent that their efforts would be facilitated by a shared view of how library services should be organised and surfaced in these new settings and contexts.

Recent discussions in a variety of areas underscore this point:

— Institutional repositories: what is the role of the library in collecting, managing, and preserving institutional scholarly output, and what services should be offered to faculty and students in this regard?

— Metasearch: how can the fragmented pieces of library collections be brought together to simplify and improve the search experience of the user?

— E-learning and course management systems: how can library services be lifted out of traditional library environments and inserted into the emerging workflows of "e-scholars" and "e-learners"?

— Exposing library collections to search engines: how can libraries surface their collections in the general Web search environment, and how can users be provisioned with better tools to navigate an increasingly complex information landscape?

In each case, there is as yet no shared picture of the library to bring to bear on these questions; there is little consensus on the specific library services that should be expected in these environments, how they should be organised, and how they should be presented.

Libraries have not been idle in the face of the changes reshaping their environments: in fact, much work is underway and major advances have already been achieved. But these efforts lack a unifying framework, a means for libraries, as a community, to gather the strands of individual projects and weave them into a cohesive whole. A framework of this kind would help in articulating collective expectations, assessing progress, and identifying critical gaps. As the information landscape continually shifts and changes, a framework would promote the design and implementation of flexible, interoperable library systems that can respond more quickly to the needs of libraries in serving their constituents. It will provide a port of entry for organisations outside the library domain, and help them understand the critical points of contact between their services and those of libraries.

Perhaps most importantly, a framework would assist libraries in strategic planning. It would provide a tool to help them establish priorities, guide investment, and anticipate future needs in uncertain environments.

It was in this context, and in recognition of efforts already underway to align library services with emerging information environments, that the Digital Library Federation (DLF) in 2005 sponsored the formation of the Service Framework Group (SFG) to consider a more systematic, community-based approach to aligning the functions of libraries with increasing automation in fulfilling the needs of information environments. The SFG seeks to understand and model the research library in today's environment, by developing a framework within which the services offered by libraries, represented both as business logic and computer processes, can be understood in relation to other parts of the institutional and external information landscape. This framework will help research institutions plan wisely for providing the services needed to meet the current and emerging information needs of their constituents.

A service framework is a tool for documenting a shared view of library services in changing environments; communicating it among libraries and others, and applying it to best advantage in meeting library goals. It is a means of focusing attention and organising discussion. It is not, however, a substitute for innovation and creativity. It does not supply the answers, but facilitates the process by which answers are sought, found, and applied.

## 9.1. A Vision for a Service Framework

This section discusses the SFG's vision of a service framework, with an emphasis on some of the key principles on which such a framework should be based.

Before proceeding further, it is useful to state explicitly the SFG's definition of a service framework:

> A service framework is a set of reference models, along with a set of concepts and vocabulary for expressing and relating them. The service framework—i.e., vocabulary and reference models—covers the range of entities relevant to the articulation of library business goals at varying levels of granularity, as well as the services that support these goals.

For the purposes of this discussion, a reference model is defined as a formal description of a library activity, expressed using consistent, well-defined terminology and relationships. The Open Archival Information System (OAIS) reference model is a useful example of what a reference model might look like, and the benefits it confers. OAIS describes a particular library activity: digital preservation. It provides a broad sketch of what digital preservation is intended to accomplish, the major processes involved, and even some of the more granular functionalities that comprise each process. It also defines some of the information objects that flow through the preservation process. OAIS provides a means of understanding and expressing the digital preservation problem space. This in turn has galvanised discussion in an extremely diverse global digital preservation community, and facilitated the development of international standards and technologies built around the understanding of digital preservation expressed by OAIS.

Just as OAIS provides a means for understanding and discussing digital preservation, a service framework for libraries would provide a similar platform for understanding and discussing the transitions shaping the general library landscape. The framework would be a tool with which to 1) understand and communicate the "business logic" needed to support library goals, and how this business logic must change as library goals and environments change, and 2) support the design and implementation of flexible, recombinant, and interoperable systems to support library goals. The framework will be a shared point of reference for libraries, and is expected to help:

— Cultivate a shared, consistent vocabulary to discuss library goals and services;

— Communicate library goals and library value to other communities;

— Encourage consensus and large-scale collaborations;

— Benchmark the current state of library service development, and identify critical needs and gaps;

— Promote the design of reusable, recombinant, and interoperable library services, and minimise reinvention of wheels across library development efforts;

— Align business planning with systems development.

It is useful at this point to mention a few things that the service framework is *not* about:

— Technology choice: the framework is not a statement about the specific ways services, applications, or library systems should be implemented;

— Application design: the framework is not about specifying the specific ways, or architectures, used to bundle services together to form more complex applications;

— "Starting from scratch": the framework will not provide an exhaustive description of all aspects of a library, but instead, concentrate on key areas of need. It will not re-invent libraries from the ground up.

The service framework is not a process modelling or systems design methodology. It is, however, a means of organising and expressing in a consistent way the *output* of process modelling or systems design activities. It is a way for libraries to organise and express their collective understanding of how library activities should be presented in changing information environments, as well as a context within which to sustain an ongoing dialogue to further that understanding.

The grand theme underpinning the framework is that library service development should be driven by library business goals, and conversely, functionality embedded in existing library systems should be "mappable" back to the business logic—i.e., the library's business processes and workflows—it is intended to support. The framework needs to encompass, therefore, concepts for expressing business logic, as well as concepts for mapping the business logic to the technical or engineering logic of library service provision. This will help decision-makers understand how the needs and goals of the library inform the design of systems.

In keeping with this theme, the SFG identified several important principles that would guide its work:

(1) *Service-orientation*: Systems development, both within the library community and beyond, is increasingly based on service-oriented concepts and design methodologies. A service is a discrete piece of functionality, manifested in the form of a technical implementation, and deployed for use, usually on a network (e.g., as a Web service). Looking ahead, there is every indication that more and more library processes and workflows will take the form of automated systems built by combining a variety of services. Service orientation is a modular approach to systems development, through the combination and recombination of component services from possibly numerous sources. This permits flexible development strategies responsive to constantly shifting information environments. It organises community-wide development efforts in ways that promote reusability and avoid duplicative effort, enhance interoperability, and ultimately, lower costs. All of these factors are essential ingredients for library system development in increasingly complex network environments, where responses to change must be rapid and economical.

(2) *Consistency and Cohesiveness*: Libraries have invested considerable effort into thinking about how their services should

be organised and presented in changing environments. However, very little has been documented in ways that promote convergence of thinking, and perhaps even standardisation. Libraries therefore lack consistent ways of presenting their services and communicating their value in new environments. The service framework aims to rectify this through the accumulation of reference models that provide a consistent view of library activities, and a shared means of expressing them. However, the service framework needs to be more than just a disjointed set of reference models. There must be a way to create useful relationships across the reference models—that is, to move both horisontally (across library activities) and vertically (across different levels of granularity within the same activity)—within the service framework. In short, the service framework must have an internal structure that supports a cohesive, "big picture" view of the library service landscape.

(3) *Outward-Facing:* Library services will not always be accessed in library-controlled environments and systems; instead, they will often be surfaced in, and accessed through, non-library environments. For example, the library catalogue may take the form of a search service embedded in a course management system; similarly, reference desk services may take the form of an "ask-a-librarian" service available with the click of a button on a Web browser tool bar. Libraries need to make their services available at the point of need, whether it be in course management systems, e-learning materials, collaboration tools, or even the general Web search environment. It is important, therefore, that the service framework facilitate communication, collaboration, and interoperability not just between libraries, but also between libraries and other domains. It needs to be outward-facing, in the sense that it serves as an aid for communicating a consistent view of library services in non-library domains, and identifying key points of contact across domain boundaries. The framework should help libraries interact seamlessly with other parts of the information landscape, and help them actively define their role in new information environments, rather than having it defined for them, or being excluded entirely.

In summary, the SFG will lay the foundations for a framework that is service-oriented, consistent and cohesive, and outward-facing. More than this however, the framework should be facilitating rather than prescriptive, flexible rather than constraining, and a catalyst for, rather than an obstacle to, understanding and innovation.

## 9.2. A Structure and Vocabulary for the Framework

The SFG's activities to date have focused on articulating the case for a service framework for libraries; compiling and reviewing related initiatives, including direct discussions with several projects (more on this below); and sketching out a structure and vocabulary for representing library business logic in the context of the service form work. The latter is illustrated in Figure 9.1.

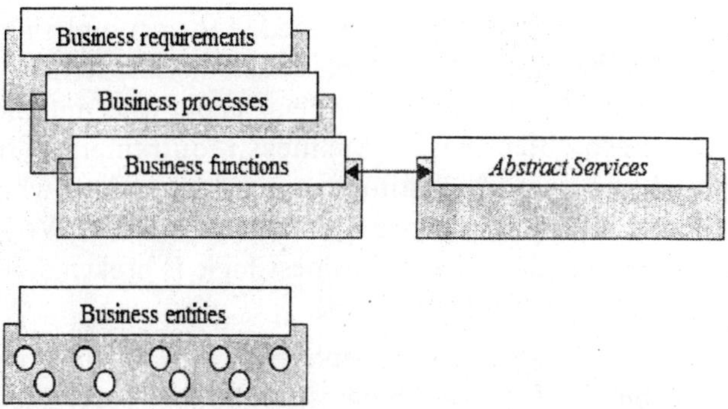


*Figure 9.1: Decomposing the Library's Business Logic*

Figure 9.1 embeds several key concepts that can be used to decompose and describe a library's business logic:

— *Business Requirement:* identifiable segment of an organisation's overall mission. Example: Preserve Digital Resources

— *Business Process*: identifiable portion of a business requirement. Example: Ingest Digital Resources into Repository

— *Business Function:* identifiable portion of a business process. Example: Validate Format of Ingested Resource

A library can be viewed as a set of activities which, taken together, define what the library is and what it is expected to do to fulfill its mission. In some instances, these activities are defined broadly—for example, "collect, organise and preserve". This may be useful in some contexts, but not in others. For instance, if the goal is to build a digital library system, simply asserting that the system must support the collection, organisation, and preservation of digital resources provides little information for the system architect. There is also little assurance that two different systems, both supporting the preservation activity, will offer the same, or even similar, functionality.

In order to cultivate a shared view of library services, it is useful to follow a process of decomposition, beginning with broad library requirements and ending with self-contained units of specific functionality. This is illustrated in Figure 9.1: the library's business logic—its broad statement of mission—is decomposed, or featured, into a set of business requirements needed to accomplish overall objectives. The business requirements attach more specificity to the library's objectives, and convey more detail about what must be done to achieve these objectives. A business requirement is in turn decomposed into a set of constituent processes, each of which are broken down into one or more business functions. With each decomposition step, the library's business logic is broken down into smaller and more specific descriptions.

Boundaries between requirements, processes, and functions can be arbitrary, but the downward progression through several levels of granularity helps simplify decomposition by allowing it to occur in stages on units of manageable size. In contrast, attempting to decompose a broad requirement into a set of "atomic" functionalities in a single step would be complex and difficult. Moreover, it is often the case that the boundaries between levels are quite natural, and in this sense, may give useful hints to system architects as they design automation logic to implement the business logic. For example, decomposition could help identify instances where the same functionality appears in multiple contexts, and can therefore be refused; it might also help isolate functionality that could be stripped out of local implementations and deployed instead as a shared service infrastructure. In either case, this would help reduce local development effort and costs.

The structure and vocabulary represented in Figure 9.1 convey a misleading sense of simplicity; in fact, while the structure and concepts were intentionally kept simple and straightforward, they were the product of much discussion and analysis. The SFG membership brought a variety of perspectives, and means of expressing these perspectives, to their work; crafting these into a single model was both a challenging and interesting process. Figure 9.1 represents a convergence of views among the membership on some basic concepts with which to express a consistent view of library services. This in turn can aid in communicating these services across a variety of boundaries—within libraries, between libraries, and between libraries and other domains—as well as inform a flexible, service-oriented approach to library systems development.

Decomposing library activities into granular, self-contained functions helps us better understand libraries, and in doing so, helps in the development of flexible, consistent library services. Recall that a service is a discrete piece of functionality, manifested in some form of technical implementation, and deployed for use, usually on a network. In this sense, a service embodies two aspects: a description of a functionality, and a technology choice for implementing that functionality. As the latter aspect suggests, there are often multiple ways to implement a given functionality, and so a service may be manifested in different ways. But there should be a way to express the underlying functionality, independent of technology choice. In the SFG's vocabulary, this is handled through the concept of an abstract service.

### 9.2.1. Abstract Service

Abstract services represent an intermediate step between defining a business function (i.e., a discrete piece of library business logic), and a technical implementation of that function. An abstract service elaborates on a business function by organising it into a set of automatable behaviors, as well as a generic description of its input and output requirements, perhaps in the form of an abstract data model. In short, an abstract service is a way of expressing a business function as a service—but independent of technology choices for its implementation. In this way, multiple service implementations can be drawn together into a single family, each implementing the same piece of library business logic, and represented by the same abstract service. By abstracting away the specificities of technical implementation, library services can be expressed in generic terms, which in turn permits a consistent view of library services across multiple, and possibly very different, technical contexts and environment.

The definition of an abstract service includes a general specification of the data requirements needed to support implementations. This is addressed in Figure 9.1 through the concept of business entities.

### 9.2.2. Business Entity

It is the entity of interest within the environment, usually represented by metadata. Examples: service, person, organisation, collection, policy, transaction.

Library services are increasingly dependent on data about important entities in the environments in which they operate. This data will usually take the form of schematised descriptions of people, places, and things within the environment. Libraries, of course, have a great deal of experience in terms of schematised descriptions of information objects, and this kind of data will continue to play a key role in supporting library services. However, automated fulfilment of many key library functions will require much more than this: consistent ways of describing users, institutions, services, policies, and a host of other business entities will also be needed, as well as consistent ways of representing relationships between various types of entities. Library services will be increasingly data-driven, and therefore business entities must be a key element of the service framework.

Figure 9.1 represents a possible structure and vocabulary for the service framework. It is service-oriented in the sense that it aims to decompose library business logic down into discrete units of functionality that can be implemented and deployed as services in a variety of environments. It is consistent and cohesive, in the sense that it supplies concepts for describing library activities at various levels of granularity, independent of specific technology choices, and provides a structure for organising and relating these concepts as a unified whole. And it is outward-facing, in the sense that it provides a means of communicating library services in non-library environments, by expressing these services in a consistent way that is independent of technical or environmental context; moreover, by taking into account key business entities library services need to understand and support—information objects, people, other services, and so on—it helps identify points of contact between libraries and other domains.

The service framework was defined above as a set of reference models, along with a structure and vocabulary for expressing them. Figure 9.1 is a partial fulfilment of the latter requirement. Reference models may be developed at all levels of the structure depicted in Figure 9.1: requirements, processes, functions, abstract services, and business entities. The structure and vocabulary is a means of expressing, organising, and linking the reference models gathered under the umbrella of the service framework.

Digital libraries are far from well-defined Definitional agreement may only extend to notions of accessible collections of information. Because of this, it is hardly surprising to note that the field does not easily converge on standards and technology. Most of the existing systems that are classified as DLs have resulted from custom-built software development projects — each the product of intensive design, implementation and testing cycles. There are many reasons why this effort is repeated for each project:

— Many DLs are built in isolation as a response to the needs of a particular community, in most cases not involving personnel with prior experience.
— Most modern DLs have WWW interfaces — thus the user interfaces and process flows are fashioned to resemble the way people use the WWW, which itself changes with time.
— Each DL is aimed at meeting the needs of a particular community—so the underlying program logic varies vastly among systems.
— Most DLs are intended to be quick solutions to urgent community needs—so not much thought goes into planning for future redeployment of the systems.
— DLs, by the very nature of being responses to user needs, can be arbitrarily complex, so new projects sometimes choose to

develop from scratch because it is cheaper than adapting what already exists to a different set of scenarios.

— As DL systems get more complex, extensibility becomes more difficult and, as a result, maintainability is compromised. As testimony to this, at the turn of the millenium, Dijkstra wrote that computing's central challenge of "how not to make a mess of it" had not been met.

— There are very few software toolkits available to build DLs.

A natural solution would be to create software toolkits. A few institutions have investigated this approach. Dienst is a DL system developed at Cornell University with tasks clearly divided and specified by a protocol based on HTTP and eventually using XML. It was developed to support distributed operation of the NCSTRL project and, while technically sound, required an investment in software, methodology, and support that some prospective users were not willing to make. The Repository-in-a-Box software from the University of Tennessee is an alternative, as is the E-Prints software from Southampton University. Both these toolkits avoid many problems related to complexity of DLs by defining workflows that are not easy to change. All of these and other systems have had varying degrees of success among archivists looking for drop-in solutions but they generally suffer from two basic problems:

— The range of possible workflows is restricted by the design of the system.

— The software is either built as a monolithic system or as components that communicate using nonstandard protocols — in both cases making understanding and modification a complex process.

Because it is widely accepted as good software engineering practice, most modern programming environments adopt some form of component model. Even in the DL community, as far back as 1994, early discussions on the future of DLs concluded that components were an integral part of the solution. The University of Michigan Digital Library Project investigated using autonomous agents as the basic components of a DL. Stanford's InfoBus project defined a set of services to support distributed digital libraries, each wrapped in an object, communicating through a remote method invocation interface.

Other scientific communities embraced component technology as an aid to rapidly and correctly solving problems—for example, the Sieve framework at Virginia Tech encapsulates scientific functionality into software components. However, in spite of the widespread use of such technology, for the reasons outlined above, the DL community did not in general adopt a single component framework.

In October of 1999 the Open Archives Initiative (OAI) was launched in an attempt to address interoperability issues among the many existing and independent DLs. The focus was on high-level communication among systems and simplicity of protocols. The OAI has since received much media attention in the DL community and, primarily because of the simplicity of its standards, has attracted many early adopters.

The OAI Protocol for Metadata Harvesting in essence supports a system of interconnected components, where each component is a DL. Also, since the protocol is simple and is becoming widely accepted, it is far from being a custom solution of a single project. The OAI protocol can be thought of as the glue that binds together components of a larger DL. However, since DLs are themselves defined only loosely, this collaborative system could be composed of individual component DLs, each with different functionality. In the extreme case, each component DL could supply the functionality of exactly one (part of a) service expected by a user.

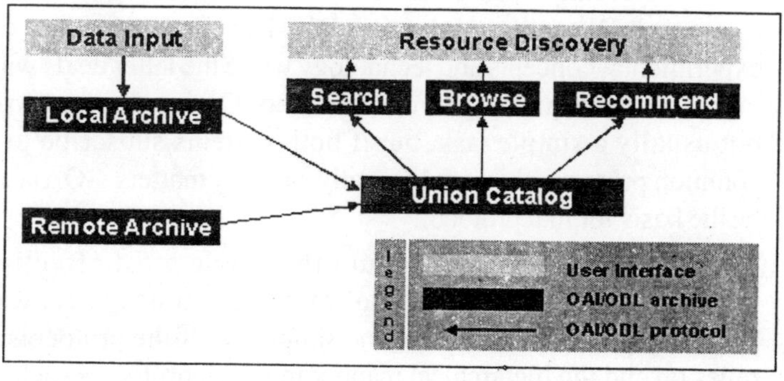


*Figure 9.2. Example networked architecture of an Open Digital Library*

This is the approach taken in this work, where Digital Libraries are modelled as networks of extended Open Archives, with each extended Open Archive being a source of data and/or a provider of services. (The "extensions" are necessary since Open Archives are optimised for the provision of data — but are generalisable to other tasks with a few minor changes.) This network of extended Open Archives, an instance of which is illustrated in Figure 9.2, is herein called an Open Digital Library (ODL). This approach to DL architecture is further motivated by the following factors:

— Componentisation and standardisation are built into the system by design if every service is delivered by an extended Open Archive. This inherently supports reuse and allows for interoperability at the level of individual services within the DL.

— The ODL approach closely resembles the way that physical libraries work. In a physical library the individual systems interoperate within their own communities. For example, the purchasing department interoperates with the booksellers and the inter-library loan department interoperates with peer departments at other libraries. A retiring head of the acquisitions department can be replaced by a peer at another institution because he or she understands a common protocol for all libraries. Interoperability is achieved at the level of individual services rather than at the level of organisations.

— There is currently a significant difference in technology between a research DL and a production DL. The former focuses on experimental concepts and technology while the latter deals with the real issues of meeting the needs of users. Connecting the two is not usually a simple task, but if both systems subscribe to a common protocol, that would greatly simplify matters—OAI can be the basis for that protocol.

— The Internet is without a doubt the single most effective information dissemination tool of current times. This was primarily possible because of the simplicity of the protocols it relies on and the hierarchical manner in which protocols such as HTTP build on more fundamental protocols such as IP and TCP. The OAI provides us with a simple protocol to transfer metadata;

building simple layered extensions to this protocol would closely follow the proven methodology of the networking community.

— While complex system interactions might support complex operations, they also raise the bar on adoption of new technology. A good example would be the hypertext community where the WWW has succeeded well beyond other projects simply because its model was always a simple one. Modelling DL services as Open Archives would enforce such a degree of simplicity.

— Scholarly communication is a rapidly changing field and many people are slow in making the transition to new forms of communication in spite of a growing number of advocates. The success of new DL systems in this arena relies on keeping pace with current thinking on how publications are created, processed, and distributed. A simple component model will greatly simplify changes in the workflow of the DL to support the gradual shift to new and improved processes.

— User interface design and workflow management are complex tasks. But common base-level services--mediators for connecting resources or middleware in three-tier client-server development—have emerged in practice, for example, supporting searching and browsing.

— Norman advocates that designs should be visible, understandable and natural in their mappings. The OAI protocol is already establishing itself in those areas so it makes an ideal foundation upon which to build.

## 9.3. Open Digital Library Design

ODLs are guided by a set of design principles and operationalised with the aid of a set of OAI-PMH extensions. By analysing some of the emerging aspects of Internet development, a set of basic design principles have been extracted to guide the construction of new protocols so that they are consistent with proven techniques in networked information systems. The observed factors that influence these include: simplicity of protocols, openness of standards, layering of semantics, independence of components, loose coupling of systems, purposeful orthogonality, and reuse wherever possible. Based on these ideas, a generalisation of the OAI protocol is possible so that it may be used for purposes that go beyond its original intention, namely to provide higher-level DL services. Formally, these principles are stated as follows:

1. All DL services should be encapsulated within components that are extensions of Open Archives.
2. All access to the DL services should be through their extended OAI interfaces.
3. The semantics of the OAI protocol should be extended or overloaded as allowed by the OAI protocol, but without contradicting the essential meaning.
4. All DL services should get access to other data sources using the extended OAI protocol.
5. Digital Libraries should be constructed as networks of extended Open Archives.

Each DL service is then designed as a self-contained component that communicates with other services using a protocol that is an extension of the OAI-PMH. A typical example of how this works in practice is illustrated in Figure 9.3, which shows a search engine's relationships to its data source and the interface that uses it as a service component.

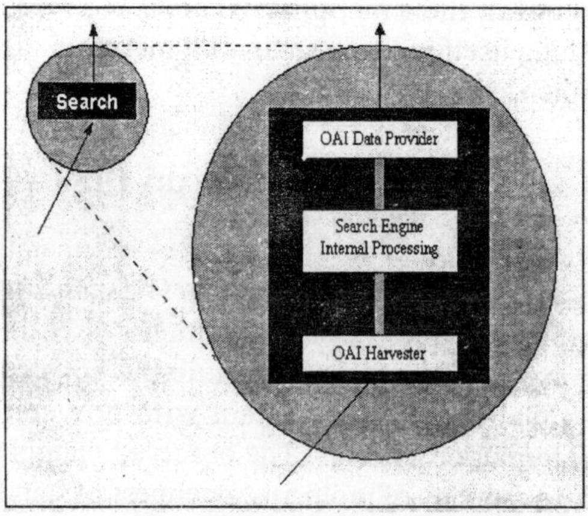


*Figure 9.3. Internal structure of a typical ODL search component.*

In this case, the OAI Harvester is used to obtain a stream of data which in turn is used to create indices for searching. Queries are then submitted through the OAI Data Provider interface. These queries overload the semantics of the OAI-PMH, by using the OAI notion of sets to correspond to the dynamically generated result sets of a search engine. Analogously, when such a request is submitted, the query is mapped to the name of a set. Thus, without making any changes, the OAI-PMH can be used to serve as the interface to a search engine. With a few minor additions to the OAI-PMH, information such as cardinality of result sets also can be returned.

An example of such an OAI request, with overloaded semantics for a search component is:

```
verb=ListIdentifiers&set=odlsearch1/computer%20science/1/10
```

This query specifies that the response should contain the identifiers of the first 10 most relevant documents with respect to the query "computer science". The response generated by the component is in the standard format returned by OAI-compliant archives.

To use this component in a typical ODL network, it must be connected to a source of metadata and a user interface, much in the same manner as UNIX pipes and filters are used to connect cooperating processes together. This is illustrated in Figure 9.4.

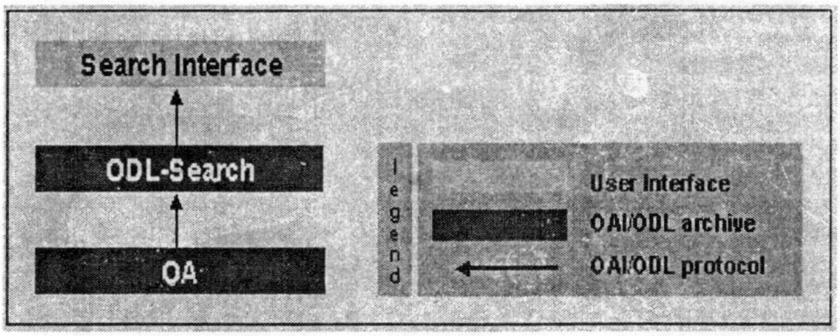


*Figure 9.4. Simple ODL network using Search component*

## 9.4. Implementation and Analysis

To test the feasibility of ODL design, a suite of components was specified, implemented, integrated into a network, and assessed for their ability to replace existing systems. These components and their functionality are specified in Table 9.1.

*Table 9.1. Components used in prototype systems*

| Component | Function |
|---|---|
| ODL-Union | Combine metadata from multiple sources |
| ODL-Filter | Reformat metadata from (non-OAI-Conforming) data sources |
| ODL-Search | Provide search engine functionality |
| ODL-Browse | Provide category-driven browsing functionality |
| ODL-Recent | Provide a sample of recently-added items |

The components were implemented individually, tested using the Repository Explorer, and combined into an ODL network to provide DL services over the union archive of metadata maintained by the Networked Digital Library of Theses and Dissertations (NDLTD). Then, to illustrate reusability, some components were integrated into the production server for the Computer Science Teaching Center. A system architecture for the former of these systems is depicted in Figure 9.5.

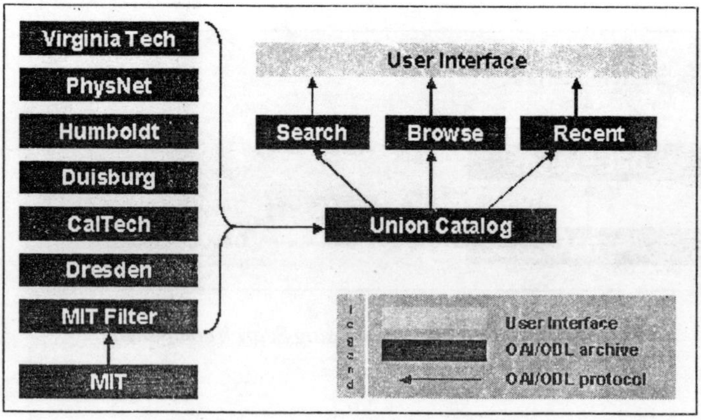


*Figure 9.5. Architecture of NDLTD ODL system*

There were seven source archives from which data was harvested through OAI-PMH interfaces, one of which required a filter because of minor differences in implementation from the others. The data was aggregated into a central archive for use by local services. Three high-level services were provided using this data: Search, Browse, and Recent Search indexed the data and exposed an OAI-like interface for specifying keyword queries. Browse sorted the data and exposed a slightly different OAI-like interface for accessing items by controlled vocabulary elements. Recent stored recent items and upon request returned a random sample of those.

The user interfaces were created using minimal scripts to translate HTML form elements into ODL requests and then convert the XML responses into human-readable displays using XSL style sheets.

It is hoped that the results of this ongoing work will change the way people build Digital Libraries. The evaluations and feedback received from users and colleagues strengthen the case for building on the OAI protocol to support high-level services, and composition of those services into complete Digital Library systems.

Building upon a foundation of extensibility, it then will be possible to work on providing more interesting services to users, thus bridging the wide gap between current research and production systems, and ultimately making information more accessible to more people.

## References

Berners-Lee, Tim and Mark Fischetti. 1999. *Weaving the Web*, Harper, San Francisco.

Birmingham, William P. 1995. "An Agent-Based Architecture for Digital Libraries", in *D-Lib Magazine*, July 1995.

Dijkstra, Edsger. 2001. "The End of Computing Science", in *Communications of the ACM*, Vol 44, No 3, March 2001, p. 92.

Fielding, R., J. Gettys, J. Mogul, H. Frystyk, L. Masinter, P. Leach, and T. Berners-Lee. 1999. *RFC2616: Hypertext Transfer Protocol - HTTP 1.1*. Network Working Group, June 1999.

Gladney, H., Z. Ahmed, R. Ashany, N. J. Belkin, E. A. Fox, and M. Zemankova. 1994. *Digital Library: Gross Structure and Requirements (Report from a Workshop)*, IBM Almaden Research Center, Virginia Tech Dept. of Computer Science, June 1994.

Harnad, S. 1999. "Free at Last: The Future of Peer-Reviewed Journals", in *D-Lib Magazine*, Vol 5, No 12, December 1999.

ISO. 1994. *ISO/IEC 7498-1:1994, Open Systems Interconnection Basic Reference Model: The Basic Model*, International Organization for Standardization.

Lagoze, C. and J. R. Davis. 1995. "Dienst - An Architecture for Distributed Document Libraries", in *Communications of the ACM*, Vol 38, No 4, p. 47.

Umar, Amjad. 1997. *Object-Oriented Client/Server Internet Environments*, Prentice Hall, New Jersey.

Van de Sompel, Herbert and Carl Lagoze. 2000. "The Santa Fe Convention of the Open Archives Initiative" in *D-Lib Magazine*, Vol 6, No 2, February 2000.

# 10

# Information Security in Digital Age

Information technology has done more than make it possible to do things faster or easier—electronic commerce has transformed and created industries. Successful companies depend on the ability to identify and contact potential customers; customer buying habits and market trends are increasingly valuable as businesses try to maximise their returns. Manufacturing is becoming increasingly dependent on receiving and making shipments "just in time" and no earlier or later to reduce inventories. Documents critical to business transactions—including electronic funds—are increasingly stored and transferred over computer networks.

Electronic information has opened new questions about copyright, ownership, and responsibility for information. Rights in paper-based and oral information have been developed through centuries of adaptation and legal precedents. Information in electronic form can be created, distributed, and used very differently than its paper-based counterparts, however. Measures to streamline operations through use of information technology and networks require careful attention to technical and institutional safeguards. For example, combining personal records into a central database, in order to improve data processing efficiency, can put privacy at risk if adequate safeguards are not also implemented. In addition, many types of information safeguards are still relatively new, and methods to balance risks and the costs of protecting information are not fully developed.

Distributed computing and open systems can make every user essentially an "insider". This means that responsibility for safeguarding information becomes distributed as well, potentially putting the system at greater risk. With the rapid changes in the industry, the responsibilities of each network provider to other providers and to customers may not be as clear as in the past.

Even though each player may be highly trusted, the overall level of trust in the network necessarily decreases, unless the accountability of each of the many intermediaries is very strict. Thus, users must take responsibility for safeguarding information, rather than relying on intermediaries to provide adequate protection.

## 10.1. Cryptography

Cryptography is a fundamental technology for protecting the confidentiality of information, as well as for checking its integrity and authenticating its origin. It was originally used to protect the confidentiality of communications, through encryption; it is now also used to protect the confidentiality of information stored in electronic form and to protect the integrity and authenticity of both transmitted and stored information.

With the advent of what are called public-key techniques, cryptography came into use for digital signatures that are of widespread interest as a means for electronically authenticating and signing commercial transactions like purchase orders, tax returns, and funds transfers, as well as for ensuring that unauthorised changes or errors are detected. These functions are critical for electronic commerce. Techniques based on cryptography can also help manage copyrighted material and ensure its proper use.

In 1987, new information security and privacy issues have resulted from advances in networking, such as the widespread use of the internet and development of the information infrastructure, and from the prospect of networking as a critical component of private and public-sector functions. These advances require appropriate institutional and technological safeguards for handling a broad range of personal, copyrighted, sensitive, and proprietary information.

The information infrastructure is already international: networks like the internet seamlessly cross national borders. Networked information is similarly borderless. Achieving consensus regarding information safeguards among the diverse stakeholders worldwide is more difficult than solving many technical problems that might arise. The federal government can help resolve many of these interrelated issues. But they must be solved systematically, not piecemeal, in order to attain an overall solution.

The internet and a strong networking and software industry in the United States has not consistently produced products equipped with affordable, easily used safeguards. In general, many individual products and techniques are currently available to adequately safeguard specific information networks—provided the user knows what to purchase, and can afford and correctly use the product. Nevertheless, better and more affordable products are needed. In particular, there is a need for products that integrate security features with other functions for use in electronic commerce, electronic mail, or other applications.

The establishment of a system of certification authorities and legal standards, in turn, is essential to the development of a public-key (PKI) infrastructure and to safeguarding business and personal transactions. Current PKI proposals need further development and review, however, before they can be deployed successfully. Ideally, the safeguards an organisation implements to protect networked information should reflect the organisation's overall objectives.

Network designers must continuously struggle to balance utility, cost, and security. Information can never be absolutely secured, so safeguarding information is not so much an issue of how to secure information as one of how much security a government agency or business can justify. There is a great need for federal agencies, as well as other organisations, to develop more robust security policies that match the reality of modern information networks. These policies should support the specific agency objectives and interests, including but not limited to policies regarding private information. The policies must also anticipate a future where more information may be shared among agencies. Finally, these policies should be mandated from the highest level.

Most important step toward implementing proper safeguards for networked information in a federal agency or other organisation is for its top management to define the organisation's overall objectives and a security policy to reflect those objectives. Only top management can consolidate the consensus and apply the resources necessary to effectively protect networked information.

Emergency response efforts are vital to safeguarding networked information, due to the relative lack of shared information about vulnerabilities on information networks. Expanding current efforts could further improve the coordination of system administrators and managers charged with protecting networked information.

Criminal and civil sanctions constitute only one aspect of safeguarding networked information. Further study is needed to determine the effectiveness of such sanctions, as opposed to improving the effectiveness of law enforcement to act on existing laws.

With the rapid expansion of the networked society, there is a great need to support re-evaluation of fundamental ethical principles—work that is currently receiving too little attention.

More resources also could be applied to study and improve the methods and materials used in education of ethical use of networked information, so that more effective packages are available to schools and organisations that train users. Finally, more resources could also be directly applied to educate users (including federal employees, students, and the public at large) about ethical behaviour. Security policy issues are divided in three areas:

i) national cryptography policy, including federal information processing standards and export controls;
ii) guidance on safeguarding unclassified information in federal agencies; and
iii) legal issues and information security, including electronic commerce, privacy, and intellectual property.

Cryptography has become a technology of broad application; thus, decisions about cryptography policy have increasingly broad effects on society. The effects of policies about cryptography are not limited to technological developments in cryptography, or even to the health and vitality of companies that produce or use products incorporating cryptography. Instead, these policies will increasingly affect the everyday lives of most Americans: cryptography will be used to help ensure the confidentiality and integrity of health records and tax returns; it will help speed the way to electronic commerce; and it will help manage copyrighted material in electronic form. Policy debate over cryptography used to be as arcane as the technology itself. Most people did not regard government decisions about cryptography as directly affecting their lives. There is also growing recognition of the potential misuses of cryptography, such as by disgruntled employees as a means to sabotage an employer's databases. Thus, export controls, intended to restrict the international availability of US cryptography technology and products, are now being joined with domestic cryptography initiatives intended to preserve US law-enforcement and signals-intelligence capabilities.

Public-key cryptography can be used for digital signatures, for encryption, and for secure distribution or exchange of cryptographic keys. The Digital Signature Standard (DSS) is intended to supplant, at least in part, the demand for other public-key cryptography by providing a method for generating and verifying digital signatures. However, while the DSS algorithm is a public-key signature algorithm, it is not a public-key encryption algorithm.

Licensing requirements vary according to the nature of the item to be exported, the end use, the end user, and, in some cases, the intended destination. For many items, no specific approval is required and a "general licence" applies. In other cases, an export licence must be applied for from either the state department or the commerce department, depending on the nature of the item.

Software and hardware for robust, user-controlled encryption are under state department control, unless state grants jurisdiction to commerce. This has become increasingly controversial, especially for the information technology and software industries.

The impact of export controls on the overall cost and availability of safeguards is especially troublesome to business and industry at a time when high-technology firms find themselves as targets for sophisticated foreign-intelligence attacks and thus have urgent need for sophisticated safeguards that can be used in operations worldwide. Moreover, software producers assert that several other countries do have more relaxed export controls on cryptography.

Information-security managers must compete for resources and support to properly implement needed safeguards. In order for their efforts to succeed, top agency management must fully support investments in cost-effective safeguards. Given the expected increase in interagency sharing of data, interagency coordination of privacy and security policies is also necessary to ensure uniformly adequate protection.

## 10.2. Use of Safeguards

Security is used generally to describe the protection against disclosure, modification, or destruction of networked information through the use of safeguards. These safeguards include hardware, software, physical controls, user procedures, administrative procedures, and management and personnel controls. The degree of security, along with the safety and reliability of a system, is reflected in the level of confidence that the system will do-what it is expected to do-that is, its trustworthiness.

Information network as any set of interconnected electronic information systems; therefore, a "network" is not restricted to the internet, corporate networks, the telephone network, and so forth. In any case, today's networks are increasingly interconnected or overlapping, and distinctions are difficult to make. To be successful, safeguards must be applied in a coordinated fashion to contain the risks from the above threats, while maintaining the functional objectives of the network. To implement such safeguards, professionals can use a top-down and ongoing process that is based on the objectives and design of each particular network.

Alternatively, many managers and users attempt to protect information through more ad hoc applications of products and services that sometimes lack even an informal consideration of an overall process. While such an informal approach may be adequate for some small networks, it can put the information in other networks at great risk. The single most important step toward implementing proper safeguards for networked information in a federal agency or other organisation is for its top management to define the organisation's overall objectives, define an organisational security policy to reflect those objectives, and implement that policy.

Reflecting their organisational objectives, different types of network providers and users emphasise different security aspects or services. Long-distance carriers, local telephone companies, cable companies, satellite providers, wireless carriers, and other providers of the telecommunications links generally place the most emphasis on the availability of their services. Availability means that core services will be operational despite threats of fire, flood, software errors, undercapacity, virus attacks, and so forth. Building on the links are value-added providers, some resellers, computer network services, and others who use the links to transport information, but also add features of their own.

Commercial internet providers primarily emphasise availability, while electronic data interchange (EDI) value-added services emphasise integrity and non-repudiation. Integrity means that the information is only altered from its original form and content for authorised reasons. Non-repudiation refers to the ability to prove that a party sent a particular message.

Subscription services, such as Compuserve, America Online, Genie, Delphi, and Prodigy, also emphasise access control. Access control refers to mechanisms based on user-identification and user-authentication procedures that restrict each user to reading, writing, or executing only the information or functions for which he or she is authorised.

Users are both providers and consumers of information; they may have little control over the overall availability of the links, but they can control other aspects. Users can assure the confidentiality of classified, proprietary, or private information through the use of cryptography and access controls. Confidentiality refers to the assurance that only properly authorised persons can view particular information.

Online publishers and corporations may use cryptography and access controls to emphasise the protection of copyrighted or proprietary information, i.e., assuring that two parties have properly exchanged payments or permissions for services or products delivered electronically. Confidentiality is distinguished here from privacy, which is less commonly used in the computer security profession. It refers to the treatment of data and is achieved when designated information is not disseminated beyond a community of authorised knowers.

The security policy of an agency or other organisation is intended to implement the overall objectives, express the organisation's view on risk, and assign responsibilities, among other things. Whether implicit or explicit, the policy is essential to define the requisite safeguards. Without a security policy, it could be argued that it is not possible to have a security violation. The business has nothing defined as confidential and no standards to meet.

In an organisation, a successful security policy is made by the top management-a chief executive officer or agency head, for example. In cooperative networks, the policy may be made by representatives of its members, standards committees, regulatory bodies, or by law. Organisational security policies range from one page to several volumes in length, but should not be overly specific.

Information networks make horizontal exchanges of information between low-level agency employees much easier, but sharing such information also brings new risks since different agencies have different objectives and policies about handling such information. Agencies and other organisations will have to work together to assure that sensitive information is handled uniformly according to privacy and computer matching laws. There is a great need for agencies and other organisations to develop sound security policies that match the reality of modern information networks. These policies should be mandated from the highest level. They should support the specific organisational objectives and interests, including but not limited to policies regarding private information.

The actual safeguards implemented to protect networked information should represent the overall objectives of the organisation, but in practice they often do not. Network designers must continually balance utility (including speed, capacity, flexibility, user-friendliness, and interoperability), cost, and security.

In any case, information can never be absolutely secured, and safeguarding information is therefore not an issue of how to secure information, but how much security an agency or business can justify. Many approaches are effective and inexpensive, but others can be very costly, for both small and large organisations. The organisation's management, therefore, must have a method to balance the cost of a safeguard with the potential loss that may occur if it does not use that safeguard.

Security professionals can use risk analyses to estimate risks and probable losses for information assets. These analyses can then be used to determine the appropriate safeguard expenditures. A crude qualitative risk analysis may simply identify the obvious holes in a system but can, nevertheless, be valuable. A rigorous quantitative analysis requires some experience with security systems and understanding of how to determine the value of information assets.

Management benefits from risk analyses only in so far as an analysis provides timely, quantifiable, and credible measurements. In practice, however, risk often can be difficult to quantify and the analysis expensive. Quantification requires statistics about the frequency and size of losses in similar organisations. Such statistics may be difficult to obtain, and the frequencies of losses may be too low to be useful or may not be applicable to a particular organisation. Incidents of loss are widely underreported or undetected. The discipline of risk analysis also is still relatively young and needs further development.

Therefore, a risk analysis does not necessarily assure that a system is effectively safeguarded, only that the organisation is following a systematic approach. New developments in risk analysis have made the process easier, however, relying on past experience and on automated tools with extensive threat, vulnerability, and safeguard knowledge bases, and user-friendly interfaces. Risk analysis performs best where the nature of losses are best understood or frequent-such as in cases of natural disasters or credit card fraud. Its shortcomings lie in cases where the losses are less understood.

Alternatively, management can use a due care (reasonalbe care) approach to determine how much security an organisation can afford. A due care approach seeks an acceptable level of safeguards relative to other businesses and agencies, as opposed to an acceptable level relative to an absolute measure of risk. This approach uses 'baseline' controls and practises, as well as risk analyses for vulnerabilities not addressed by the baseline.

The baseline varies depending on the application or industry; for example, the baseline for the banking industry would be different from that of an information publisher. The baseline is also intended to be flexible and incorporate changes in technology. The due care approach is intended to build on the experience of others in the field and, therefore, to lower the cost of managing networked information. The due care approach to safeguarding information assets is not well established, however, and has relatively little precedent or experience to build on. The establishment of generally accepted principles is integral to providing standards for due care, but detailed principles will take some time to develop.

The tools and techniques alone will not safeguard an organisation's information; they require expert personnel to apply and maintain them. They also must be combined in a coordinated fashion to meet the organisation's objectives, whether they emphasise confidentiality, integrity, availability, or any other attributes of security.

Even small networks require users to identify themselves through a user name and a confidential password. These passwords are usually stored in an encrypted file in a central computer, and few people or perhaps no one has the key to the file that contains the passwords. An intruder might guess a password by trial and error, however, using typical passwords such as names, nicknames, names of spouses or children, and so forth. An intruder might also monitor and copy passwords that are sent to the central computer as the user logs on, or that are written on scraps of paper left near the user's computer. This latter type of attack can be deterred by 'challenge-response' systems that never actually send the password over the network.

When the user enters his or her account name at a terminal, the central computer issues the user a random challenge. The user sees the challenge, and transcribes it and a password into the keypad of a hand-held authenticator. The authenticator calculates a unique response; the user enters that response into the terminal and sends it to the central computer. The central computer repeats the calculation and compares its result with the user's result. An intruder cannot imitate the user without access to the identical authenticator and its associated password. The user's token can generate a response based on a card-unique secret key and the local time, instead of the challenge sent by the central computer.

Other technologies perform similar functions in different forms. Smart cards are plastic cards the size of bank cards that have a microprocessor chip embedded in the plastic, sometimes with a magnetic stripe also on the back. The SmartDisk is a token in the shape of a 3.5-inch diameter magnetic disc with a connectionless interface that communicates with the disc drive head.

A firewall provides a focus for managing network safeguards by restricting communication into and out of the network. The firewall itself is a dedicated computer that examines and restricts mainly incoming, but sometimes outgoing, communications. The form of the firewall restriction may be simple; for example, electronic mail may be allowed while other services are not. Or the restriction may be more elaborate, perhaps requiring individual user authentication as a prerequisite for communication through the firewall. Firewalls are particularly important for networks connected to the internet, to assure that computers on a smaller network are less vulnerable to intruders from the much larger internet.

Virus checkers are software programmes that automatically search a computer's files for known viruses. The checker scans files every time the computer is turned on or when new memory disks are inserted into the computer. The virus checker looks for patterns of code that resemble the code used in known viruses, and alerts the user when it finds a resemblance. Since new viruses are discovered every month, virus checkers must be updated often, although many viruses cause no damage or are not relevant to most users.

Auditing is the act of automatically monitoring certain transactions that occur in a network over a period of time. Such transactions include transfers of files, and the local time when a user accesses the network. Auditing features on a network can quickly generate volumes of information about network use, however, that can overwhelm busy security personnel. Auditing, therefore, is often a passive activity where records are only kept for later examination. It is also a passive deterrent to authorised users who might fear getting caught should an investigation arise. Integrated, dynamic auditing systems not only record information, but also act to restrict use or to alert security personnel when possible safeguard violations occur-not just violations from intruders but also from insiders.

One feature might alert security personnel if users are accessing certain files after hours or if a user (or possible intruder) repeatedly but unsuccessfully attempts to access a certain computer. The security officer might then closely monitor the user's actions to determine what further actions should be taken (simply denying access might alert an intruder to use a more reliable or more covert method, confounding the security staff). Some sophisticated systems use expert systems that "learn" users' behaviour.

Encryption, Electronic Mail, and Digital Signatures can be integrated to provide multiple safeguards. Encryption is used for a variety of applications, including the protection of confidentiality and integrity, authentication, and nonrepudiation. Different methods are used to assure these properties, and each method has its strengths and weaknesses. One widely used network application is electronic mail (email). Large and small networks can transfer electronic mail messages from workstation to workstation, holding the message for the addressee until he accesses it on a computer.

Historically, electronic mail has not used encryption to protect the confidentiality of the message contents. PEM—or Privacy-Enhanced Mail—is a specific set of proposed standards that specifies how to encrypt the contents of electronic mail messages for the internet. Unauthorised users cannot read a PEM encrypted message even if they were to obtain access to it. PEM can also digitally "sign" the message to authenticate the sender. Although PEM can protect the confidentiality of the message, it cannot protect the confidentiality of the address, since that information must be understood by network providers in order to send the message. Privacy-enhanced mail requires that both the sender and the receiver of the electronic mail message have interoperable software programmes that can encrypt and decrypt the message, and sign and verify the digital signature. Therefore, widespread adoption is still far off.

Biometric devices can be effective in many cases, but are expected to be less effective for protecting networked information due to their generally higher cost. Biometric signatures also can be intercepted and imitated, just as unchanging passwords can, unless encryption or an unpredictable challenge is used. Characteristics that might be analysed by biometric devices include retinal scans of the eye, fingerprints, handprints, voice 'prints', signature dynamics, and the typing of keystroke patterns.

Safeguards need not be based in only hardware or software. They can also include administrative and other procedures like those used in accounting practices. As only one example, the authority and capacity to perform certain functions to networked information should be separated and delegated to different individuals. This principle is often applied to split the authority to write and approve monetary transactions between two people. It can also be applied to separate the authority to add users to a system and other system administrator duties from the authority to assign passwords, review audits, and perform other security administrator duties. The separation of duties principle is related to the "least privilege" principle, that is, that users and processes in a system should have least number of privileges and for the minimal period of time necessary to perform their assigned tasks.

### 10.2.1. Safeguarding Networks

Safeguarding networks collectively amounts essentially to safeguarding the so-called information infrastructure. The Information infrastructure includes the public-switched telephone network, satellite and wireless networks, private networks, and the internet and other computer and data networks. The infrastructure is continually and rapidly evolving as technology advances and as users find new applications. Individuals, corporations, governments, schools and universities, and others own components of the infrastructure, but no one owns or controls it as a whole. Moreover, the numerous stakeholders have diverse and often conflicting goals. The transportation infrastructure is similar: better freeways favour the interests of suburban living and private transportation, for example, but conflict with the interests of inner cities and public transportation.

The information infrastructure and its associated safeguards also cannot be built "from the ground up". Instead, the infrastructure must be steered by its stakeholders, including users and the federal government, by strengthening its institutions and assuring that there are adequate products and services available to users. By strengthening the roles of each of these interdependent institutions, the overall marketplace gains by more than the sum of the parts.

The overall information infrastructure is not a well-defined or closed system and cannot be strengthened through technical solutions alone. Rather, the infrastructure is changing and growing, and its vulnerabilities are not well understood. The federal government must work together with the many stakeholders to assure robust solutions that will automatically accommodate changes in technology and that can provide feedback for steadily strengthening safeguards overall. The information infrastructure is already international. Networks like the internet seamlessly cross national borders.

Networked information is also borderless and affects many different stakeholders worldwide. Achieving consensus regarding safeguards among these diverse, international stakeholders is more difficult than achieving technical breakthroughs. Nevertheless, the federal government has the capacity for resolving many of the issues that inhibit or facilitate the use of quality safeguards by diverse communities. These issues are interrelated, however, so solving them piecemeal may not provide an overall solution.

Information has become as much of an asset to a business or government agency as buildings, equipment, and people. The information in a corporate database is as crucial to one business, for example, as manufacturing equipment is crucial to another. Once the value of information is recognised, it follows that an organisation's management should protect it in the same manner as other corporate or government assets; for example, using risk analyses, contingency plans, and insurance to cover possible losses. Managers and accountants often do not recognise electronic information as an asset, however, because of its less tangible nature, its relatively recent prominence, and the lack of documentation of monetary losses arising from loss or theft of information.

Paper-based information and money can be protected in a safe inside a secured building. Destruction of the building in a fire is a very tangible and easily documented event. In contrast, loss or duplication of electronic information may not even be noticed, much less reported publicly. The losses that are reported or that reach the public consciousness also do not necessarily represent the overall losses.

Until now, most losses in corporate networks arise from human errors and authorised users. Media attention, however, most often highlights virus attacks or teenage and adult "crackers"—important, but often unrepresentative, sources of lost information, time, and money.

Management may perceive that the corporate or agency network is safe from these sensational threats, while ignoring other important threats. Management may also be reluctant to make changes to the network that can cause disruptions in productivity. Experts note that information is never adequately safeguarded unless the responsibility for information assets is placed directly on top management, which can then assign the necessary resources and achieve consensus among diverse participants within the organisation. Information security then becomes a financial control feature subject to audit in the same manner as other control functions.

Insurance helps spread and manage risk and therefore, in principle, protect an organisation's information assets from losses. Insurance policies exist to protect against the loss of availability of networks in a disaster, threats from computer viruses, toll fraud, or claims made by a third party as a result of an error made by the organisation. Users can also purchase computer disaster recovery services that can restore services in the event that the main computer centre is incapacitated.

Insurance for information losses does not cover the great majority of security threats, however, including losses arising from human or software errors from within the organisation. Organisations must continue to self-insure against monetary losses due to loss, theft, or exposure of networked information, using appropriate safeguards. To justify a market for broader insurance coverage, risks must be assessable, the losses must be detectable and quantifiable, and the insurer must have confidence that the insured is acting in good faith to report all relevant information and is exercising reasonable care to avoid and mitigate losses.

Network security is a dynamic field, however; losses are not necessarily detectable or quantifiable. The standards for due care and concepts of risk analysis for protecting networked information also are not necessarily adequately developed or dependable to allow insurance companies to make underwriting decisions. Moreover, policies too high, reflecting their uncertainty about the magnitude of losses, as well as their inability to verify the safeguards undertaken.

Insurance companies are most likely to accommodate risks to networked information into policies by modifying traditional coverage, but these risks are not always comparable with traditional risks such as the loss of availability from a natural disaster. Information can be "stolen" without removing it from the premises, for example.

Ideally, broader insurance coverage for information assets may help stabilise the marketplace by forcing policy-owners to meet minimum standards of due care or generally accepted principles and to perform risk analyses. The underwriters could audit the policyowners to ensure that they are following such methods. As more companies buy insurance, the standards could become better developed, helping to improve the level of safeguards overall.

Software developers sell new software packages with few or no guarantees that the programmes are secure or free of undesirable characteristics, some of which are intentionally built-in for various reasons, and some of which are unintentional ("bugs").

Moreover, the customer or client generally must pay for upgraded versions that repair the "bugs" in original versions or add new features such as security. Products are also not necessarily shipped with security features already switched "on". If products are not user-friendly or fully secure, users have no other choice except to write their own software, go without the safeguards, or make do with what is available.

The buyers cannot necessarily articulate what features they want, and the developers are ultimately responsible for designing new and useful products. Given society's growing dependence on networked information, the question of the developers' responsibilities for secure and safe products will be increasingly important in coming years.

Vendors and product developers often claim that buyers do not strongly demand safeguards. In a very competitive market for software, safeguards often add development cost and may require trade-offs in functionality, compatibility, or capacity for which users are not willing to sacrifice. Indeed, buyers are often accustomed to thinking of computers as isolated machines, and that security violations "won't happen to me."

Users, therefore, often make computer operation simpler by disabling the safeguards that are provided with the product. Users may not perceive that threats are real, may lack the expertise to use the products, or may simply be willing to assume the associated risk. For whatever reason, the majority of safeguard failures in information networks is attributable to human errors in implementation and management of existing systems.

Encryption technology has moved beyond the security market into the commercial market. Today, intelligence and law-enforcement agencies are concerned about strong encryption incorporated into integrated hardware and software products (including commercial, public-domain, and shareware products). Much of the controlled encryption is already available as stand-alone products developed legally overseas, or pirated, transported, or developed overseas illegally.

Moreover, since security features are usually embedded inside of other hardware and software products, foreign companies could capture more of the overall information technology market. On the other hand, buyers may not be demanding as much encryption protection for confidentiality as vendors claim. Further study into this issue is needed to determine more fully the effects of export controls on the ability of vendors and developers to supply affordable and user-friendly safeguards.

Safeguards can be weakened as well as strengthened through the standards-setting process. Designers must often make compromises so that different protocols can work together. Maintaining the safeguarding features is only one aspect of these modifications; other important features include user-friendliness, flexibility, speed or capacity, and cost. The lack of any standards or too many standards, however, significantly limits the effectiveness of many safeguards.

In particular, safeguards that require each user of either end of a communication to have compatible schemes—for sending messages, for example, or encrypting and decrypting telephone calls-benefit from the widest possible distribution of that product so that the users can communicate with more people. Even market-driven *de facto* standards, in such a case, are better than well-protected users who cannot communicate with but a few other users because of a wide variety of incompatible standards. Standards are most effective when applied to relatively narrow, well-defined areas where there is a clear need for them. Policy-makers and others must therefore consider carefully the balance between setting *de jure* standards versus allowing the market to diversify or drift to its own *de facto* standards.

Broader efforts to protect networked information will be frustrated by cryptography-standards issues unless the process for establishing cryptography policy is clarified and improved. Product evaluations in general are intended to help assure buyers that off-the-shelf computer and network equipment and software meet contract requirements and include certain acceptable safeguards free of defects. Even relatively simple systems require that all but experts place a significant amount of trust in products and their vendors. Independent experts can evaluate these products against minimum qualifications and screen for defects, saving buyers the cost of errors that might result from making their own evaluations or from relying on the vendors.

Increasingly, computers are becoming connected via networks and are being organised into distributed systems. In such environments a much more thorough system security analysis is required, and the product rating associated with each of the individual computers is in no way a sufficient basis for evaluating the security of the system as a whole. This suggests that it will become increasingly important to develop methodologies for ascertaining the security of networked systems, not just evaluations for individual computers. Product evaluations are not applicable to whole systems in general, and as "open systems" that can be interconnected relatively easily become more the rule, the need for system security evaluation, as distinct from product evaluation, will become even more critical.

The subsequent step of accreditation refers to the formal approval by a designated authority to use the system in that particular environment. The accreditation should take account of the results of the certification, but may not necessarily reflect it; the accreditation also takes account of nontechnical (business and political) considerations and is the ultimate decision regarding the system.

Generally accepted practices can be documented and adopted to help guide information security professionals and vendors. These practices would act much as generally accepted accounting principles standardise practices for accountants. Such practices could help advance professional examinations; provide standards of due care to guide users, managers, and insurance companies; and give vendors design targets. To be comprehensive, however, the generally accepted practices must be defined at several levels of detail, and different sets of standards would apply to different users and applications.

The Organisation for Economic Cooperation and Development (OECD) has developed general guidelines to help member countries in information-security issues. The guidelines were adopted in 1992 by the OECD Council and the 24 member nations. These guidelines list nine general principles and several measures to implement them. The guidelines are intended to serve as a framework for both the private and public sectors.

The Information Systems Security Association (ISSA) is in the process of developing a comprehensive set of Generally Accepted System Security Principles (GSSPs) for professionals and information-technology product developers to follow. The ISSA effort includes members from the federal government (through NIST), and representatives from Canada, Mexico, Japan, the European Community, and industry. The ISSA has divided the principles into two sets.

The first—the Information Security Professional GSSPs—is aimed at professionals, including managers, developers, users, and auditors and certifiers of users. The second group—the GSSPs for Hardware and Software Information Products—is aimed at products and the auditors and certifiers of products. Each of these sets of GSSPs has a three-tier hierarchy of pervasive principles, broad operating/functional principles, and detailed security principles.

The pervasive principles adapt and expand on the OECD principles described above. The broad operating/functional principles are more specific and are based on many documents such as the NSA Rainbow Series, FIPS, Electronic Data Processing Auditor's Association Control Principles, and the United Kingdom's Code of Practice for Information Security Management. The detailed principles address the practical application of the other principles, and are expected to change frequently to stay current with evolving threats. The detailed principles will include step-by-step procedures of common security tasks, prevalent practices, and so forth. Generally accepted principles have strategic importance to other aspects of networked information, such as for establishing due care guidelines for cost-justifying safeguards, as targets for training and professional certification programmes, and as targets for insurance coverage.

The educational and career paths for information-security practitioners and managers are not so mature as in other fields, such as accounting or law. The field could benefit from the professional development of security practitioners and managers. Security professionals enter the field from widely diverse disciplines, and managers cannot necessarily compare the expertise of applicants seeking positions as security professionals.

Professional recognition credits individuals who show initiative and perform well against a known standard. University computer science departments lack programmes specialising in information safeguards; but professional examinations provide a target for institutions that graduate computer scientists or provide continuing education in safeguards.

The International Information Systems Security Certification Consortium (ISC2) is developing an information security certification in cooperation with the US federal government (through NIST and NSA), the Canadian government, Idaho State University, the Data Processing Management Association, Electronic Data Processing Auditors Association, the Information Systems Security Association, the International Federation for Information Processing, the Canadian Information Processing Society, the Computer Security Institute, and others.

Efforts to "professionalise" the information security field are important steps, but will not produce significant results for some time. Their success is also related to the success of generally accepted system security principles and their adoption in industry and government. It is unclear whether professional examinations and certifications will ever have a strong impact in an industry that is as dynamic and evolutionary as information networking.

Engineers in the information industry, for example, have not widely adopted the licensing of professional engineers. Engineering examinations and licences are more effective in relatively stable fields, such as the construction and oil industries. Examinations and certifications are also effective, however, where liability and the protection of assets is involved, as in accounting and construction.

The most prominent of these is the Computer Emergency Response Team (CERT), sponsored since 1988 by the Software Engineering Institute at Carnegie Mellon University and the Department of Defence's Advanced Research Projects Agency (ARPA). CERT provides a 24-hour point of contact available by telephone, facsimile, or electronic mail. It collects information about vulnerabilities; works with vendors and developers, universities, law-enforcement agencies, NIST, and NSA to eliminate the vulnerabilities and threats; and disseminates information to systems administrators and users to eliminate vulnerabilities where possible.

According to its policy, CERT does not disseminate information about vulnerabilities without an associated solution (called a "patch") since malicious users could exploit the vulnerability before the majority of users had time to develop their own repairs. Some claim, however, that CERT could be more effective by readily disseminating information about vulnerabilities so that users can design their own patches, or perhaps if no solutions are found after a fixed period of time. CERT is not the only emergency response team.

The Defence Data Network (DDN) Security Coordination Centre, sponsored by the Defence Communications Agency and SRI International, is a clearinghouse for vulnerabilities and patches on the MILNET. The Computer Incident Advisory Capability was established at Lawrence Livermore Laboratory to provide a clearinghouse for classified and unclassified information vulnerabilities within the Department of Energy, including those relating to the Energy Science Network (ESnet).

These and other emergency response teams form the Forum of Incident Response and Security Teams (FIRST), created by ARPA and NIST. The forum is intended to improve the effectiveness of individual and overall response efforts. Its members include groups from industry, academia, and government, both domestic and international. The Administration has proposed that NIST, in coordination with the Office of Management and Budget and NSA, develop a governmentwide crisis response clearinghouse. This clearinghouse would serve existing or newly created agency response teams to improve the security of agency networks. Emergency response efforts are vital to safeguarding networked information, due to the relative lack of shared information about vulnerabilities in information networks. Expanding current efforts could further improve the coordination of system administrators and managers charged with protecting networked information.

Ethical and legal use of computers and information is not clearly defined, however. Computer networks are entirely new media that challenge traditional views of ownership of information, liability, and privacy. As the internet reaches more people, commercial enterprises are exploring it for uses other than education and research. Using the internet for unsolicited commercial promotions has historically met great opposition from users, but recent events indicate a desire on the part of some to change this tradition.

Now that more commercial enterprises are attaching to the internet and the "backbones" for the large part are removed from the oversight of the National Science Foundation, the old rules for acceptable use of the internet could change. Experts note that users generally want to know where the line is drawn regarding ethical use of information, and may only need some simple but memorable guidelines. For example, relatively few users probably know what constitutes fair use of copyrighted information, but would appreciate knowing what they can legally copy and what they cannot. Children are taught early on that writing in library books is an unethical practice; straightforward, ethical computer practices can also be taught to children at an early age. Training in the workplace also can help users to understand ethical principles, but such programmes are only effective if they are well-developed, do not appear superficial or insincere, and are repeated.

Group behaviour is particularly important since groups of users do not necessarily behave in the same manner as individuals. Even relatively secure networks rely on the cooperation of users to alert system managers to problems or threats. A strategic employee who never takes a vacation, for example, may be a worker who cannot leave work for a single day without risk of becoming discovered in a security violation. An unannounced change in a programme's operation may indicate that it has been altered.

## 10.3. Digital Archives and Copyright Issues

Digital technology yields additional, effective means of access. In full text documents, a reader can retrieve needed information by searching for words, combinations of words, phrases or ideas. Readers can also manipulate the display of digital materials by choosing whether to view digital materials on a screen, store them on their computer or external media, or to print them. Digital technology, however, poses new threats and problems as well as new opportunities. Its functionality comes with complexity. Anyone with a compass could theoretically set up or repair a sundial. A digital watch is more useful and accurate for telling time than a sundial, but few people can repair it or even understand how it works. Rapid changes in the means of recording information, in the formats for storage, and in the technologies for use threaten to render the life of information in the digital age. Today, information technologies that are increasingly powerful and easy to use, especially like those that support the world wide web, have unleashed the production and distribution of digital information.

If we are effectively to preserve for future generations the portion of this rapidly expanding corpus of information in digital form that represents our cultural record, we need to understand the costs of doing so and we need to commit ourselves technically, legally, economically and organisationally to the full dimensions of the task. Failure to look for trusted means and methods of digital preservation will certainly exact a stiff, long-term cultural penalty. The question of preserving or archiving digital information is not a new one and has been explored at a variety of levels over the last five decades.

Archivists responsible for governmental and corporate records have been acutely aware of the difficulties entailed in trying to ensure that digital information survives for future generations. Far more than their library colleagues, who have continued to collect and organise published materials primarily in paper form, archivists have observed the materials for which they are responsible shift rapidly from paper objects produced on typewriters and other analogue devices to include files created in word processor, spreadsheet and many other digital forms.

Early attention to the difficulties in preserving digital information focused on the longevity of the physical media on which the information is stored. Even under the best storage conditions, however, digital media can be fragile and have limited shelf life. Moreover, new devices, processes and software are replacing the products and methods used to record, store, and retrieve digital information on breathtaking cycles of two to five years. Given such rates of technological change, even the most fragile media may well outlive the continued availability of readers for those media. Efforts to preserve physical media thus provide only a short-term, partial solution to the general problem of preserving digital information. Indeed, technological obsolescence represents a far greater threat to information in the digital form than the inherent physical fragility of many digital media.

In the face of rapid technological obsolescence and to overcome the problem of media fragility, archivists have adopted the technique of "refreshing" digital information by copying it onto new media. Copying from medium to medium, however, also suffers limitations as a means of digital preservation. Refreshing digital information by copying will work as an effective preservation technique only as long as the information is encoded in a format that is independent of the particular hardware and software needed to use it and as long as there exists software to manipulate the format in current use.

Otherwise, copying depends either on the compatibility of present and past versions of software and generations of hardware or the ability of competing hardware and software product lines to interoperate. In respect of these factors—backward compatibility and interoperability—the rate of technological change exacts a serious toll on efforts to ensure the longevity of digital information. Digital information today is produced in highly varying degrees of dependence on particular hardware and software. Moreover, it is costly and difficult for vendors to assure that their products are either "backwardly compatible" with previous versions or that they can interoperate with competing products.

Refreshing thus cannot serve as a general solution for preserving digital information and this conclusion has prompted discussion of other kinds of solutions. Refreshing digital information by copying it from medium to medium and the possibility of maintaining a complex set of emulators describe two distinct points on a continuum of approaches to preserving digital information. However, neither refreshing nor emulation sufficiently describes the full range of options needed and available for digital preservation.

Instead, a better and more general concept to describe these options is migration. Migration is the periodic transfer of digital materials from one hardware/software configuration to another, or from one generation of computer technology to a subsequent generation. The purpose of migration is to preserve the integrity of digital objects and to retain the ability for clients to retrieve, display, and otherwise use them in the face of constantly changing technology.

Migration includes refreshing as a means of digital preservation but differs from it in the sense that it is not always possible to make an exact digital copy or replica of a database or other information object as hardware and software change and still maintain the compatibility of the object with the new generation of technology.

Compounding the technical challenges of migrating digital information is the problem of managing the process in a legal and organisational environment that is in flux as it moves to accommodate rapidly changing digital technologies. Consider, for example, the barriers to decisive preservation action caused by widespread uncertainty about legal and organisational requirements for managing the intellectual property that digital information represents. Addressing and resolving the legal and practical questions of migrating intellectual property in digital form necessarily involves a complex set of interested parties, including the creators and owners of intellectual property, managers of digital archives, representatives of the public interest, and actual and potential users of intellectual property.

Owners of intellectual property are unsure about how to price access to their information and worry, given the ease of copying, that the first digital copy of a work they sell may be the only copy they sell. Users of intellectual property are unsure about what rights are conveyed with the use of a particular digital information object and about how much such use is worth.

The state of the copyright law, which was generated and developed in an analogue world but is applied in an increasingly digital universe, is itself confusing and uncertain. The costs and the technical, legal and organisational complexities of moving digital information forward into the future raise our greatest fear about the life of information in the digital future, namely, that owners or custodians who can no longer bear the expense and difficulty will deliberately or inadvertently, through a simple failure to act, destroy the objects without regard for future use.

Even after more than forty years of growth, the digital world of information technology and communication is still relatively young and immature in relation to the larger information universe, parts of which have been under development for centuries. Viewed developmentally, the problem of preserving digital information for the future is not only, or even primarily, a problem of fine tuning a narrow set of technical variables. It is not a clearly defined problem like preserving the embrittled books that are self-destructing from the acid in the paper on which they were printed.

Rather, it is a grander problem of organising ourselves over time and as a society to manoeuvre effectively in a digital landscape. For digital preservation, the organisational effort—the process of building deep infrastructure—necessarily involves multiple, interrelated factors, many of which are either unknown or poorly defined. One of the biggest unknowns is the full impact on traditional information handling functions of distributed computing over electronic networks. The effort to meet the cultural imperative of digital preservation thus requires a complex iteration and reiteration of exploration, development and solution as the relevant factors and their interrelationships emerge and become clearer and more tractable.

Digital archives are distinct from digital libraries in the sense that digital libraries are repositories that collect and provide access to digital information, but may or may not provide for the long-term storage and access of that information. Digital libraries thus may or may not be, in functional terms, digital archives and, in fact, much of the recent work on digital libraries is notably silent on the archival issues of ensuring long-term storage and access.

Conversely, digital archives necessarily embrace digital library functions to the extent that they must select, obtain, store, and provide access to digital information. Many of the functional requirements for digital archives overlap those for digital libraries. Many traditional libraries, archives and museums, as institutions, have taken and may well continue to assume digital library and archival functions.

Digital archives will have available to them a critical fail-safe mechanism. Such a mechanism, supported by organisational will, economic means and legal right, would enable a certified archival repository to exercise an aggressive rescue function to save digital information that it judges to be culturally significant and which is endangered in its current repository. The current repository may be a digital library, another digital archives, or some other individual, organisational, public or private source of digital information.

Information objects in digital form, like those in other forms, move through lifecycles. They are created, edited, described and indexed, disseminated, acquired, used, annotated, revised, recreated, modified and retained for future use or destroyed by a complex, interwoven community of creators and other owners, disseminators, value-added services, and institutional and individual users.

Knowledge cannot advance without consistent and reliable access to information sources, past and present. It is the archival function in the system of knowledge creation and use that serves to identify and retain important sources of information and to ensure continuing access to them. How reliable the archival process proves to be in the emerging digital environment hinges on the trustworthy operation of digital archives and on their ability to maintain the integrity of the objects they are charged to preserve. For digital objects, no less than for objects of other kinds, knowing how operationally to preserve them depends, at least in part, on being able to discriminate the essential features of what needs to be preserved. Digital technologies increasingly serve to integrate information resources. Text, numeric data, images, voice, and video have heretofore resided in print or other analogue media for storage and transmission. When they are encoded digitally, either by conversion or at the point of creation, these various kinds of resources share layers of technology—a common means of storage and transmission—that allows them to be brought together and used in both old and new ways.

Multimedia and hyperlinked objects on the world wide web represent some of the new kinds of information and new ways of knowing in the digital realm that bring together the traditional forms of information and transform their use. The application of computer hardware and software has also generated other new kinds of information objects, including the products of simulation, remote sensing, computer-aided design (CAD) and geographic information (GIS) systems. These objects come into being and exist as creatures of the digital environment; if nurtured well, digital technologies will certainly beget still other kinds of information objects, which we can now only anticipate.

The processes of preserving digital information will vary significantly with the different kinds of objects—textual, numeric, image, video, sound, multimedia, simulation and so on—being preserved. Whatever preservation method is applied, however, the central goal must be to preserve information integrity; that is, to define and preserve those features of an information object that distinguish it as a whole and singular work.

In the digital environment, the features that determine information integrity and deserve special attention for archival purposes include the following: content, fixity, reference, provenance, and context. What digital archives are trying to preserve after all is the intellectual substance contained in information objects. The notion of content, however, is itself a complex idea that operates at several different levels of abstraction. To preserve the integrity of objects in their charge, digital archives must decide at which level, or levels, of abstraction they are defining information content.

In the digital environment, ideas are typically embedded in particular formats and structures that are dependent on hardware and software technologies subject to rapid change. Conceived at this higher level of abstraction-that is, in terms of format and structure-the definition of content poses considerable difficulties for managing information integrity in an archival context, and we are just beginning to come to terms with the expression of these problems in the digital environment.

Word processing and desktop publishing systems still dominate the market for the creation of documents with complex structure and layout, and the software for such use typically models and stores document structure and layout in proprietary terms. Although software may provide mechanisms for converting documents to common interchange formats, use of such mechanisms often results in the loss or inadequate rendering of content such as page structures and the layout of headers, footers and section headings.

The preservation of images comprises another example of the ways in which content, defined in terms of structure and format, poses integrity problems for digital archives. Image resolution, accuracy of colour representation and compression for storage all require attention, but the interaction of these structural factors tends to pit judgements about the quality of content against the need for its efficient archival storage and use.

At the highest level of abstraction, digital archives define content in a way that transcends the limits of the hardware and software systems needed for reading and interpreting the bits of an information object and for rendering it for use in a specific format and structural representation; that is, they define content in terms of the knowledge or ideas the object contains.

The preservation challenge for digital archives is to migrate intellectual content using standard interchange algorithms and other appropriate migration strategies so that the ideas available in the end are identical to those contained in the original object. The measure of integrity in the preservation process thus turns, at least in part, on informed and skilful judgements about the appropriate definition of the content of an digital information object—about the extent to which content depends on its configuration of bits, on the structure and format of its representation, and on the ideas it contains—and for what purposes.

The process of identifying and preserving a digital information object as a whole and singular work goes well beyond considerations of content. It also depends, for instance, on the way that the content is fixed as a discrete object. If an object is not fixed, and the content is subject to change or withdrawal without notice, then its integrity may be compromised and its value as a cultural record would be severely diminished.

A wide range of cryptographic techniques, such as watermarking, already exist for various kinds of digital information objects. These could serve well to mark and identify specific, canonical versions and editions of textual, audio and visual works, and to establish trusted, protected channels of distribution for those objects. However, the standards and infrastructure and the policies and practices for applying such techniques to the creation of fixed versions of digital information objects still need considerable development. Absence of such development and the fixity of information that would result, digital archives face considerable challenges in trying to preserve the integrity of digital objects.

Some kinds of digital objects present the problem of fixity of information in yet another way. An increasing number of networked information resources are better modelled, not in terms of versions or editions of works, but as continuously updated databases. As the networked environment for digital information expands and matures, intense interactions among the parties with stakes in digital information are providing the opportunity and stimulus for new stakeholders to emerge and add value, and for the relationships and division of labour among existing stakeholders to assume new forms.

Moreover, all of the stakeholders, including the new ones who are emerging, are exercising their various functions simultaneously in relation to particular digital information objects. That is, for example, the creator of an object may retain a financial or other stake in its dissemination and use for an extended period, just as a publisher/disseminator of the object exercises the same or similar interest.

Similarly, stakeholders acting as collectors/disseminators may retain an interest in the continuing use of the object, at the same time as they or other stakeholders acting as digital archives take steps to preserve it for future use. In a time of such sustained flux and change, during which these various divisions of labour are taking shape, the most effective and affordable strategy for developing a system of digital archives is to assume a distributed, rather than centralised, structure for collecting digital information objects, protecting their integrity over the long term, and retaining them for future use.

A distributed structure, built on a foundation of electronic networks, places archival responsibility with those who presumably care most about and have the greatest understanding of the value of particular digital information objects. Moreover, such a structure locates the economic and cultural incentives where they are most likely to prompt those preserving digital information to respond with the greatest agility to the changing digital landscape and to the shifting tides of technology. Effective structures for digital archives in a distributed network will surely take various forms and will include corporations, federations and consortia, each of which may specialise in the archiving of digital information and range over regional and national boundaries.

In the end, existing archival organisations may successfully adapt their current roles and responsibilities to changing needs, existing archival roles and responsibilities may be redistributed among other kinds of organisations with stakes in digital information, and focused attention on the division of labour in the digital information economy will lead to the emergence and growth of new kinds of archival structures.

Information creators/providers/owners have initial responsibility for archiving their digital information objects and thereby ensuring the long-term preservation of those objects. The creator/provider/owner may engage other parties, such as certified digital archives, to take over some or all of the archival responsibility. Libraries and archival organisations may interact with creators/providers as subcontractors for maintaining digital archives during and after the active life of their information objects.

Certified digital archives have the right and duty to exercise an aggressive rescue function as a fail-safe mechanism to preserve information objects that become endangered because the creator/provider/owner does not accept responsibility for the preservation function and does not take steps formally to convey responsibility, or because there is no natural institutional home for the objects. The conditions of creating digital information and giving it a useful life are essentially the same as those required for the information to persist over time.

A variety of factors budgetary constraints, reorganisation of priorities or focus, change of business, the need to go out of existence, or expiration of copyright—might prompt custodians to neglect, abandon or destroy their collections of digital information. No distributed system of digital archives will afford effective protection of electronic information unless it provides for a powerful rescue function allowing one agency, acting in the long-term public interest of protecting the cultural record, to override another's neglect of or active interest in abandoning or destroying parts of that record.

Digital archives operating normally and those operating in fail-safe mode differ mainly in the rights and obligations they have with respect to rescuing materials that have fallen in jeopardy because a custodian no longer accepts preservation responsibility. Section 108 of the 1976 Copyright Act of the United States defines the rights and obligations for libraries and archives operating normally to preserve copies of printed materials. The proposed revision of the copyright law reserves to libraries and archives similar rights and duties for digital materials.

However, neither in its present form nor in its proposed revision does the Copyright Act provide a legal foundation defining the rights and duties that must come into play to facilitate and encourage an aggressive rescue function. The Copyright Act, in fact, may not provide the best legal and institutional framework for establishing fail-safe mechanisms for digital archives. Users of archived information in electronic form and of archival services relating to that information need to have assurance that a digital archives is what it says that it is and that the information stored there is safe for the long term.

Archives cannot save all information objects; they must appraise and select for retention the most valuable items. Selection processes for archives of all kinds—paper and digital—are matters of intellectual judgement about what to include and save and what to exclude. Selection for digital archives must be a continuing process. Given the need to migrate digital information regularly from its hardware and software environment, the stimulus and occasion will recur to reappraise the value of the material being migrated. Materials may lose value over time and may need to be withdrawn and discarded.

Digital archives thus need to formulate and implement policies and practices for ongoing appraisal. Once an information object is identified for inclusion in a digital archives, it needs to be accessioned, that is, prepared for the archives. The accession process involves both describing and cataloguing selected objects, including their provenance and context, and securing them for storage and access. Standards for description are well developed for certain kinds of materials that are likely to appear in digital archives, such as monographs and serials.

For other kinds of materials, such as WWW pages, motion video and multimedia, relevant attributes are less well understood. Standards of description are less well practised and one cannot reasonably expect satisfactory descriptive material to accompany the digital object. In all cases, special attention is needed in the accession process to creating, describing and tracking the versions of the object in the digital archives to satisfy the various requirements for display and other forms of access and for long-term storage.

A digital archives may need to establish access controls for its information objects and the means for authenticating them to future users. Establishing access controls involves setting terms and conditions for authorised use by specific users or classes of users. In any digital archives, there may be multiple levels of storage graded to levels of expected use and needed performance in retrieval. Little used material may be stored most efficiently off-line, usually in tape format. For objects in high demand, where retrieval time is at a premium, online storage in magnetic media may serve best.

In a distributed network, they may need to be stored online in multiple locations. An intermediate solution is near-line storage, where information objects may be stored on optical or tape media and loaded in a jukebox. Retrieval time in near-line storage systems suffers by comparison to on-line storage, but is considerably more responsive to user demand than off-line storage. Digital archives may use any or all of these methods. The most sophisticated systems combine the resources so that objects in use or recent use are stored online and, as they age from the time of most recent use, they move to near-line storage and then eventually off-line.

Effective storage management thus means providing for redundant copies of the archived objects as an insurance against loss. Depending on the copyright status of the objects, digital archives may choose to make backup copies on their own or to make arrangements for other sites, which hold the same object, in the network of digital archives to serve as backup, or they may choose to do both. Providing access to digital information in a distributed network environment means above all that digital archives are connected to networks using appropriate protocols and with bandwidth suitable for delivering the information their control.

Digital archives have an obligation to maintain the information in a form so that users over the network can find it with appropriate retrieval engines and view, print, listen to or otherwise use it with appropriate output devices. In the descriptions of the resources they hold, responsible digital archives must provide to their users what they know about the provenance and context of their digital objects so that users can make informed decisions about the reliability and quality of the evidence before them.

With respect to access, digital archives also have the responsibility to manage intellectual property rights by facilitating transactions between rights-holders in the information and users and by taking every reasonable precaution to prevent unauthorised use of the material. Since so many of the operational responsibilities of the digital archives are functionally identical to those of more traditional permanent repositories, they may successfully extend their scope to include digital materials.

Many traditional archives have already embraced digital materials, and libraries and museums are not far behind. Wherever digital archives may reside organisationally, their operation is highly distinctive in one crucial respect. That is, they need, at least now and for the foreseeable future, a high level of systems engineering skill to manage the interlocking requirements of media, data formats, and hardware and software on which the operation of the digital archives essentially depends.

There are a variety of migration strategies for transferring digital information from obsolete systems to current hardware and software systems so that the information remains accessible and usable. No single strategy applies to all formats of digital information and none of the current preservation methods is entirely satisfactory. Migration strategies and their associated costs vary in different application environments, for different formats of digital materials, and for preserving different degrees of computation, display, and retrieval capabilities.

Although migration should become more effective as the digital preservation community gains practical experience and learns how to select appropriate and effective methods, migration remains largely experimental and provides fertile ground for research and development efforts. Enhancements are technologically possible through clean-up, mark-up, and linkage, or by adding indexing and other features. These technological possibilities in turn impose serious new responsibilities for presenting digital materials to users in a way that allows them to determine the authenticity of the information and its relationship to the original object.

One migration strategy is to transfer digital materials from less stable to more stable media. The most prevalent version of this strategy involves printing digital information on paper or recording it on microfilm. Paper and microfilm are more stable than most digital media, and no special hardware or software are needed to retrieve information from them. Another migration strategy for digital archives with large, complex, and diverse collections of digital materials is to migrate digital objects from the great multiplicity of formats used to create digital materials to a smaller, more manageable number of standard formats that can still encode the complexity of structure and form of the original.

A digital archives might accept textual documents in several commonly available commercial word processing formats or require that documents conform to standards like Standard Generalised Markup Language (SGML). Databases might be stored in one of several common relational database management systems, while images would conform to a tagged image file format and standard compression algorithms. Changing format as a migration strategy has the advantage of preserving more of the display, dissemination, and computational characteristics of the original object, while reducing the large variety of customised transformations that would otherwise be necessary to migrate material to future generations of technology.

Digital archives will benefit from the widespread adoption of data and communication standards that facilitate reference to digital information objects and enable their interchange among systems. Organisations that create, use and maintain Geographic Information Systems (GIS), for example, are trying to reduce data conversion and maintenance costs by creating data that conform to widely accepted standards so that they can be exchanged, reused, or sold.

Digital archives must keep abreast of standards developments and make sure that their own technological infrastructure conforms to widely adopted standards. Planning for long-term preservation is a critical element of digital preservation. To the extent that creators/providers/owners of digital information accept initial responsibility for archiving their objects, they may begin to see the wisdom of incorporating migration paths or other provisions for preservation as an integral part of the process or system that generates digital information.

Healthy demand for particular information objects will push the digital archives that provide them to shift delivery to more costly online storage or to sophisticated and expensive systems of hierarchical storage. The costs of software and intellectual property may also be pegged to demand. Another usage factor affecting costs is the high variability in the kinds of user access devices. For many types of information objects, modes of access are still closely tied to the type of workstation available to the user. The tradeoff for the digital archives is either to limit access only to "approved" devices or to support multiple platforms and incur the added associated costs in hardware, software, intellectual property and systems engineering.

### 10.3.1. Issues of Digital Copyrights

As the world increasingly makes use of digital and online technologies to create and distribute knowledge and culture, questions of digital copyright become increasingly important. Copyright can be defined as a person's exclusive right to authorise certain acts such as reproduction, publication, public performance, adaptation, etc., in relation to his or her original work of authorship. The creator of the work typically owns the copyright, at least initially. However, copyright is often sold or assigned, in whole or in part, to a commercial publisher, a filmmaker, a recording studio or to someone else who will exploit the work commercially. As a consequence, copyright often benefits commercial interests more than individual authors. Copyright law has long emphasised that copyright protection does not exist for its own sake but rather to serve the public interest. The greater public interest is served in two ways:

i) By giving authors an incentive to create;

ii) By encouraging the dissemination of new knowledge.

Creators enjoy the right to control, and to be remunerated for, subsequent dissemination. Without these incentives some authors might not be motivated to spend their time and effort in creating valuable original expression. However, it should also be noted that a significant number of creators place a far higher value on dissemination of their creative work rather than direct reimbursement for the use of the work. In addition, new ideas and knowledge will not readily benefit a society if their transmittal is limited. Only when knowledge is learned, discussed and added to by students, researchers, scientists and the ordinary citizen, is its value truly appreciated. The means of furthering the public interest are frequently under tension: on the one hand, the rights owner is given control of the dissemination of his or her works, while on the other hand, the rapid and widespread dissemination of information contained in these works is also to be encouraged. It is only by consciously and properly balancing these two competing concerns that a copyright regime will maximise both the creation and communication of new knowledge and ideas.

This need for balance can be seen in the Universal Declaration of Human Rights, which recognises both sides of the equation as vital to humanity. The protection of the labour of authors is guaranteed by Article 27(2): "Everyone has the right to the protection of the moral and material interests resulting from any scientific, literary or artistic production of which he is the author." The right of all to share in the cultural and scientific output of humanity is similarly guaranteed by Article 27(1): "Everyone has the right freely to participate in the cultural life of the community, to enjoy the arts and to share in scientific advancement and its benefits."

The International Federation of Library Associations (IFLA) is concerned that the increased use of licensing and technological protection is distorting the balance toward commercial interests and away from information users. IFLA strongly endorses the notion that copyright must be balanced. The *IFLA Position on Copyright in the Digital Environment* states:

> Librarians and information professionals recognise, and are committed to support the needs of their patrons to gain access to copyright works and the information and ideas they contain. They also respect the needs of authors and copyright owners to obtain a fair economic return on their intellectual property. Effective access is

essential in achieving copyright's objectives. IFLA supports balanced copyright law that promotes the advancement of society as a whole by giving strong and effective protection for the interests of rightsholders as well as reasonable access in order to encourage creativity, innovation, research, education and learning.

Libraries are major purchasers of copyright protected works, both analogue and digital, and make such works available for patrons to browse, read and use. Librarians and information professionals do, where possible and to the best of their ability, protect against copyright abuse of library material in collections. Access to knowledge is vital and many reasons are given below:

i) A full and comprehensive exchange of information is necessary for the functioning of a healthy democracy. A society which is unable to access the knowledge required for a proper discussion of political, social, environmental or economic issues will not be able to achieve the kind of broad consensus upon which a healthy society is based;

ii) A rich public domain and fair access to copyright protected material enhances creativity and the production of new works. It is often assumed that economic growth benefits from ever-stronger intellectual property rights while some concession must be made to copyright exceptions for purely social reasons. In fact, this is a false dichotomy. Many industries require access to copyright material for the purposes of research and development, education, software or hardware interoperability.

iii) Fair access to material in copyright can help to mitigate the digital divide. If access to knowledge is dependent upon an individual's capacity to pay, then the less privileged will be placed at a significant disadvantage. In particular, this can play a part in perpetuating poverty and the lack of educational opportunities.

A balance between the interests of copyright owners in receiving fair reward for their efforts and the interests of copyright users in receiving reasonable access to copyright materials has been traditionally maintained in a number of ways. One of the most important of these is the implementation of a series of limitations and exceptions to the exclusive rights of copyright owners, which is the subject of this submission. However, there are other important limits, besides exceptions, on the control over knowledge that copyright imposes, some of which are being weakened in the digital environment. These limits are:

i) Duration of copyright
ii) Limited suite of rights
iii) Subject matter

*Duration of copyright:* Copyright has a limited duration, after which copyright material enters the public domain and may be freely used by anyone for any purpose. This is a very important aspect to copyright as it guarantees an enormous treasure trove of resource material that is permanently available to education, research and the development of new creative works. However, the entry of copyright works into the public domain has been restrained by successive increases in the duration of copyright.

Since then the duration of copyright has increased in many jurisdictions to the life of the author plus 70 years, which is far beyond any reasonable window of commercial exploitation. While the duration of copyright provides the author with a definite period of protection, extending the term progressively is unfairly prejudicing users of information. The reasoning given for an extended term of protection is that life expectancy is increasing and hence the period of protection should be extended accordingly. Moreover, extended terms of protection are even more prejudicial to some developing countries where adult life expectancy is low. Essentially, what the extension of the term does is benefit rights owners and their future generations in developed nations, at the expense of users of information and potential new creators in both developed and developing nations.

The extension of the copyright term is occurring at the same time that many governments are promoting increased access to local content through digitisation. Much of this content is perceived by copyright owners to have no economic value. Nevertheless, it will continue to remain broadly inaccessible, as it will not enter the public domain until the expiry of its allotted span—well beyond the lifetime of the author.

*Limited suite of rights:* A copyright owner's capacity to control the use of his or her work is limited to the suite of rights, which is specifically granted by the copyright regime. These rights typically include the right to reproduce, the right to communicate to the public, the right to publish, etc. Uses that fall outside these rights are not subject to the copyright owner's control. For example, copyright permission is required to print copies of a book; however, once a legitimately-printed copy has been sold, the copyright owner may not control what is done with that copy. The purchaser is free to read the book multiple times, lend, borrow, sell or destroy it. Again, the digital environment has very much weakened the value of this limit; most uses of a digital work will constitute either reproduction or communication or both. Access to copyright works in the digital environment requires a reproduction even of a temporary nature, e.g., a cache copy. If the right to control reproduction is not limited, a rights owner has the right to total control of every access.

*Subject-matter:* Copyright historically applied only to books. It has been expanded ever since to include an ever-widening set of creative and non-creative material. Due to the reduced impact of these limitations on the scope of copyright in the digital environment, other exceptions and limitations have become more important than ever.

Technological copyright protection measures are a significant issue for the world's library and education communities, because they can override and effectively eliminate any copyright exceptions. This is because such technological measures do not distinguish between uses which are not authorised by the copyright owner but are permitted by law, on the one hand, and those uses which are not authorised by the owner and also infringing. For example, the same copy-control mechanism which prevents a person from making infringing copies of a copyright work may also prevent a student or a visually impaired person from making legitimate fair use/fair dealing copies.

Besides intellectual property laws and the increasing use of digital rights management technology, contractual licensing also shapes the digital environment and is being used to limit user rights. Unlike paper materials, digital information generally is not purchased by consumers or the library; rather it is licensed by the library from information providers. A licence usually takes the form of a written contract or agreement between the library and the owner of the rights to distribute digital information. Licences for libraries frequently take one of three forms:

i) standard-form
ii) paper licences,
iii) shrink-wrap or click-through licences.

In most cases there is no opportunity to actually negotiate the terms of these licences, and even if there were, the relative bargaining power between the purchaser and the manufacturer is grossly uneven. Shrink-wrap licences are so-called because they are contained inside shrink-wrapped plastic around a physical article embodying intellectual property. 'Click-through' licences are typically used with respect to copyright material that is acquired online; before the user can access any part of the copyright material, they must first signal their agreement with a licence agreement. Standard-form agreements may or may not be negotiable, however, shrink-wrap or click-through licences never are.

Licences can involve a wide range of terms and conditions, but, unlike copyright law, licencors are not statutorily obliged to consider the public interest in accessing information when setting such terms and conditions. As most digital information is distributed by licence, public policy considerations such as fair use, fair dealing or exceptions to the author's rights are likely to become null and void. It is therefore essential that limitations and exceptions are carefully considered in the digital realm to protect access to information. Some examples of the types of restrictions that licence agreements often impose include:

i) restrictions on users printing or downloading or emailing copies of (parts of) the material;
ii) restrictions on the number, location, and organisational affiliation of users;
iii) restrictions on libraries performing interlibrary loan/document supply;
iv) restrictions on libraries copying the work for preservation purposes;
v) restrictions on the use of a work beyond a certain date;

vi) restrictions on libraries networking the work across the premises of the library;

vii) restrictions on lending or otherwise disposing of a digital work.

viii) restrictions on the right to quote, analyse and even to index a work.

The combination of protected technological measures and licences can lead to an absolutely unlimited protection of the interests of the rights owners, who benefit from several cumulative layers of protection: copyright protection, technological protection, legal protection of the technological measures, and contract law.

Most copying of print-based material in libraries is for educational, research or private study purposes or for preservation. The reasons usually given for copying are because users are unable to read the material in the library or because the user wishes to read it at a more convenient time. Despite rights owner concerns about loss of sales there is no evidence that copying reasonable amounts from copyright protected works displaces sales. Those who copy would not necessarily buy a work if prevented from copying it. There is no reason to believe that this pattern will not also be true of copying from digital works.

Not only must traditional copyright exceptions be preserved both in the print environment but also in the digital environment, and this must be addressed at the same time as the issues of the increasing use of copyright protection technologies and contractual licence agreements. It is of little use for national legislatures to guarantee fair use rights if these rights are promptly overridden by non-negotiated click-through licence agreements or technological protection systems in almost every case.

If exceptions allowed in national legislations conform to the Berne Convention three-step test, the interests of rights owners will not be harmed and, therefore, no further permission or compensation payment for uses should be required. However, it should be borne in mind that the needs of the users in developing countries are greater than those in developed countries. More exceptions are necessary, particularly in the transformation from illiteracy to literacy, e.g., in literacy programmes, basic adult education training, etc.

Unless libraries and citizens are granted exceptions which allow reasonable access and fair use for purposes which do not harm the interests of rights owners, and which are in the public interest and in line with fair practice such as education and research, there is a danger that only those who can afford information will be able to take advantage of the benefits of the information society. If there were no effective public interest exceptions, especially in the digital environment, this would lead to an even greater divide than already exists between the information rich and the information poor in both the developed and the developing nations. This is not to say that rights owners should be persuaded to give their works away freely. Further, there should be no discrimination in copyright laws against visually, aurally or learning disabled persons. Reformatting of material to make it accessible should not be considered an infringement of copyright and should be considered as reasonable access. In countries with many languages and dialects, there is a greater need for exceptions to allow translation and reproduction of materials for literacy and learning purposes.

### 10.3.2. Copyright Infringement

Copyright infringement is determined without regard to the intent or the state of mind of the infringer; "innocent" infringement is infringement none the less. Moreover, although the exclusive rights refer to such rights with respect to "copies" (plural) of the work, there is no question that under the Act the making of even a single unauthorised copy may constitute an infringement. Courts generally use the term "copying" as shorthand for a violation of any of the exclusive rights of the copyright owner (not just the reproduction right). Courts usually require a copyright owner to prove ownership of the copyrighted work and "copying" by the defendant to prevail in an infringement action. A copyright owner may prove copying through circumstantial evidence establishing that the defendant had access to the original work and that the two works are substantially similar. Other indications of copying, such as the existence of common errors, have also been accepted as evidence of infringement.

The copying of the copyrighted work must be copying of protected expression and not just ideas; likewise, the similarity between the two works must be similarity of protected elements (the expression), not unprotected elements (the facts, ideas, etc.). The similarity between the two works need not be literal (i.e., phrases, sentences or paragraphs need not be copied verbatim); substantial similarity may be found even if none of the words or brush strokes or musical notes are identical. Various tests have been developed to determine whether there has been sufficient non-literal copying to constitute substantial similarity between a copyrighted work and an allegedly infringing work.

The ability to manipulate works in digital form raises an issue with respect to infringement of the reproduction and derivative works rights. A copyrighted photograph, for instance, can be manipulated in the user's computer in such a way that the resulting work is not substantially similar to the copyrighted work. The initial input of the copyrighted work into the user's computer may be an infringement of the copyright owner's reproduction right, but the infringing nature of the resulting work is less clear. Although courts traditionally rely on a substantial similarity test to determine infringement liability—including with regard to the derivative works right—neither the meaning of derivative work nor the statutory standard for infringement appears to require an infringing derivative work to be substantially similar.

The US Copyright Act grants to copyright owners not only the right to exercise the exclusive rights, but also the right "to authorise" the exercise of those rights. The inclusion of the right "to authorise" was "intended to avoid any questions as to the liability of contributory infringers"—those who do not directly exercise the copyright owner's rights, but "authorise" others to do so. Other than the reference to a copyright owner's right "to authorise" exercise of the exclusive rights, however, the Copyright Act does not mention or define "contributory infringement" or "vicarious liability", the standards for which have developed through case law.

If someone has the "right and ability" to supervise the infringing action of another, and that right and ability "coalesce with an obvious and direct financial interest in the exploitation of copyrighted materials—even in the absence of actual knowledge" that the infringement is taking place—the "supervisor" may be held vicariously liable for the infringement. Vicarious liability is based on a connection to the direct infringer. The best known copyright cases involving vicarious liability are the "dance hall" cases, where vicarious liability was found when dance hall owners allowed the unauthorised public performance of musical works by the bands they hired, even when the owners had no knowledge of the infringements and had even expressly warned the bands not to perform copyrighted works without a licence from the copyright owners.

"Contributory infringement" may be found when "one who, with knowledge of the infringing activity, induces, causes or materially contributes to the infringing conduct of another." Contributory infringement is based on a connection to the infringing activity (not necessarily to the direct infringer). A contributory infringer may be liable based on the provision of services or equipment related to the direct infringement.

Courts have found contributory infringement liability, for instance, when a defendant chose the infringing material to be used in the direct infringer's work, and vicarious liability when a defendant was responsible for the day-to-day activities where the infringement took place. Infringement liability may also be based on the provision of equipment or other instrumentalities or goods used in or related to the infringement. The Court also held that in an action for contributory infringement against a manufacturer of copying devices, "the copyright holder may not prevail unless the relief that he seeks affects only his programs, or unless he speaks for virtually all copyright holders with an interest in the outcome."

Online service providers, such as bulletin board operators, should be exempt from liability or given a higher standard for liability, such as imposing liability only in those cases where infringement was wilful and repeated or where it was proven that the service provider had both "actual knowledge" of the infringing activity and the "ability and authority" to terminate such activity. The latter proposed standard would combine the contributory infringement standard with the requirements for vicarious liability and apply it to all infringements of the service provider. Altering the standards of liability for infringement would be a significant departure from current copyright principles and law and would result in a substantial derogation of the rights of copyright owners. It is a difficult issue, with colourable arguments on each side.

Online service providers can certainly investigate and take appropriate action when notified of the existence of infringing material on their systems and thus limit their liability for damages to those for innocent infringement. Again, this problem has been a part of the cost of doing business for many other distributors of material that is provided to them by others.

Online service providers have a business relationship with their subscribers. They are in the position to know the identity and activities of their subscribers and to stop unlawful activities. And, although indemnification from their subscribers may not reimburse them to the full extent of their liability and other measures may add to their cost of doing business, they are still in a better position to prevent or stop infringement than the copyright owner. Between these two relatively innocent parties, the best policy is to hold the service provider liable.

The online services provide subscribers with the capability of uploading works because it attracts subscribers and increases usage—for which they are paid. Service providers reap rewards for infringing activity. It is difficult to argue that they should not bear the responsibilities. The cost/benefit analyses have prompted service providers to discontinue such services.

The risk of infringement liability is a legitimate cost of engaging in a business that causes harm to others, and that risk apparently has not outweighed the benefits for the more than 60,000 bulletin board operators currently in business. There has been tremendous growth in the online service industry over the past several years, and it shows no signs of reversing the trend under current standards of liability. Other entities have some of the same costs of doing business, have instituted practices and taken appropriate precautions to minimise their risk of liability, such as indemnification agreements and insurance.

Online service providers currently provide a number of services. With respect to the allowance of uploading of material by their subscribers, they are, in essence, acting as an electronic publisher. In other instances, they perform other functions. No one rule may be appropriate. If an entity provided only the wires and conduits, such as the telephone company, it would have a good argument for an exemption if it was truly in the same position as a common carrier and could not control who or what was on its system. The same could be true for an online service provider who unknowingly transmitted encrypted infringing material.

It would be unfair to allow one class of distributors to self-determine their liability by refusing to take responsibility. This would encourage inten-tional and wilful ignorance. Whether or not they choose to reserve the right to control activities on their systems, they have that right. Service providers expect compensation for the use of their facilities and have the ability to disconnect subscribers who take their services without payment. They have the same ability with respect to subscribers who break the law.

Exempting or reducing the liability of service providers prematurely would choke development of marketplace tools that could be used to lessen their risk of liability and the risk to copyright owners, including insuring against harm caused by their customers, shifting responsibility for infringement to the infringing subscriber through indemnification and warranty agreements, licensing (including collective license agreements), educating their subscribers about infringement and using technological protections, such as tracking mechanisms.

Circumstances also vary greatly among service providers. A bulletin board is simply a computer that the owner allows to be accessed by others using their computers and modems. One needs only a personal computer, a modem, a phone line, and some software to go into business. There are small, non-profit and large, commercial operators. There are those that try to prevent and react when notified and those that encourage infringing activity.

Different service providers play different roles and these roles are changing and being created virtually every day. At this time in the development and change in the players and roles, it is not feasible to identify *a priori* those circumstances or situations under which service providers should have reduced liability. However, it is reasonable to assume that such situations could and should be identified through discussion and negotiation among the service providers, the content owners and the government. Service providers should have the incentive to make their subscribers more aware of copyright law and to react promptly and appropriately to notice by copyright owner that infringing material is available on their systems. Service providers should make clear that infringing activity is not tolerated on the system and reserve the right to remove infringing material or disconnect the subscriber who participated in the placement of it on the system.

A copyright owner may seek a preliminary or permanent injunction to prevent or restrain infringement. Courts generally grant permanent injunctions where liability is established and there is a threat of continuing infringement. Courts may also order the impounding of all copies or phonorecords at any time an action is pending. As part of a final judgment, the court may order the destruction of the infringing copies or phonorecords. At any time before final judgment is rendered, a copyright owner may elect to recover actual damages and profits of the infringer or be awarded statutory damages. Actual damages may be awarded in the amount of the copyright owner's losses plus any profits of the infringer attributable to the infringement. Criminal sanctions are levied against infringers if the infringement was wilful and for purposes of commercial advantage or private financial gain.

## 10.4. Intellectual Property Issues

Digital libraries, information highways, and virtual communities are the metaphors that shape public dialogue about social justice in an information society, shaping intellectual property law and information policy for a digital age. Intellectual property law narrowly understood consists of rules about when and how expressions of ideas should be treated as private property. These boundaries between the public and private use and ownership of ideas will become problematic in an information society if, as we are frequently told, intellectual property is the new form of capital driving a global knowledge economy. If so, all of the traditional questions about economic and social justice in an industrial society will now apply to information and knowledge in an information society.

Information highways and libraries are useful metaphors, but are taken from an industrial society, and related to networked information only in their functions of transportation and information management. The term community originally referred to social relationships in feudal villages, and if anything, modern life in an urban industrial society is marked by the absence of community.

The information highway is a very powerful and useful metaphor, for it reminds us that computer networks are a means of transportation, one that instantly carries a new kind of economic commodity around the world. As social theory reminds us, transportation technology has always controlled the scope of control of organisations, from the state to markets, to corporations, thus it is a vital subject for information theory.

Unlike printed information, digital information is a signal, not a thing, thus it is easy to copy and distribute, and difficult to protect. The first efforts to regulate information technology were royal licenses to use printing presses, but it was found to be easier to regulate printing itself, the making and distribution of copying. Universal access may guarantee equal access, information itself is to be distributed by fee for service, ultimately on the basis of wealth, creating a new kind of inequality, and perhaps this will be particularly pernicious in an information society.

The virtual community concept frames our interpretation around digital networks as a mode of communication, and upon the new kinds of social relations and civic life that may now be possible in cyberspace. It is striking that the word community is used in relation to computer mediated communications, given that urban life in a technological society is often criticised precisely for the absence of community, but it is a useful metaphor precisely because it defines the need for community as a social goal. The evidence about the existence or nonexistence of virtual communities is still very incomplete, and very dependent upon what one thinks a community might be.

The great virtues of the virtual community metaphor— whether or not virtual communities actually exist—are:

i) It reminds us that ideas are not commodities, although they may usefully be treated as commodities in some contexts, they are the medium of social and cultural life;

ii) It reminds us that the market is not the only important social institution, must also think about the role of information technology in the family, in education, in civil society, and in political life.

iii) There is a specific finding about virtual community that may challenge the traditional foundation of intellectual property—the idea of the author. The idea of property tends to be founded on natural right theory. Natural right theory begins with the idea of an author, who in creating an original expression of an idea creates value and thereby a property right, ownership of which may then be transferred.

The digital library metaphor—as distinct from the many kinds of online information that are called digital libraries reminds us that the library might serve as a model for an institution which can mediate between two truths defined by the information highway and virtual community metaphors. One truth is that information has economic value and must be treated as property, and the other truth that information is only valuable when it is learned and used by human communities.

The digital library metaphor is helpful because in industrial society the library has been a boundary management institution between markets and communities: it buys information in the marketplace; it subsidies free use of information by communities. As a theory of justice, the digital library metaphor represents a claim that intellectual property must sometimes be a public good, particularly for educational purposes, and more generally as a means of providing for equality of opportunity in a society in which access to information is increasingly important.

The value of the digital library metaphor is that market economies and gift exchange economies are symbiotic, not opposites, must have pragmatic laws and institutions that manage the boundary between private and public property. Granted, this may be difficult when regulating the flow of information on a global information network, in which no one nation has sufficient jurisdiction to enforce its laws.

### 10.4.1. Computer Database

The computer database is a new type of intellectual property of growing importance in today's world. Essentially it is a collection of information stored so that it can be selectively searched and the desired information retrieved using a computer. As society moves further into the informational age the significance and dollar volume of database products should increase. Since this is a relatively new type of property, American law is having to rapidly evolve and create new standards and legal principles to try and protect against its misuse and theft. Databases have long existed in manual or book form. Contemporary examples of manual databases still abound, such as the phone book and many reference books, including legal reporters.

The computer database is essentially an information compendium like a phone book which has been placed in a computer and thereby automated. When information is computerised, however, there are many more ways for the information to be accessed, manipulated and used; the value of the database to users is thereby greatly enhanced. Some popular examples of computer databases include legal databases such as Westlaw and Lexis, and various business and scientific databases such as those found on Dialogue and internet.

An automated database is a body of facts, data, or other information assembled into an organised format suitable for use in a computer and comprising one or more files. The US Copyright Office considers a computer database to be copyrightable as a 'compilation'. The federal copyright law defines compilation as a work:

> Formed by the collection and assembling of preexisting materials or of data that are selected, coordinated or arranged in such a way that the resulting work as a whole constitutes an original work of authorship.

The law extends copyright protection to compilations as a form of literary work. Computer databases, a compilation can be a collective work such as a periodical, anthology and encyclopedia, or a reference work such as a directory, index, map, telephone book, guide book, law reporter, catalogue, chart, or racing guide. The 'literary work' in a computer database which may be protected is composed of four parts:

i) Selection of the contents;

ii The coordination of the contents internally;

iii) The arrangement of all of all elements of the database; and,

iv) The contents itself. The copyright of a compilation may extend to one of these parts without including the others.

Under traditional concepts of literary copyright, the data contained in a compilation, and the selection of the data, may sometimes not be protected from copying. Only the coordination and arrangement of the database may be protected, and even then there must be some originality to the collection and arrangement for it to be protected. When a database is composed of facts, these facts frequently cannot be copyrighted, for otherwise the public's right to use information in the public domain would be unreasonably limited.

Protection of raw data is legally tricky, and the first pioneer can frequently lose out if he is not careful. There are essentially three ways to legally protect computer databases are given below:

i) copyright,
ii) trade secret
iii) contract.

Ideally, all three of these legal means can be employed, along with practical non-legal methods, to provide the maximum protection against the piracy of a database programme. There are, of course, other legal theories that could be argued in a law suit to protect databases, such as unfair competition and conversion; however, these theories may be preempted by copyright law.

Copyright law originates in Article 1, of the Constitution of the United States which says that Congress shall have the power:

> To promote the Progress of Science and useful Arts, by securing for limited Times to Authors and Inventors the exclusive Right in their respective Writings and Discoveries.

To implement this constitutional right Congress enacted copyright and patent laws. The copyright law was written to protect 'original works of authorship'.

Over the centuries courts have examined whether or not a work has 'originality' to determine if it may receive copyright protection. Under traditional copyright doctrine a work must show some 'creativity' in order to meet the originality test, and it is not subject to copyright if the work merely copies an existing work. This essential element of creativity is weak or completely absent in many manual reference works or computer databases.

Copyright law can only provide protection to the arrangement and coordination of facts in a database. Even then, there must be some originality to the collection and arrangement for it to be protected. Typically the preparation of a database requires a significant expenditure of time, effort and money to cull and select information from many different sources, but little or no original creativity to express the facts, or arrange them. In these circumstances, where the compiler gathers and compiles raw facts, he did not create the facts, he just discovered or uncovered them, sometimes at great expense and trouble.

In order to lend copyright protection to merely factual databases, some courts have tried to move away from a strict application of the creativity test, to also employ an 'industriousness' or 'sweat of the brow' test to determine if the database is an 'original' enough work to be afforded copyright protection. Under the sweat of the brow doctrine, copyright could prevent the unauthorised copying of facts in a database, if the compiler could show that sufficient effort went into the acquisition and selection of the data to make it original. The protection would lie even if the information compiled was public knowledge or otherwise not protected. Other courts, however, continued to analyse a database dispute by using traditional concepts of creativity, and criticised the 'sweat of the brow' standard. To grant copyright protection based merely on the 'sweat of the author's brow' would risk putting large areas of actual research material off limits and threaten the public's unrestrained access to information.

Now that the sweat of the brow doctrine is dead, it is clear that raw facts in a database may not be protected by copyright, regardless of the time or expense that went into locating them. Still, in many databases the data itself, or the particular expressions of the facts, may have been created by the author. In such cases the data has originality and can be protected.

Copyright law prevents the copying of the coordination and arrangement of the facts, the format of data presentation and manipulation, provided that the format and means are original. This entails a consideration as to whether the coordination and arrangement are novel and unique, or whether the arrangement itself contains information. Not all compilations will meet the minimal originality standard.

There are a number of other drawbacks and limitations to copyright protection. For instance, if not properly perfected and registered a copyright can be waived and the work may enter the public domain. Also, there are certain exceptions to copyright, such as exceptions based on the 'fair use' rule. Another drawback pertains to the deposit requirements of copyright registration. Printouts of the programme source code and the database must be included with the registration. Another practical problem with the deposit requirement is that some databases are continually changing and being updated, and thus the deposits and registrations must continue.

With copyright law providing only limited protection to databases, and with all of the other problems inherent in copyright protection of a database, contract and trade secret law become all the more important to try and prevent the unauthorised copying of factual data in a database.

Adding trade secrecy protection to a database can provide significantly greater legal rights. Essentially a trade secret is knowledge which a person or company acquires through its own efforts and which has some value to it. Typically, this knowledge is kept secret from competitors because it is felt that this information provides some type of competitive ad 'antage. The Uniform Trade Secrets Act has now been enacted by most of the states in the country. Unif. Trade Secrets Act, 14 U.L.A. 541 (1980). Section 1(4) of the Act defines a trade secret to mean:

> Information, including a formula, pattern, compilation, programme, device, method, technique or process that: (a) derives independent economic value, actual or potential, not being generally known to, not being readily ascertainable by proper means by, other persons who can obtain economic value from its disclosure or use; and (b) is the subject of efforts that are reasonable under the circumstances to maintain its secrecy.

Apart from state statutes, trade secrecy protection has long existed as part of the common law. Since a computer database is a compilation which derives economic value, it is a type of intellectual property which has frequently received trade secrecy protection. Whether or not a court will find that a database is legally a trade secret frequently depends upon whether the compiler made reasonable efforts to maintain its secrecy. Many of the trade secret cases involve a dispute between an employer and former employee over a compilation of data, namely, a customer list.

Many employers consider their customer list to be their most valuable trade secret. Thus, when an employee leaves and takes the list with him to compete against an employer, a suit frequently follows to have an injunction entered to make the employee return the list and not use those trade secrets. Information will be protected as a trade secret, even where there is no express contract requiring non-disclosure of the information, where based upon the nature of the information and the confidential relationship between the parties, such as employer-employee, equity should imply such an agreement. Conversely, if parties have a written contract to treat certain information as a trade secret, and not to disclose it, then even if the information does not legally qualify as a trade secret, the parties may still be required to keep it secret. Without such an agreement, however, the information in question must legally qualify as a trade secret to be entitled to protection. When a database is licensed to others, and there is no confidential relationship, the data may still have and retain a trade secrecy status, if it is sold with the express condition that the purchaser of the database maintain the secrecy of the information.

A seller of the database can require that any purchaser enter into a written contract as a condition of purchase of the database. The purveyor of the computer lawyer database could refuse to sell this information to anyone unless they first sign a written contract. That written agreement could expressly provide that the purchaser will not disclose the list of computer lawyers to anyone but authorised users, nor make any copies or unauthorised use of the information. Typically this takes the form of a Licence Agreement between the preparer/licensor of the database and the user/licencee of the database.

A Licence Agreement is unlike a typical purchase and sale agreement in that ownership of the product involved, the programme, remains in the licensor. The licensee merely purchases the right to use the programme. The licencee's right to use the programme can be limited in any number of ways. The most important limitations typically are that the licensee can only use the programme on one or a select number of computers, he may not make any copies of the programme, and he has to keep confidential certain information about the programme or the database. Many other types of limitations or rights and reservations can be contained within the licence agreement between the parties.

Since the law and courts in general are struggling to keep up with the rapid changes in technology, a preparer of a database is well advised to try and strengthen his legal hand as much as possible with certain practical protection measures. There are methods which a programme can employ to try and prevent someone from simply copying his work, or if they do, to make proof of this copying in court far easier. Without the conscious employment of these methods it may be difficult to know whether or not a competitor has 'cheated', and simply copied your information, or has come up with the same information on his own. The solution to this problem is the deliberate placement of errors or omissions in your database. If your competitor's database contains the same errors or omissions, then you have pretty good evidence that your database was copied.

## References


Frey, D. and R. Adams, *A Directory of Electronic Mail Addressing and Networks*, O'Reilly and Associates, Inc., Sebastopol, CA, January 1990.

Harvery, Ross, *Preservation in Libraries: Principles, Strategies and Practices for Librarians*, London: Bowker-Saur, 1993.

Hentoff, Nat, *The First Freedom: The Tumultuous History of Free Speech in America*, New York, Delacorte Press, 1980.Englewood Cliffs, N. J: Prentice Hall, 1964.

Hildreth, Charles, *On-line public access catalogue: the user interface*, Dublin, Ohio, On-line Computer Library Centre, 1982.

Johnson, C.A., "Retrospective Conversion of Three Library Collections", *Information Technology and Libraries*, 1982.

Raitt, David, (ed.), *Libraries for the New Millennium: Implication for Managers*, London, Library Association Publishing, 1987.

Wusteman, J., "Electronic Journal Formats", *Programme* 30, October 1996.

# Bibliography


Andrews, J. & Law, D. G. *Digital libraries: policy, planning and practice.* Aldershot, Hants, England; Burlington, VT: Ashgate. 2004.

Bailey, C.W., 'Public-Access Computer Systems', *Information Technology and Libraries*, 12, March 1993.

Baker, Thomas. A Grammar for Dublin Core. *D-Lib Magazine,* Vol. 6 No. 10 .

Bawden, D., *User-oriented Evaluation of Information Systems and Services,* Aldershot: Gower, 1990.

Berners-Lee, Tim and Mark Fischetti. 1999. *Weaving the Web*, Harper, San Francisco.

Birmingham, William P. 1995. "An Agent-Based Architecture for Digital Libraries", in *D-Lib Magazine*, July 1995.

Bishop, A. P., Van House, N. A. & Buttenfield, B. P;, eds. *Digital library use: social practice in design and evaluation.* Cambridge, MA: MIT Press. 2003.

Borgman C.L. What are digital libraries? Competing visions. *Information Processing and Management*, 35(3):227-243, 1999.

Brogan, M. L. *A survey of digital library aggregation services. Washington,* D.C.:; Digital Library Federation, Council on Library and Information Resources. 2003.

Chapman, S. *Techniques for creating sustainable digital collections.* Chicago: ALA TechSource. 2004.

Chowdhury, G. G. & Chowdhury, S. *Introduction to digital libraries.* London: Facets Publishing. 2003.

Conway, Paul , *Preservation in the Digital World,* Washington, D.C.: Commission on Preservation and Access, 1996.

Dekkers, Makx and Stuart Weibel. Dublin Core Metadata Initiative Progress Report and Workplan for 2002. *D-Lib Magazine,* Volume 8, #2 February 2002.

Del Bimbo, A.; Gradmann, S.; Ioannidis, Y. (Eds.) *Future Research Directions*. 3rd DELOS Brainstorming Workshop Report, Corvara, Italy, July, 2004.

Dijkstra, Edsger. 2001. "The End of Computing Science", in *Communications of the ACM*, Vol 44, No 3, March 2001, p. 92.

Duval, Erik. Metadata standards: What, who & why. *Journal of Universal Computer Science,* 7(7):591-601, July 2001. Special Issue: I-Know 01 - International Conference on Knowledge Management.

Fielding, R., J. Gettys, J. Mogul, H. Frystyk, L. Masinter, P. Leach, and T. Berners-Lee. 1999. *RFC2616: Hypertext Transfer Protocol - HTTP 1.1*, Network Working Group, June 1999.

Fox, E. A., *Source Book on Digital Libraries*, Virginia Tech, Department of Computer Science, 1993.

Frey, D. and R. Adams, *A Directory of Electronic Mail Addressing and Networks*, O'Reilly and Associates, Inc., Sebastopol, CA, January 1990.

Gladney, H., Z. Ahmed, R. Ashany, N. J. Belkin, E. A. Fox, and M. Zemankova. 1994. *Digital Library: Gross Structure and Requirements (Report from a Workshop)*, IBM Almaden Research Center, Virginia Tech Dept. of Computer Science, June 1994.

Gonçalves, M.A.; Fox, E. 5SL - A Language for Declarative Specification and Generation of Digital Libraries. In *Proceedings of the 2nd ACM/IEEE-CS Joint Conference on Digital Libraries (JCDL '02)*, Portland, Oregon, USA, 2002.

Gopal Krishan, *Digital Libraries in Electronic Information Era*, Authorspress, New Delhi, 2000.

Gore, Albert. The digital earth: Understanding our planet in the 21st century. Speech delivered at the California Science Center, Los Angeles, California. January 31. 1998.

Harnad, S. 1999. "Free at Last: The Future of Peer-Reviewed Journals", in *D-Lib Magazine*, Vol 5, No 12, December 1999.

Harvery, Ross, *Preservation in Libraries: Principles, Strategies and Practices for Librarians*, London: Bowker-Saur, 1993.

Hentoff, Nat, *The First Freedom: The Tumultuous History of Free Speech in America*, New York, Delacorte Press, 1980.Englewood Cliffs, N. J: Prentice Hall, 1964.

Hickey, T. B. 2003. *Web services for digital libraries*. European Library Automation Group, ELAG 2003: Cross language applications and the Web, 27th Library systems seminar, Bern (Switzerland) 2-4 April 2003.

Hildreth, Charles, *On-line public access catalogue: the user interface*, Dublin, Ohio, On-line Computer Library Centre, 1982.

Hulser, Richard P., Digital Library: Condent Preservation in a Digital World, *DESIDOC Bulletin of Information Technology*, 17 (6), 1997.

Ioannidis Y. (Ed.) *Digital Libraries: Future Directions for a European Research Programme*. DELOS Brainstorming Report, San Cassiano, Italy, June 2001.

ISO. 1994. *ISO/IEC 7498-1:1994, Open Systems Interconnection Basic Reference Model: The Basic Model*, International Organization for Standardization.

Johnson, C.A., "Retrospective Conversion of Three Library Collections", *Information Technology and Libraries*, 1982.

Kahle, B., *Archiving the Internet*, Paper submitted to Scientific American for March 1997 issue, 1997.

Kantor, P.B., *Objective Performance Measures for Academic and Research Libraries*, Washington, DC: Association of Research Libraries, 1984.

Kelleher, J., E. Sommerlad, and E. Stern, *Evalution of the Electronic Libraries Programmes: Guidelines for e-Lib Project Evaluation*, London: Tavistock Institute, 1996.

Lagoze, C. and J. R. Davis. 1995. "Dienst - An Architecture for Distributed Document Libraries", in *Communications of the ACM*, Vol 38, No 4, p. 47.

Lynn, M.S., "Digital Preservation and Access", *Collection Management* 22, nos. 1998.

Ma, Y. *A., Semiotic Analysis of Icons on the World Wide Web*, Paper presented at the Annual Conference of the International Visual Literacy Association, Chicago, 1995, (ERIC Document Reproduction Service, ED 391481).

MacKenzie, M.; Laskey, K.; McCabe, F.; Brown, P.; Metz, R. *Reference Model for Service Oriented Architecture*. OASIS Committee Draft 1.0, February 2006.

Malwad N. M., *et al* (ed.), *Digital Libraries: Dynamics storehouse of digitised information*, New Delhi, New Age International, 1996.

Mitchell, A. M. & Surratt, B. E. *Cataloging and organizing digital resources: a how-to-do-it manual for librarians*. New York: Neal-Schuman Publishers. 2005.

MITI. *Program for advanced information infrastructure*. Japan Ministry for International Trade and Industry. May. 1994.

Moy, Naomi, *CyberSpace Reference Library: the Virtual Reference Collection*. Carson, CA: CA State University at Dominguez Hills, 1997.

Paepcke, Andreas, Chen-Chuan K. Chang, Terry Winograd, and Hector Garcia-Molina. Interoperability for digital libraries worldwide. *Communications of the ACM*, 41(4):33-42, 1998.

Philip, H. Young, "Visions of Academic Workplace in a Brave New Future", *Library and Future: Essays on Library in the Twenty-First Century*, New York, Haworth Press, 1993.

Prudlo, M. E-archiving: an overview of some repository management software tools. *Ariadne*, 43. 2005.

Raitt, David, (ed.), *Libraries for the New Millennium: Implication for Managers*, London, Library Association Publishing, 1987.

Rajashekar, T.B., *Digital Libraries, Information Studies,* October, 1995.

Rhyno, A. *Using open source systems for digital libraries*. Westport, CT: Libraries Unlimited. 2004.

Rydberg-Cox, J. A. *Digital libraries and the challenges of digital humanities*. Oxford: Chandos Publishing. 2005.

Schek, H.-J.; Schuldt, H. DelosDLMS - Infrastructure for the Next Generation of Digital Library Management Systems. *ERCIM News*, No. 66, July 2006.

Snowdon, D.N.; Churchill, E. F.; Frecon, E. (Eds.) *Inhabited Information Spaces - Living with your Data*. Springer, London 2004.

Sproull, L., and S. Kiesler, *Connections: New Ways of Working in the Networked Organisation*, MIT Press, Cambridge, MA, 1991.

Sutton, Stuart, and Jon Mason. The Dublin Core and Metadata for Educational Resources. *Proceedings: International Conference on Dublin Core and Metadata Applications 2001,* pp 25-31. (2001)

Tedd, L. A. & Large, A. *Digital libraries: principles and practice in a global environment*. Germany: K.G. Saur. 2005.

Tennant, R. *Managing the digital library*. New York: Reed Press. 2004.

Theng, Y. L. & Foo, S., eds. *Design and usability of digital libraries: case studies in the Asia-Pacific.* Hershey, PA: Idea Group Publishing. 2004.

Umar, Amjad. 1997. *Object-Oriented Client/Server Internet Environments*, Prentice Hall, New Jersey.

Van de Sompel, Herbert and Carl Lagoze. 2000. "The Santa Fe Convention of the Open Archives Initiative" in *D-Lib Magazine*, Vol 6, No 2, February 2000.

Wusteman, J., "Electronic Journal Formats", *Programme* 30, October 1996.

# Index